COLLEGE IN CANADA
2007 – 2008 EDITION

GUIDE TO

College

IN

Canada

FOR AMERICAN STUDENTS

2007 – 2008 EDITION

NANCY & GREG VIS

AVOCUS
PUBLISHING

Gilsum, New Hampshire

Avocus Publishing
4 White Brook Road
Gilsum, NH 03448
800-345-6665
www.avocus.com

Vis, Nancy & Greg
Guide to College in Canada for American Students 2007–2008 edition
p. cm.   includes indexes

ISBN-10: 1-890765-12-0
ISBN-13: 978-1-890765-12-5

1. Universities and colleges- Canada- Directories
2. College choice- Canada- Directories I. Title: College in Canada

Printed in Canada

CONTENTS

CANADA

LIST OF SCHOOLS BY PROVINCE

Chapter 1

WHY STUDY IN CANADA?

Welcome to the second edition of *College in Canada for American Students*. Since the first edition was published in 2003 the landscape of higher education in Canada has changed substantially. Over the last several years enrollments have grown steadily at Canadian universities and a new era of capital improvements and expansions to the schools has begun. Every school profile in the book has been updated to reflect the many changes over the last several years. *College in Canada* has been created to serve as an introduction for American students to the universities of Canada. While in close geographical proximity to us, there exists a wide gap in knowledge about the Canadian higher education system here in the US. We believe that Canada offers many attractive and practical higher education choices based on the criteria of academic quality, cost and variety. Those willing to broaden their search horizons will find a world of new options, institutions rich in tradition and cities of learning with worldwide reputations for excellence, waiting to be discovered by a new generation. As your list of colleges to apply to is drawn up, close examination of one or more Canadian options can fill important slots in your selection strategy. Whether as your first choice or as a safety selection, the time may be right to have a Canadian school in the mix.

This guide will help you begin your exploration of prospective colleges in Canada. Introductory sections will give you a feel for the country and the things you should consider in making your decision. The main part of *College in Canada* is the profiles of individual universities and colleges. Essential information such as size, type of school, costs and programs offered make up this section. Lastly, a comprehensive majors index section will allow you to quickly search for schools offering programs of interest.

Exceptional Value and High Standards

The quality of higher education in Canada is in keeping with the prevailing standards across the rest of North America. Students receive the same degrees that they would in the United States.

Canadian schools are also attractive from a financial perspective. The majority of Canadian universities are state-run non-profit organizations and costs are very reasonable in comparison with average US costs. Almost all Canadian universities are accredited by the US Department of Education as eligible institutions for Federal Student Aid.

FAFSA eligibility information is included in the individual school profiles.

On a practical level, most Canadian schools are within 100 miles of the US-Canada border and are easily accessbile.

Choice and Quality of Life

College in Canada covers close to 100 different schools and locations to study. Each university has its own personality. Are you looking for a small liberal arts institution in a quiet community? Are you looking to prepare for a specific career? Maybe you are attracted to a large urban area and campus. Perhaps you know exactly what you want to study and can select a school based on its reputation in your area of interest. If location and student life are important criteria for you, Canadian schools offer a wide variety of choices. Within every profile we have tried to give you a feel for the immediate vicinity of each school. Large Canadian cities are statistically much safer than their US counterparts. From the mountainous West, to the cosmopolitan cities of Montreal and Toronto, to unique college towns scattered here and there, Canada has excellent universities to match every selection criteria.

International Perspective

American students who gain the experience of international study improve their job prospects upon graduation. The spirit of adventure that characterizes students who seek to broaden their experiences is an attractive trait to most employers. Canada is the United States's largest trading partner and holds vast natural resources of oil, water, timber and minerals, which will become increasingly important to the American economy in a turbulent world.

The benefits to both countries of having many close ties is clear. These benefits apply on a personal level as well. Time spent away from the US will allow you to more fully appreciate your home and it will also allow you to see things from a new perspective. The gifts from a university education are enjoyed long after the school days are over. The value of study in Canada is a well-kept secret. We hope to make this secret more widely known and hope that this guide will encourage more Americans to explore the wonderful opportunities that lie on our doorsteps.

Chapter 2

ABOUT CANADA

As you investigate colleges in Canada you will want to learn more about the country and also find out what is similar to life in the US and what are some of the differences in perspectives, customs and day-to-day living that will enrich your stay. Much about Canada remains unknown to Americans and this is a shame for there is much that Americans would find attractive and familiar in their northern neighbor. In this chapter we will give you a broad overview of the country covering its people and culture, geography, history, politics and economics. The chapter ends with suggestions for planning campus visits and includes links to important travel planning information.

People/Culture

Canada is a multicultural society of 31,000,000 people. The makeup of Canadian society has been compared to a mosaic with each culture retaining its unique characteristics within the larger whole. This is in contrast to the melting pot analogy often used to describe the US. Canada's cultural makeup today reflects the influence of the original native people as well as successive waves of immigrants.

The largest ethnic groups within Canada are: British 28%, French 23%, other European 15%, Asian/Arab/African 6%, indigenous Amerindian 2%, mixed background 26%. Canada is an officially bilingual country, the two official languages are English and French. The French population is concentrated in the province of Quebec. Canada is the refuge the British Loyalists fled to after the Revolutionary War and their influence as well as continued close ties to Britain have been key factors which have shaped the Canadian outlook on life. This wide mix of cultures and languages combine to give Canada a slightly more international feel than one gets in the US.

Canada is a heavy exporter of cultural talent to the United States, from songwriters like Avril Lavigne, Celine Dion, Shawnia Twain, Neil Young to actors like Michael J. Fox, William Shatner, comedians Mike Myers and Dan Aykroyd. In the sports realm Canadian hockey players dominate the NHL. Canada has 2 NBA teams, the Grizzlies and the Raptors, and 2 Major League Baseball franchises, the Blue Jays and the Expos. Overall much of the popular culture, TV and radio are very similar in the two countries. Distinctiveness can be found in the regions where local talent is first nurtured before appearing on the North American stage.

Canada enjoys one of the highest standards of living in the world. It has consistently earned the number one spot from the United Nations in terms of quality of life throughout the world. Canadians have very high life expectancy, a low infant mortality rate, and a high level of literacy. Canadians have a comprehensive social welfare system that includes universal healthcare as well as strong public education.

Geography

Canada is a vast, beautiful country covering close to 4,000,000 miles. It is the second largest country in the world after Russia. The geography of Canada is diverse and ranges from Mountains in the West, plains and prairie in the center, and lowlands and old forest in the eastern parts, to Arctic tundra in the North. The climate also varies from temperate to arctic. This rich land supports many natural resources, has a rich cultural industry and contains a significant proportion of the world's fresh water.

Canada is subdivided into ten provinces and three territories in the North. The newest territory, Nunavit, enjoys Native self-government. The Atlantic provinces of Newfoundland, Prince Edward Island, Nova Scotia and New Brunswick have close connections to the sea and a way of life that retains historical traditions. The province of Quebec, predominantly French, has a distinct cultural and social structure compared to the rest of Canada. The province of Ontario is the largest in population and is the economic powerhouse of Canada. Ontario enjoys a strong manufacturing-based economy and its largest city, Toronto, is the fifth largest urban center in North America. The Prairie provinces of Manitoba, Saskatchewan, and Alberta are known for their agricultural exports. The region is also rich in natural resources with abundant oil and natural gas being found there. On the Pacific Coast, British Columbia occupies mountainous terrain.

The urban centers in Canada are a mix of large metropolitan areas and small smaller rural ones. Large cities include: Toronto 4,000,000; Montreal 3,000,000; Vancouver 2,000,000; and Ottawa 1,000,000. The majority of the population lives within a two-hour drive of the US border. The vast northern regions reaches of Canada are sparsely populated.

History

The French initially colonized Canada. Jacques Cartier claimed this vast territory for the French crown in the 1500's. Colonization began in earnest during the early 1600's with Samuel de Champlain's first settlement in Quebec City. Much of the seventeenth and eighteenth century saw a continental rivalry between France and Britain. Most of what is today Canada was French. The thirteen English colonies in the US clung to the Atlantic seaboard. Both countries formed alliances with Native American tribes and fought sporadic wars. The American Revolution followed the final defeat of the French forces in North America in 1759. For a brief time all of what is today Canada and the US was under British Dominion.

The cause of the American Revolution found sympathetic ears in some parts of Canada, mainly among the common folk. During the American Revolution the city of Montreal was occupied by American troops for six months early in the war. After the war 40,000 British loyalists moved to Canada mainly in the eastern townships of Quebec and in Nova Scotia. These loyalists had a major impact on the development of Canada and on that development taking a separate path from that of America. During the war of 1812, the Canadians briefly occupied Washington DC before the war came to a tie. Canada officially became a country and not a colony of Britain on July 1, 1867. This date is now celebrated as a national holiday. The history of Canada and the United States followed similar paths during the late 1800's and early 1900's. Both countries enjoyed increasing prosperity and industrialization, both countries welcomed waves of immigrants from Europe, and both countries fought in the two world wars. The early 1960's brought a quiet revolution to Quebec, leading to a new assertiveness and heightened sense of identity among the French speaking Quebeckers, who make up about one fourth of Canada's population. In 1976, a government committed to forming an independent Quebec won the provincial election and began to explore a course towards greater independence from the rest of Canada. Two referendums, one in 1980 and one in 1995, resulted in narrow victories for the federalists over the sovereignists. Quebec's status within Canada remains a serious political issue. Canada is still seeking a constitutional settlement that will satisfy the aspirations of the French-speaking province of Quebec. In typical Canadian fashion this issue is likely to be settled peacefully and by compromise.

The passing of the US-Canada Free Trade Agreement in 1989 and the superseding North American Free Trade Agreement (NAFTA) in 1994 have had a profound impact on the economic relations between the two countries. The reduction of trade barriers has led to significantly higher levels of trade between the two countries. On the world stage Canada has played an important role as a peacekeeper for the United Nations in the world's hot spots during the second half of the 20th century.

Government

Canada is a parliamentary democracy as well as a constitutional monarchy. The federal structure resembles the US system in many ways. Queen Elizabeth the Second, as Queen of Canada, serves as a symbol of the nation's unity. She appoints a Governor General as her representative on the advice of the Prime Minister of Canada, usually for a five-year term. The prime minister is the leader of the political party in power and appoints his cabinet. The cabinet remains in office as long as it retains majority support in the House of Commons. Canada's Parliament consists of an elected House of Commons and an appointed Senate. Legislative power rests with the 301 member of the House of Commons who are selected during general elections with terms not to exceed five years. Federal elections were last held in November 2000. Prime Minister Jacques Chretien's Liberal Party won a majority victory in the 2000 elections. Chretien became the first Prime Minister to lead three consecutive majority governments since 1945. The liberals won 57% of the seats. The Canadian Alliance Party won the second highest net totals of seats and forms the official opposition.

A premier governs each province with a single elected legislative chamber. Federal provincial interplay is a central feature of Canadian politics. Quebec wishes to preserve and strengthen its distinctive nature, western provinces desire more control over their abundant natural resources, industrialized Central Canada is concerned with economic development and the Atlantic provinces have resisted federal claims to fishing and mineral rights off their shores. The central government has responded to these different regional needs by seeking once again to rebalance the Canadian Confederation.

US – Canada Relations

Canada maintains very close relations with the United States. In fields ranging from environmental cooperation to free trade the two countries have set the standard by which other countries measure their own progress. US Defense arrangements with Canada are more extensive than with any other country. The United States and Canada share mutual NATO security commitments. In addition, US and Canadian military forces have cooperated since 1958 on

Continental Air defense within the framework of the North American Aerospace Defense Command—NORAD.

Although Canada views its relationship with the US as crucial to a wide range of interests, it also occasionally pursues policies at odds with the United States. This is particularly true of Cuba, where the US and Canada have pursued divergent policies for nearly 40 years, even while sharing the common goal of a peaceful democratic transition.

Canada maintains an embassy in the United States in Washington, DC. A number of consulates are also maintained throughout the US. The Canadian ambassador to the US is Michael Kergin.

The United States maintains an embassy in the Canadian capital of Ottawa. The American Ambassador to Canada is Paul Celucci, the former governor of Massachusetts.

Economy

Canada is one of the leading industrialized countries in the world. It is a member of the G7, the grouping of the largest economies. The Canadian economy is diversified, with strengths in manufacturing, agriculture, natural resources, the service sectors and tourism. Canadian researchers have made important contributions in the field of medicine and high technology. As befits a country with huge distances, Canada is a world leader in telecommunications. Alexander Graham Bell did some of his pioneering research in Nova Scotia and today such telecom giants as Nortel, JDS Uniphase and others call Canada home.

The volume of trade between Canada and the US is the most extensive in the world—a staggering $1.4 billion worth of merchandise crosses the border each day. Over 200,000,000 people also cross the border each year. Canada is by far the United States largest trading partner. US trade with Canada exceeds that of all Latin American countries combined; US exports to Canada exceed those to all members of the European Union combined. The two-way trade that crosses the Ambassador Bridge between Michigan and Canada is greater than all US exports to Japan. Canada is the leading export market for 35 of 50 US states. Canada is the largest US energy supplier in the world. Canada provides about 16% of US oil imports and 14% of total US consumption of natural gas.

The US is Canada's largest foreign investor. Canada is the third largest foreign investor in the United States. It is hard to overstate the mutual dependence of these two countries. A knowledge of our most important partner through education can certainly lead to open doors in the future.

Visiting and Studying Canada

Visiting a university is one of the best ways to get to know a school. Spending some time on campus, talking with current students, attending some classes and visiting with admissions staff and professors can provide you with a sense of what it's like to study and live at a particular school. Ideally you will want to visit while classes are in session. Spring break and early fall are traditional school visit times. You should begin planning your trip a few months ahead of when you plan to visit. Once you've determined which schools you would like to visit, contact their admissions department to coordinate your trip. We have included the admissions contact information for each school profiled in this guide.

Admission department personnel can help you get as much out of your visit as you can. They can save you a lot of time finding what is important to you and also save you from missing anything you should see. Ask your admissions contact whether the school will be in session when you plan to attend, about the availability of tours and how much advance notice is needed to book a tour. Apart from the guided tour you will want to set up an appointment with an admissions counselor and perhaps a professor or coach.

Leave yourself time for free exploration while at a school. Plan on spending at least three hours for each school you plan to visit. This will allow you to visit two schools in close proximity to each other in a day. Be sure to set aside some time to get to know the surrounding community. We've included some points of interest in each school's profile and the web sites listed below as well as any good tour guide will provide you with more information on planning a productive and fun trip.

The relationship between the United States and Canada is perhaps the closest and most extensive between any two countries in the world. The differences between the two countries are such that you can gain a new perspective on the world from spending time in Canada and yet are able to stay in touch with many of the comforts of home. The opportunities for exploration outside of the classroom are rich and will form an important part of your stay and the memories you keep.

References:

U.S. Department of State: www.state.gov

Additional information:
Canadian Tourism Commission: www.travelcanada.ca

Chapter 3

ADMISSIONS AND FINANCES

As in the US, the application process to a Canadian school requires you to assemble a great deal of information. The first step in the process is to obtain the appropriate application forms from the schools where you hope to study. These forms must be thoroughly studied, all the necessary information assembled and sent along with the application fee to the appropriate location by the application deadline. Once you've been accepted to the school of your choice you will need to put in place the financial plan that will pay the cost of your studies. This chapter will examine all of these considerations in detail.

Application Procedure

You should contact the admissions or registrar's offices of universities that interest you in the fall of your senior year to request application packages. Application forms are often available online. An American high school curriculum meets the application requirements of Canadian universities provided that students successfully complete any admission requirements to the program of their choice. Check with the school and faculty to which you are applying to determine what specific admission requirements are and what prerequisites may exist for specific degree programs. Read the materials you receive and compile a list of the materials you will need to submit. Complete the forms carefully as errors may result in a delay of your application. Every school will want an official transcript from your previous school. In addition to grades, class standing and teacher recommendations are strongly recommended. Many Canadian universities require American students to report their SAT I and/or SAT II scores. You must check with the admissions office and the specific faculty to which you are applying to see if this is the case. Many Canadian universities will recognize results from Advanced Placement exams. Contact the admissions departments to see which specific exams are recognized by each university.

Application deadlines can range from January to June with most typically falling between April and May. We have indicated general admission dates in this guide, however, it is absolutely necessary that you contact each university's admissions office to inquire about its policy and any changes which may have been made since the printing of this guide. Applying early is strongly advised.

In most cases you should submit your application to the universities directly. Many schools will now allow you to apply online. Be sure to include the non-refundable application fee. Applications which are received without payment will not be processed. The fee is payable by certified check, money order or credit card.

Applications to Ontario and British Columbia universities should not be made directly to the schools. Applications to Ontario universities go to the Ontario Universities' Application Center. Non-Canadian applicants use the OUAC 105F common form, which can be completed online at www.ouac.on.ca. Universities in the province of British Columbia accept paper applications by mail as well as online submissions via the Postsecondary Application Service of British Columbia, www.pas.bc.ca.

You will receive a letter acknowledging your application within 3-5 weeks after applying. Many schools make an effort to offer admissions to applicants before May 1.

Graduate Studies Application

The graduate admissions process generally takes longer than the undergraduate process. Students should contact the department to which they wish to apply directly to obtain information on specific graduate programs, program availability, financial information and a complete list of admission requirements.

Finances

The incredible value that a Canadian university education offers is one of the principal reasons for considering college in Canada. If you require financial assistance to fund your education, you have several options.

U.S. residents are eligible to apply for US federal government loans while studying at a Canadian university. The majority of Canadian universities are accredited by the U.S. Department of Education as eligible institutions for the HOPE Scholarship and Lifetime Learning tax credits, and the Student Financial Assistance Programs including Stafford Loans. We have included eligible schools' Federal School Code within the finance section of their descriptions. The US Department of Education website offers a complete source of information for federal loan programs, www.ed.gov.

The application process for student loans guaranteed by the US federal government is similar for students attending school in the US or Canada. The first step in the process is to complete a Free Application for Student Aid (FAFSA), at www.fafsa.ed.gov. This form is available online or by calling (800) 433-3243.

Many states have extensive student aid programs and some offer need-based grants for out-of-state study, merit awards, low interest loans, and other assistance packages. Students should contact their state's higher education agency to obtain complete information.

Many schools will also be able to help with innovative tuition payment plans. These may include installment plans, prepayment discounts or other financial arrangements depending on your circumstances.

In addition to government and school programs, there are private sources which will lend you the money necessary to fund your education. Your school's admissions office can supply contact information.

Scholarships

A wide variety of scholarships and grants are available from individual universities. Some schools have specific scholarships to encourage American students to attend. Bishop's University, located near Montreal, awards five entrance scholarships valued at $2000 CDN annually to American students. You should contact a university's student financial services office for details on general or program specific awards available to you. The deadline for scholarship applications is generally earlier than the general admission deadline. Check deadlines and apply as soon as possible for your best chances.

Chapter 4

LIVING IN CANADA

Upon acceptance by the school of your choice, you will need to make arrangements for obtaining a student visa and health insurance. Housing plans will also be high on your pre-departure checklist. You should plan on starting the student visa application process three months before the start of studies. Your school's international student advisors will usually send you information on each step listed below. Get to know your advisors and ask them any questions you may have about the process. They have advised hundreds of students in your situation and are happy to help.

Student Visa – Canada

To study in Canada you will need to obtain a Student Authorization, the official term for a student visa, from Citizenship and Immigration Canada (CIC). CIC is the Canadian equivalent of the INS in the US. This visa is issued outside of Canada. Upon acceptance into a Canadian university you may apply for your Student Authorization at a CIC office in the US or at any Canadian port of entry (border crossing). CIC offices are located in: Buffalo, Detroit, New York, Seattle, Los Angeles and Washington, D.C.

When applying you must supply: 1) a valid form of identification, examples include a current passport or an original birth certificate; 2) the original letter of acceptance from the Canadian educational institution; and 3) evidence of adequate funds to cover tuition and living costs for your entire stay in Canada, examples may include a letter from your bank, your parents' bank statements for the past several months and/or your parents' and your latest tax returns.

Application forms and additional information can be found at the CIC website—www.cic.gc.ca. The current processing fee is $125 CDN. The processing fee must be sent along with your application. Acceptable payment forms include money orders, cashier checks or bank drafts.

Student Visa – Quebec

Students studying in Quebec must obtain a separate approval from the Government of Quebec in addition to the CIC Student Authorization. The Quebec Certificate of Acceptance (CAQ) is obtained from the Quebec Ministry of Citizenship and Immigration—www.immigration-quebec.gouv.qc.ca.

The CAQ requirements are similar to those of the Student Authorization. CAQ applications are sent to regional offices in Montreal, Sherbrooke or Quebec City, depending on where your school is located. The current processing fee is $100 CDN. The processing fee must be sent along with your application. Acceptable payment forms include cashier's checks or certified checks.

Working in Canada

Canadian immigration rules allow full-time international students to work part-time on campus and also to work as part of a course of study such as in a cooperative program. Although work allows students to supplement their income, it is not possible to earn enough money to cover all tuition and living expenses. Upon graduation, if students can obtain employment in their field, they can remain in Canada for one year to gain practical work experience.

Health Care Insurance

A significant difference between the US and Canada is the health care system in each country. In the US health care is a private system while in Canada the system is government-run and all citizens are covered. The Canadian system offers high quality care from one end of the country to another. As a student in Canada you will be covered by this system once you make the required applications and pay the required fees.

Depending on where you study, applications will be made through your school, the provincial health department or a private insurance company. In the provinces of Saskatchewan and Alberta, the provincial government covers the bulk of the fee for international students. In the other provinces the fees are in the very reasonable range of $500-$1000/year. This figure is listed in each school profile in College in Canada.

Housing

Your school will provide you with information for both on- and off-campus living options once you are accepted. Individual school listings in College in Canada will detail whether residence spaces are guaranteed to first-year students as well as the cost ranges.

Residence life can be an important part of your college experience. It is a wonderful way to meet people and to be close to campus life. Students planning to live on campus in residence must reserve a room as soon as possible once they have been accepted.

Most colleges and universities operate a housing service for students who prefer to rent a room or an apartment off-campus. Finding affordable, comfortable and convenient housing requires time and effort. Allow yourself sufficient time before the start of classes to begin your search. In addition to finding a location, you must allow time to furnish the apartment and to arrange for all utilities setups. The school housing service can advise you on the length of time this will typically take.

Banking

Shortly after your arrival in Canada you should open an account at a Canadian bank. This is an important step in getting settled as most of your payments will need to be made in Canadian funds. There are several ways of getting money transferred from the US to Canada. Cashier's checks and wire transfer are two very economical methods of transferring funds. In exchanging funds you will want to search for the best exchange rate and lowest service charges. A credit card from a US bank will allow you to access small amounts of cash at a very favorable exchange rate as well. Upon your initial arrival, traveler's checks are a good second option to credit cards until you have your Canadian account established.

Settling In

We recommend that you plan on arriving on campus one to two weeks before classes start in order to get settled and familiarize yourself with the new environment. You may experience culture shock upon your initial arrival. Take this time to enjoy the many offerings of your new location and to get to know your fellow students.

Chapter 5

ABOUT THIS GUIDE

Organization of the Guide

This book this book has been designed to give you an overview of the Canadian higher education system and allow you to easily compare many fine schools based on criteria that are important to you. The Guide has been designed specifically for American students and uses criteria that will be familiar to US readers. Schools are placed in categories that closely reflect the Carnegie Classification of Institutions of Higher Education. The classification of instructional programs reflect the US Department of Education descriptions. Schools that are accredited for US FAFSA assistance are noted and dollar figures reflect both Canadian and US dollars. Our goal is to provide you with useful information and help you explore schools you may not normally have considered.

College in Canada is divided into three main sections: introductory reference chapters, individual school profiles and a comprehensive majors index. The introductory reference section contains five chapters:

1. Why Study in Canada
2. About Canada
3. Admissions and Finance
4. Living in Canada
5. About this Guide

These chapters will help you gain an understanding of the Canadian educational system, introduce you to the people and customs, and explain the many steps involved in evaluating, applying to, and studying at a Canadian university. The individual school profiles cover close to 100 accredited Canadian universities using a mix of narrative and factual data such as admissions requirements, entry dates and tuition costs. Schools included grant degrees at the bachelor's, master's and doctoral levels. Generally a bachelor's degree is a four-year program and the schools listed in this directory can be called four-year schools. It should be noted however that some bachelor's degrees can be completed in three years. The format of all the entries are consistent allowing for quick comparison between schools. The Majors Index section at the back of the text allows user to quickly search for schools offering a particular program of study.

School Profiles

Individual school profiles are grouped by province. The provinces are organized from east to west, starting with

Newfoundland and going to British Columbia. Within each province individual schools are organized alphabetically. The layout of each school's information has been carefully designed to make information retrieval as efficient as possible. Comparisons between schools is much easier with this layout.

Key to the School Profiles

School Name
City, Province

At-A-Glance Information: This prominent black band includes important information about a school that will allow you to quickly categorize a school based on School Category, Total Enrollment, Setting and City Population.

School Category: Schools are classified into one of the following 5 categories—Doctoral/Research, Master's, Bachelor's/Liberal Arts, Bachelor's/General, Specialized. These categories closely approximate the Carnegie Classification of Institutions of Higher Learning. The Carnegie Classification system is the most commonly used standard for categorizing American Colleges and Universities (www.carnegiefoundation.org).

Doctoral/Research: These schools offer a wide range of baccalaureate programs, graduate programs at the master's and doctoral levels as well as medical schools.

Master's: These schools offer a wide range of baccalaureate programs and graduate education primarily at the master's level.

Bachelor's/Liberal Arts: These schools are primarily focused on undergraduate education at the baccalaureate level. At least half of their programs are in liberal arts fields.

Bachelor's/General: These schools are primarily focused on undergraduate education and offer a wide range of baccalaureate programs.

Specialized: These schools offer a wide range of academic options including specialized training in a single academic area or non-traditional delivery of courses. Included are schools specializing in fine arts, agriculture and distance learning.

Total enrollment: This is the total number of full-time undergraduate and graduate students as well as part-time students attending a school. School size is an important criterion in school selection.

Setting: Schools can be classified as either Urban, Suburban or Rural. The setting of a school is an important indicator of its character.

City Population: This number indicates the population of the city or town where a school is located. For schools located in suburbs of large metropolitan areas, the population of the greater metropolitan is indicated.

Narrative Section: In this section we have attempted to give you a brief overview of the school, answer some basic questions, and capture some of the school's atmosphere in a few paragraphs. This section is easy to read and will help you determine whether a university should be examined more closely. Areas covered in this section include a general introduction to the school and its setting, an indication of whether the school is affiliated to a larger school, interesting facts about the school's history as well as a description of the campus setting. The accomplishments, new research initiatives or traditions that the school is known for are also listed here. Next, we describe the range of academic programs offered and general information on admissions. Student life, recreational opportunities and a brief description of the surrounding cities or areas are also covered.

General Information

This section will provide readers with a general overview of the school.

Year founded: Year when school began granting degrees

Undergraduate enrollment, full-time

Graduate enrollment, full-time

Faculty, full-time

Number of international students

Male/female ratio (%)

Residence spaces available

Residence space guaranteed for 1st year-students: Yes/No

Student media website: URL for student paper or radio station if available online

Undergraduate Admissions

This section contains information needed at the time of application, dates, fees and materials required for submission. Always verify dates and dollar amounts with schools prior to application.

Admissions Office Contact Information: Address, phone number and e-mail for this important office

Minimum High School Average: Depending on the program, students must often have maintained a minimum high school grade point average in order to be considered for admission.

Applications: Number of applications received, number accepted and number enrolled.

Rolling Admissions: Yes/No

International fall application deadline: Most schools operate on a strict deadline and applications need to be submitted prior to the deadline for consideration.

Application fee: This is a non-refundable fee that is submitted with the application.

Domestic fall application deadline: Most schools operate on a strict deadline and applications need to be submitted prior to the deadline for consideration.

Electronic application accepted: Yes/No

Admission notification by: Date by which school notifies applicants of acceptance.

Required with application: Many schools may require students to submit some of the following with their application: high school transcript, SAT I, SAT II, ACT, essay, recommendations, interview, portfolio.

Recommended with application: Many schools recommend that students submit some of the following with their application: SAT I, SAT II, ACT, essay, recommendations, interview, portfolio.

Undergraduate Finances

This section contains information relating to the cost of attending a school. **Note regarding dollar figures:** where appropriate Canadian and US dollar figures are noted. The exchange rate used was $0.90 US for every $1 Canadian which was slightly above the current rate at the time of publication in early 2006 and was meant to reflect the inclusion of exchange fees. This rate may vary up or down from month to month and year to year.

Undergraduate tuition
International students: Fee paid by visa students for 2 semesters at full course load, does not include miscellaneous ancillary fees.
Canadian students: Fee Canadian residents of a school's province pay for 2 semesters at full course load, does not include miscellaneous ancillary fees.

Estimated annual health insurance: Fee for a single person

Estimated annual books & supplies

Financial aid available for international students: Yes / No

Application deadline: Most schools operate on a strict deadline and applications need to be submitted prior to the deadline for consideration.

Scholarships available for international students: Yes / No

Application deadline: Most schools operate on a strict deadline and applications need to be submitted prior to the deadline for consideration.

Annual room/board cost for students in residence

Average monthly rent for students living off campus

Federal School Code: Code given to schools accredited by the US Department of Education as eligible institutions for US federal government financial aid programs. (www.fafsa.ed.gov)

Undergraduate Instructional Program

This section contains an A-Z listing of the majors offered at a school. We have used the terminology of the US Department of Education from the publication *Classification of Instructional Programs* to name the majors available (www.ed.gov). Schools may use a slightly different terminology for similar fields of study.

Most popular majors

Percentages by program: Listed in 6 broad categories- Liberal Arts and Science / General Studies / Humanities; Science and Mathematics; Computer Science and Engineering; Business and Economics; Professional Studies; Health Professions and Related Sciences.

Special study options: Choices available are: co-op programs, internships, study abroad, language programs, special summer programs, distance learning programs.

Majors available: A-Z list in 6 broad categories.

Graduate Admissions

This section contains general information needed at the time of admission. For graduate studies it is very important to contact individual departments.

Admissions Office Contact Information: Address, phone number and email for this important office.

International fall application deadline: Most schools operate on a strict deadline and applications need to be submitted prior to the deadline for consideration.

Application fee: This is a non-refundable fee that is submitted with the application.

Domestic fall application deadline: Most schools operate on a strict deadline and applications need to be submitted prior to the deadline for consideration.

Application fee: This is a non-refundable fee that is submitted with the application.

Electronic application accepted: Yes/ No

Required with application: Many schools require students to submit the following with their application: college transcript, GRE, essay, recommendations, interview, portfolio.

Recommended with application: Many schools recommend that students submit the following with their application: GRE, pre-admission tests for special programs such as MCAT, essay, recommendations, interview, portfolio.

Graduate student housing: Yes/No

Graduate Finances

This section contains information relating to the cost of attending a school.

Graduate tuition
International students: Fee paid by visa students for 2 semesters at full course load, does not include miscellaneous ancillary fees.
Canadian students: Fee Canadian residents of a school's province pay for 2 semesters at full course load, does not include miscellaneous ancillary fees.

Financial aid available for international students: Yes / No

Application deadline: Most schools operate on a strict deadline and applications need to be submitted prior to the deadline for consideration.

Scholarships available for international students: Yes / No

Application deadline: Most schools operate on a strict deadline and applications need to be submitted prior to the deadline for consideration.

Graduate Instructional Program

This section contains an A-Z listing of the majors offered at a school. We have used the terminology of the US Department of Education from the publication *Classification of Instructional Programs* to name the majors available. Schools may use a slightly different terminology for similar fields of study. Majors are listed in 6 broad categories: Liberal Arts and Science / General Studies / Humanities; Science and Mathematics; Computer Science and Engineering; Business and Economics; Professional Studies; Health Professions and Related Sciences.

Majors Index

This section of the book offers a quick guide to over 300 majors available at Canadian universities. The majors are listed alphabetically and within each major the schools that offer that major are listed alphabetically. The terminology used for the majors has been adapted from the US Department of Education publication, *Classification of Instructional Programs*. Schools may use a slightly different terminology for similar fields of study. While the information contained in this book reflects the most current available information at the time of publication, readers are advised to check with individual schools for the latest information for the specific programs to which they intend to apply as this information changes regularly. Following the Majors Index is a School by Category Index and an A-Z Index.

Research Procedures

The information in this publication is based on data gathered from detailed surveys which were sent prior to the 2006-2007 academic year to each school listed. School's were contacted directly by the authors to verify facts and to gather additional information when necessary. When specific information was unavailable from a particular school this is indicated with the abbreviation N/A. The information listed is intended as a general profile of each school. While every effort was made to ensure accuracy, readers should always verify information with the colleges directly as dates, fees and course offerings are subject to change from year to year.

Criteria for Inclusion

College in Canada includes schools which grant bachelor's, master's and doctoral degrees and have full accreditation and degree-granting status from the appropriate provincial government. The majority of schools listed are members of the Association of Universities and Colleges of Canada. Affiliated and federated member institutions of larger universities are listed individually when their course offerings and structures merit special consideration.

Contact Schools Directly

The information provided in this guide will have provided you with a good overview of your Canadian study options as well as helped you identify a few schools that you may want to research in greater detail. The next step would be to contact the schools you are interested in directly for more information. The contact information you need is located within each profile and in Chapter 2 we have provided suggestions for arranging a campus visit. All of the schools listed in the guide will be happy to provide you with more information and answer any questions you may have. Visiting a school's website is a natural starting point for the next phase of research. We have listed each school's website address within the school profile and we also provide a quick set of links to each school on our own site, www.canadacollege.com.

Continue Your Search Online

Throughout the book we have provided web site addresses where appropriate for further research on schools, Canada and other background information. The internet is a wonderful information gathering tool for in-depth examination and most schools have created very informative sites to answer your questions. Make sure to visit the student media web sites listed to get a feel for campus issues and activities. Visit our site, www.avocus.com, often as we will continue to add valuable information and resources that can help you explore your study decisions. We wish you success in your search and hope that you enjoy the process.

PROFILES BY PROVINCE

Newfoundland

Nova Scotia

Prince Edward Island

New Brunswick

Quebec

Ontario

Manitoba

Saskatchewan

Alberta

British Columbia

NEWFOUNDLAND

MEMORIAL UNIVERSITY of NEWFOUNDLAND

St. John's, Newfoundland

SCHOOL CATEGORY: Doctoral/Research   **TOTAL ENROLLMENT: 16,000**   **SETTING: Urban**   **CITY POPULATION: 175,000**

Memorial University of Newfoundland is a medium-sized comprehensive university. Established in 1925, it is one of Canada's leading academic institutions. The university has four campuses: two in Newfoundland, one on the French island of St-Pierre, and another in Harlow, England. Memorial's main campus is on 200 acres in St. John's, the capital of Newfoundland, one of North America's oldest cities, with roots going back to the sixteenth century.

Memorial offers a wide selection of undergraduate, graduate, and professional degree programs. Some of Memorial's most distinguished programs are in the study of the ocean in all it's aspects—scientific, technological, economic and cultural. The Marine Institute in St. John's, one of the world's outstanding centers for ocean studies, is the chief location for Memorial's maritime programs. The Sir Wilfred Grenfell College campus is located in western Newfoundland in the city of Corner Brook. This campus offers degree programs in a variety of disciplines, including environmental studies and forestry. French language and culture immersion are taught at the Institute Frecker on St-Pierre.

Residence spaces are limited. The university's location ensures that there are a variety of conveniently located houses and apartments available for renting off campus. The university has a full range of athletic facilities and numerous social and cultural clubs. The province offers extensive opportunities for both recreational and cultural activities. The region's close proximity to the Atlantic Ocean and its rugged terrain offer opportunities for sporting activities such as hiking, fishing and sailing. The people of St. John's are known for their friendliness, and that warmth, combined with Memorial's academic credentials, makes for a compelling combination.

GENERAL INFORMATION

Year founded:	1925
Undergraduate enrollment, full-time:	13,184
Graduate enrollment, full-time:	1375
Faculty, full-time:	920
Number of international students:	864
Male/female ratio (%)	40:60
Residence spaces available:	1990
Residence space guaranteed for 1st-year students:	N/A
Student media website:	www.mun.ca/muse/

UNDERGRADUATE ADMISSIONS

Office of the Registrar
P.O. Box 4200 Station C
St. John's, NL A1C 5S7
PH: 709.737.3200   FAX: 709.737.2337
WEBSITE: **www.mun.ca**

Minimum high school average:	70
Applications, 2005:	N/A
Rolling admissions:	Yes
International fall application deadline:	Mar 1
Application fee:	$80
Domestic fall application deadline:	Mar 1
Application fee:	$40
Electronic application accepted:	Yes
Admissions notification by:	N/A
Required with application:	Varies

UNDERGRADUATE FINANCES

Undergraduate tuition:		
International students:	$8800	(US $7900)
Canadian students:	$2550	(US $2300)
Estimated annual health insurance:	$610	(US $540)
Estimated annual books & supplies:	$1000	(US $900)
Financial aid available for international students:	No	
Scholarships available for international students:	Yes	
Application deadline:	None	
Annual room/board cost for students in residence:	$4826	(US $4343)
Average monthly rent for students living off campus:		
1 bedroom: $450+, 2 bedroom: $550+		
Federal School Code: G09500		

UNDERGRADUATE INSTRUCTIONAL PROGRAM

Most popular majors: Business, Education, Engineering, Nursing
Percentages by program: N/A
Special study options: Co-op programs, internships, study abroad, language programs, special summer programs, distance learning programs

Liberal Arts and Sciences, General Studies, and Humanities

Anthropology, Canadian Studies, Classics & Classical Languages & Literature, Drama/Theater Arts, English Language & Literature, Fine/Studio Arts, Folklore, French Language & Literature, German Language & Literature, Greek Language & Literature, History, Humanities/Humanistic Studies, Italian Language & Literature, Linguistics, Medieval & Renaissance Studies, Native Studies, Newfoundland Studies, Philosophy, Political Science, Psychology, Religion/Religious Studies, Russian & Russian Languages & Literature, Scandinavian Languages & Literatures, Sociology, Spanish Language & Literature, Visual & Performing Arts, Women's Studies

Science and Mathematics

Biochemistry, Biology, Chemistry, Earth & Planetary Sciences, Geography, Marine/Aquatic Sciences, Environmental Studies, Mathematics, Microbiology, Oceanography, Physics, Statistics

Computer Science and Engineering

Computer & Information Sciences, Engineering Science

Professional Studies

Education, Human Kinetics/Kinesiology, Leisure & Recreational Activities

Business and Economics

Accounting, Business Administration & Management/Commerce, Economics

Health Professions and Related Sciences

Nursing, Pharmacy

GRADUATE ADMISSIONS

School of Graduate Studies
Memorial University of Newfoundland
Office of Student Recruitment & Promotion
Arts & Administration Bldg room A3039
St. John's, Newfoundland A1C 5S7
PH: 709.737.2445
WEBSITE: www.mun.ca/sgs/

Fall application deadline:	Varies
Application fee:	$40
Required with application:	College Transcripts, Recommendations
Graduate student housing:	Available, single and family residences

GRADUATE FINANCES

International Graduate tuition:	$2500-4000	(US $2250-3600)
Financial aid & Scholarships available for		
international students:	Yes	
Application deadline:	Varies	

GRADUATE INSTRUCTIONAL PROGRAM

Liberal Arts and Sciences, General Studies, and Humanities

Anthropology, Archaeology, Classics & Classical Languages & Literature, English Language & Literature, Folklore, French Language & Literature, German Language & Literature, Gerontology, Greek Language & Literature, History, Humanities/Humanistic Studies, Linguistics, Philosophy, Political Science, Religion/Religious Studies, Social Work, Sociology, Women's Studies

Science and Mathematics

Aquaculture Operations, Biochemistry, Biology, Biopsychology, Chemistry, Environmental Sciences, Earth & Planetary Sciences, Food Science, Geography, Geology, Geophysics & Seismology, Marine/Aquatic Sciences, Mathematics, Physics, Physical Oceanography

Computer Science and Engineering

Civil Engineering, Computer & Information Sciences, Electrical/Electronics & Communication Engineering, Engineering Sciences, Mechanical Engineering, Ocean & Naval Architectural Engineering, Environmental Engineering

Professional Studies

Counseling, Education, Leisure & Recreational Activities, Physical Education Teaching & Coaching

Business and Economics

Business Administration & Management/Commerce

Health Professions and Related Sciences

Community Health, Immunology, Cardiovascular & Renal Sciences, Human Genetics, Medicine, Neurosciences, Nursing, Pharmacology, Toxicology

NOVA SCOTIA

ACADIA UNIVERSITY

Wolfville, Nova Scotia

SCHOOL CATEGORY: Bachelor's/Liberal Arts **TOTAL ENROLLMENT: 4000** **SETTING: Suburban** **CITY POPULATION: 4000**

Acadia is a small comprehensive university devoted primarily to undergraduate education. Founded in 1838, the school enjoys an idyllic setting in Wolfville, a friendly small town just one hour from the provincial capital, Halifax.

Acadia offers more than 30 programs of study. Every student receives a laptop computer upon enrollment, with the cost built into the tuition as part of a program called the Acadia Advantage that is designed to equip students with the tools necessary for success in the digital age. In 1999 the Acadia Advantage program was recognized by the Smithsonian Institution in Washington, D.C., for innovation in education.

Acadia also prides itself on small class sizes: Nearly half of first- and second-year classes have fewer than 50 students, and more than three-quarters of third- and fourth-year classes have fewer than 25. This low student–faculty ratio allows for close attention to individuals.

Close to half of the students live in residence, and this helps to foster a strong sense of community at the school. Campus life is active, with more than 60 clubs for students to join and excellent athletic facilities. The school is located in the beautiful Annapolis Valley, which offers abundant outdoor recreational activities. Nearby Halifax provides the opportunity to take advantage of city shopping and cultural activities.

Acadia's unique combination of innovation and tradition make it a popular choice for both Canadian and international students.

GENERAL INFORMATION

Year founded:	1838
Undergraduate enrollment, full-time:	4074
Graduate enrollment, full-time:	92
Faculty, full-time:	248
Number of international students:	710
Male/female ratio (%)	46:54
Residence spaces available:	1708
Residence space guaranteed for 1st-year students:	Yes
Student media:	www.acadiau.ca

UNDERGRADUATE ADMISSIONS

Office of Admissions
Wolfville, NS B4P 2R6
PH: **902.585.1222** FAX: **902.585.1081**
WEBSITE: **www.acadiau.ca**

Minimum high school average:	80
Applications, 2000–2001:	N/A
Rolling admissions:	Yes
International fall application deadline:	N/A
Application fee:	$25
Domestic fall application deadline:	Mar 1 (for scholarship consideration)
Application fee:	$25
Electronic application accepted:	Yes
Admissions notification by:	Rolling decisions
Required with application:	HS transcript, SAT, letter of reference

UNDERGRADUATE FINANCES

Undergraduate tuition:		
International students:	$13,810	(US $12,429)
Canadian students:	$7760	(US $6984)
Estimated annual health insurance:	$800	(US $720)
Estimated annual books & supplies:	$700	(US $630)
Financial aid & Scholarships available for		
international students:	Yes	
Application deadline:	Mar 1-Mar 15	
Annual room/board cost for students in residence:	$6014-6525	(US $5400-5870)
Average monthly rent for students living off campus:		
1 bedroom: $400, 2 bedroom: $500		
Federal School Code: G08449		

UNDERGRADUATE INSTRUCTIONAL PROGRAM

Most popular majors: Biology, Business, Computer Science, Kinesiology, Psychology
Percentages by program: N/A
Special study options: Co-op programs, internships, study abroad, language programs, special summer programs, distance learning programs

Liberal Arts and Sciences, General Studies, and Humanities

Canadian Studies, Classics & Classical Languages & Literature, Drama/Theatre Studies, English Language & Literature, Environmental Arts, French Language & Literature, German Language & Literature, History, Latin Language & Literature, Music, Philosophy, Political Science, Psychology, Sociology, Spanish Language & Literature, Theology/Theological Studies, Women's Studies

Science and Mathematics

Biology, Chemistry, Environmental Sciences, Geology, Mathematics, Physics, Statistics

Computer Science and Engineering

Engineering Science, Computer & Information Sciences

Professional Studies

Education, Kinesiology/Human Kinetics, Leisure & Recreation Activities

Business and Economics

Accounting, Business Administration & Management/Commerce, Economics, Finance, Human Resources, Information Sciences & Systems, Marketing Management & Research

Health Professions and Related Sciences

Nutritional Sciences

GRADUATE ADMISSIONS

Division of Research & Graduate Studies
Acadia University
206 Horton Hall/ 18 University Avenue
Wolfville, NS B4P 2R6
PH: **902.585.1498**   FAX: **902.585.1096**
WEBSITE: **www.acadiau.ca/gradstud/**

International fall application deadline:	Feb 1
Application fee:	$50
Domestic fall application deadline:	Feb 1
Application fee:	$50
Required with application:	College transcript, recommendations
Graduate student housing	N/A

GRADUATE FINANCES

Graduate tuition:

International students:	$13,147/1st yr	(US $11,832)
	$5520/2nd yr	(US $4968)
Canadian students:	$3127-6940	(US $2814-6245)

Financial aid & Scholarship available for

International students:	Yes
Application deadline:	Feb 1

GRADUATE INSTRUCTIONAL PROGRAM

Liberal Arts and Sciences, General Studies, and Humanities

English Language & Literature, Political Science, Psychology, Theology/Theological Studies (Acadia Divinity College)

Science and Mathematics

Biology, Chemistry, Computer & Information Science, Geology

Professional Studies

Education, Leisure & Recreation Activities

CAPE BRETON UNIVERSITY

Sydney, Nova Scotia

SCHOOL CATEGORY: Bachelor's/General | **TOTAL ENROLLMENT: 3700** | **SETTING: Suburban** | **CITY POPULATION: 120,000**

Cape Breton University is a small university that was founded in 1974. The school is located near Sydney, the second largest city in Nova Scotia with a population of 120,000.

The University offers programs in the arts, science, and business areas. Learning success is enhanced through small class sizes and a low faculty-student ratio. CBU offers a wide range of co-op programs allowing students to gain valuable work experience that complements classroom study.

Residence spaces are limited. The university's location ensures that there are a variety of conveniently located houses and apartments available for renting off-campus. The university has a full range of athletic facilities and numerous social and cultural clubs.

Cape Breton is a world-renowned tourist destination, coupling rugged scenery and rich cultural heritage of Celtic, French, and Native American traditions. Popular attractions include hiking in the Cape Breton Highlands National Park as well as visits to the reconstructed 18th-century French garrison and village of Louisbourg.

GENERAL INFORMATION

Year founded:	1974
Undergraduate enrollment, full-time:	2800
Graduate enrollment, full-time:	100
Faculty, full-time:	170
Number of international students:	67
Male/female ratio (%)	45:55
Residence spaces available:	275
Residence space guaranteed for 1st-year students:	No
Student media website:	N/A

UNDERGRADUATE ADMISSIONS

Student Service Centre
1230 Grand Lake Road
P.O. Box 5300, Station A
Sydney, NS B1P 6L2
PH: **902.583.1330** FAX: **902.583.1371**
WEBSITE: **www.uccb.ns.ca**

Minimum high school average:	60
Rolling admissions:	Yes
International fall application deadline:	Mar 31
Application fee:	$100
Domestic fall application deadline:	Aug 1
Application fee:	$30
Electronic application accepted:	Yes
Admissions notification by:	N/A
Required with application:	HS transcript

UNDERGRADUATE FINANCES

Undergraduate tuition:		
International students:	$9500	(US $8550)
Canadian students:	$5550	(US $4950)
Estimated annual health insurance:	$550	(US $485)
Estimated annual books & supplies:	$1000	(US $900)
Financial aid available for international students:	No	
Application deadline:	N/A	
Scholarships available for international students:	Yes, after 1st yr	
Application deadline:	Mar 28	
Annual room/board cost for students in residence:	$5000	(US $4500)
Average monthly rent for students living off campus:		
1 bedroom: $600+, 2 bedroom: $700+		

UNDERGRADUATE INSTRUCTIONAL PROGRAM

Most popular majors: Psychology, Business, Environmental Studies, Information Technology, Sociology
Percentages by program: 38% Liberal Arts, 21% business, 17% Science, 6% Engineering/Computer Science, 1% Health Professions
Special study options: Co-op programs, internships, study abroad, language programs, distance learning programs

Liberal Arts and Sciences, General Studies, and Humanities

African Studies, Celtic/Irish Studies, Communications, English Language & Literature, History, Mi'kmaq Studies, Native American Studies, Philosophy, Political Science, Psychology, Sociology

Science and Mathematics

Agriculture Science, Applied Science, Biology, Chemistry, Chemical Technology, Environmental Sciences, Geology, Physics

Computer Science and Engineering

Civil Engineering, Computer & Information Sciences, Electrical/Electronics & Communication Engineering, Environmental/Environmental Health Engineering, Industrial/Manufacturing Engineering, Mechanical Engineering, Motive Power Engineering, Petroleum Engineering

Professional Studies

Community Studies, Education, Hospitality/Administration Management, Tourism, Physical Education Teaching & Coaching

Business and Economics

Accounting, Actuarial Science, Canadian Studies in Business, Business Administration Management/Commerce, Economics, Finance, Geographical Information Systems, Information Sciences & Systems, Marketing Management & Research, Organizational Behavior Studies

Health Professions and Related Sciences

Nursing

GRADUATE ADMISSIONS

Departments of Business & Education
University College of Cape Breton
Sydney, NS   B1P 6L2

Fall application deadline:	May 31
Application fee:	$80
Required with application:	College transcript, essay, interview, (GRE, GMAT for MBA)
Graduate student housing:	N/A

GRADUATE FINANCES

International Graduate tuition:	$15,440	(US $13,900)
Financial aid & scholarships available for		
International students:	N/A	
Application deadline:	N/A	

GRADUATE INSTRUCTIONAL PROGRAM

Professional Studies

Education

Business and Economics

Business Administration & Management/Commerce

DALHOUSIE UNIVERSITY

Halifax, Nova Scotia

SCHOOL CATEGORY: Doctoral/Research	TOTAL ENROLLMENT: 14,500	SETTING: Urban	CITY POPULATION: 350,000

Dalhousie University is a medium-sized university with a long tradition of excellence in research and teaching. Dalhousie was founded in 1818, and the main campus has a blend of modern and historic architecture that reflects both the school's rich past and its vibrant present. A state-of-the-art Computer Science building and a central Arts and Social Sciences building are a reflection of significant new expansion at the school.

Dalhousie offers over 175 undergraduate, graduate and professional degree programs. Traditional strengths in Health Science and Ocean Studies are now being joined by an expanded list of new focus areas such as technical research, information management, materials science, and genomics. DalTech, a newly merged institution, provides advanced technical education and research opportunities to students. The University of King's College is an affiliated liberal arts college. Dalhousie boasts a global alumni network and has produced many famous alumni, including two Canadian prime ministers and numerous Rhodes scholars.

Campus life is very active, with over 150 campus clubs and a strong sports scene. The university's location in a residential area of Halifax ensures that there are a variety of conveniently located houses and apartments available for renting off campus.

Halifax is the commercial and educational center of the Atlantic provinces. Founded in the 1700s as a military base, the city retains a historic central core that is easy to explore on foot. Parts of the blockbuster movie *Titanic* were filmed here. Halifax is a very lively social and cultural center.

GENERAL INFORMATION

Year founded:	1818
Undergraduate enrollment, full-time:	10,000
Graduate enrollment, full-time:	2017
Faculty, full-time:	965
Number of international students:	N/A
Male/female ratio (%)	43:57
Residence spaces available:	2100
Residence space guaranteed for 1st-year students:	Yes (for 80%)
Student media website:	www.thedsu.com

UNDERGRADUATE ADMISSIONS

Registrar's Office
1236 Henry Street
Halifax, NS B3H 3J5
PH: **902.494.6572** FAX: **902.494.2319**
WEBSITE: **www.dal.ca**

Minimum high school average:	70
Applications, 2000-2001:	N/A
Rolling admissions:	No
Fall application deadline:	May 1
Application fee:	$40
Electronic application accepted:	N/A
Admissions notification by:	N/A
Required with application:	HS transcript
Recommended:	SAT/ACT

UNDERGRADUATE FINANCES

Undergraduate tuition:		
International students:	$12,000	(US $10,800)
Canadian students:	$6200	(US $5600)
Estimated annual health insurance:	$600	(US $540)
Estimated annual books & supplies:	$1000	(US $900)
Financial aid available for international students:	N/A	
Application deadline:	N/A	
Scholarships available for international students:	Yes	
Application deadline:	Mar 15	
Annual room/board cost for students in residence:	$7600	(US $6840)

Average monthly rent for students living off campus:
   1 bedroom: $300-350, 2 bedroom: $300-500
Federal School Code: G06838

UNDERGRADUATE INSTRUCTIONAL PROGRAM

Most popular majors: Computer Science, Engineering, Marine Biology
Percentages by program: N/A
Special study options: Co-op programs, internships, study abroad, language programs, special summer programs, distance learning programs

Liberal Arts and Sciences, General Studies, and Humanities

African Studies, Arts, Canadian Studies, Classics & Classical Languages & Literature, Drama/Theater Arts, English Language & Literature, French Language & Literature, German Language & Literature, History, Humanities/Humanistic Studies, International Relations & Affairs, Linguistics, Music, Philosophy, Political Science, Psychology, Religion/Religious Studies, Social Work, Sociology, Visual & Performing Arts, Women's Studies

Science and Mathematics

Biology, Biochemistry, Chemistry, Earth & Planetary Science, Environmental/Environmental Health Engineering, Environmental Sciences, Marine/Aquatic Biology, Mathematics, Microbiology, Neuroscience, Oceanography, Physics, Statistics

Computer Science and Engineering

Bioengineering & Biomedical Engineering, Chemical Engineering, Civil Engineering, Computer & Information Sciences, Computer Engineering, Electrical/Electronics & Communication Engineering, Food Science & Technology, Industrial/Manufacturing Engineering, Mechanical Engineering, Metallurgical Engineering, Mining & Mineral Engineering

Professional Studies

Contemporary Studies, Costume Studies, Film Studies, Kinesiology/Human Kinetics, Leisure & Recreational Activities

Business and Economics

Business Administration & Management/Commerce, Economics, Human Resources Management, Public Administration

Health Professions and Related Sciences

Disability Management, Health & Human Performance, Health Education, Health Sciences, Health Services Administration, Nursing, Occupational Therapy, Pharmacology, Physiology & Biophysics, Physiotherapy

GRADUATE ADMISSIONS

Faculty of Graduate Studies
Rm 314, A & A Building
Halifax, NS   B3H 4H6
PH: **902.494.2485**   FAX: **902.494.8797**
WEBSITE: **www.dalgrad.dal.ca**

International fall application deadline:	Mar 1-Jun 1
Application fee:	N/A
Domestic fall application deadline:	Apr 1
Application fee:	N/A
Required with application:	College transcript & departmental requirements
Graduate student housing:	4 residence housing for mature students; apartments available for singles & married students at Fenwick Place

GRADUATE FINANCES

Graduate tuition:		
International students:	$13000	(US $11,700)
Canadian students:	$6600	(US $5940)
Financial aid & Scholarships available for		
international students:	Yes	
Application deadline:	Mar 1	

GRADUATE INSTRUCTIONAL PROGRAM

Liberal Arts and Sciences, General Studies, and Humanities

Anthropology, Classics & Classical Languages & Literature, English Language & Literature, French Language & Literature, German Language & Literature, History, Political Science, Psychology, Social Work, Sociology, Women's Studies

Science and Mathematics

Agriculture Sciences, Applied Mathematics, Atmospheric Sciences & Meteorology, Biological Sciences/Life Sciences, Biochemistry, Biology, Biophysics, Biotechnology Research, Chemistry, Earth & Planetary Science, Marine/Aquatic Science, Mathematics, Physics, Physiology, Statistics

Computer Science and Engineering

Bioengineering & Biomedical Engineering, Chemical Engineering, Civil Engineering, Computer & Information Sciences, Computer Engineering, Industrial/Manufacturing Engineering, Mechanical Engineering, Mining & Metallurgical Engineering, Electrical/ Electronics & Communication Engineering, Engineering Physics, Engineering Science, Geological Engineering

Professional Studies

Architecture, City/Urban/Community & Regional Planning, Food Science & Technology, Leisure & Recreational Activities

Business and Economics

Business Administration & Management/Commerce, Economics, Internetworking, Library & Information Studies, Public Administration

Health Professions and Related Sciences

Anatomy & Neurobiology, Community Health & Epidemiology, Dentistry, Health Education, Health Services Administration, Human Kinetics/Kinesiology, Medicine, Microbiology & Immunology, Neuroscience, Nursing, Occupational Therapy, Oral Maxillofacial Surgery, Pathology, Pharmacology, Physiotherapy, Speech-Language Pathology & Audiology

MOUNT SAINT VINCENT UNIVERSITY

Halifax, Nova Scotia

SCHOOL CATEGORY: Bachelor's/Liberal Arts   **TOTAL ENROLLMENT: 4000**   **SETTING: Suburban**   **CITY POPULATION: 350,000**

Mount Saint Vincent University is a small university dedicated to the education of women, who make up more than 75 percent of the university's students. The school has an attractive suburban campus overlooking the port of Halifax.

The university offers a strong core of liberal arts and science as well as a limited number of professional disciplines. Numerous special centers enrich the learning experience: the Catherine Wallace Center for Women in Science, the Institute for the Study of Women, and the Center for Women in Business. Mount Saint Vincent is a leader in distance learning, with more than 1,000 students enrolled in various programs leading to certificates, or to bachelor's or master's degrees. Co-op education is also a strong focus of the school.

Residence spaces are limited. The university's location ensures that there are a variety of conveniently located houses and apartments available for renting off campus. The school has excellent on-campus athletic facilities and numerous social and cultural clubs.

Halifax, with a population of 350,000, is the largest city in Nova Scotia and a cultural and business center for the Atlantic provinces. The city and port have enjoyed a colorful history since their founding 250 years ago as a British military center. With its gleaming waterfront, beautiful parks, and unique blend of modern and historic architecture, Halifax is a fascinating medium-sized city.

The university's picturesque setting, emphasis on programs for women, and innovative programs make it a very strong choice.

GENERAL INFORMATION

Year founded:	1873
Undergraduate enrollment, full-time:	2130
Graduate enrollment, full-time:	60
Faculty, full-time:	160
Number of international students:	N/A
Male/female ratio (%)	20:80
Residence spaces available:	250
Residence space guaranteed for 1st-year students:	N/A
Student media website:	www.msvu.ca/studentsunion/

UNDERGRADUATE ADMISSIONS

Admissions Office
166 Bedford Highway
Halifax, NS B3M 2J6
PH: 902.457.6128   FAX: 902.457.6455
WEBSITE: www.msvu.ca

Minimum high school average:	65
Applications, 2000-2001:	N/A
Rolling admissions:	No
International fall application deadline:	June 17
Application fee:	$30
Domestic fall application deadline:	Aug 1
Application fee:	$30
Electronic application accepted:	Yes
Admissions notification by:	N/A
Required with application:	HS transcript, SAT

UNDERGRADUATE FINANCES

Undergraduate tuition:		
International students:	$10,800	(US $9720)
Canadian students:	$5600	(US $5000)
Estimated annual health insurance:	$500	(US $450)
Estimated annual books & supplies:	$1000	(US $900)
Financial aid available for international students:	Yes	
Application deadline:	Varies	
Scholarships available for international students:	Yes	
Application deadline:	Mar 15	
Annual room/board cost for students in residence:	$4300-7200	(US $3900-6500)
Average monthly rent for students living off campus:		
1 bedroom: $400-500, 2 bedroom: $550-750		
Federal School Code: G08363		

UNDERGRADUATE INSTRUCTIONAL PROGRAM

Most popular majors: Business, Family Studies, Tourism, Women's Studies
Percentages by program: N/A
Special study options: Co-op programs, internships, study abroad, language programs, special summer programs, distance learning programs

Liberal Arts and Sciences, General Studies, and Humanities

Anthropology, Art, Art History, Canadian Studies, Cultural Studies, Curriculum Studies, English Language & Literature, Gerontology, History, Liberal Arts, Linguistics, Peace & Conflict Studies, Philosophy, Political Science, Psychology, Public Relations, Religion/Religious Studies, Spanish Language & Literature, Sociology, Visual & Performing Arts, Women's Studies

Science and Mathematics

Biology, Chemistry, Mathematics, Physics

Professional Studies

Child Growth/Care/Development Studies, Education, Family & Community Studies, Leisure & Recreational Activities, Tourism

Business and Economics

Information Sciences & Systems, Management

Health Professions and Related Sciences

Nutrition

GRADUATE ADMISSIONS

Graduate Admissions Office
Mount Saint Vincent University
166 Bedford Highway
Halifax, NS B3M 2J6
PH: **902.457.6128**   FAX: **902.457.6498**
WEBSITE: **www.msvu.ca/calendar/graduate**

International fall application deadline: June 15
   Application fee: N/A
Domestic fall application deadline: Mar-May
   Application fee: N/A
Required with application: GRE, college transcript, essay, recommendations, portfolio required for some programs
Graduate student housing: Townhouses for international & mature students

GRADUATE FINANCES

Graduate tuition:

International students:	$12,800	(US $11,500)
Canadian students:	$7400	(US $6700)

Financial aid & Scholarships available for
   international students: Yes
   Application deadline: N/A

GRADUATE INSTRUCTIONAL PROGRAM

Liberal Arts and Sciences, General Studies, and Humanities
School Psychology, Gerontology, Women's Studies

Professional Studies
Child & Youth Study, Adult Education, Curriculum Studies, Educational Foundations, Educational Psychology, Elementary Education, Family & Community Studies, Human Ecology, Literacy Education

Health Professions
Nutrition

NOVA SCOTIA AGRICULTURAL COLLEGE

Truro, Nova Scotia

SCHOOL CATEGORY: Specialized   **TOTAL ENROLLMENT: 950**   **SETTING: Rural**   **CITY POPULATION: 45,000**

The Nova Scotia Agricultural College (NSAC) is an internationally respected teaching and research institution providing education in the science and management of agriculture and related disciplines. The rural campus is located less than two miles from the town of Truro in central Nova Scotia and within an hour's drive of Halifax. The school's extensive fields, experimental plots, and scenic location along the Salmon River combine to create an idyllic learning environment.

NSAC grants bachelor and graduate degrees in conjunction with Dalhousie University. The school offers a Bachelor of Science in Agriculture program as well as a Bachelor of Technology in Landscape Horticulture. Moderate class sizes, excellent facilities, and dedicated professors foster a challenging and supportive learning environment.

The school offers limited residence space, but off-campus housing is available in nearby Truro. The school offers a good mix of recreational and cultural activities.

The province offers extensive opportunities for both recreational and cultural activities. The region's close proximity to the Atlantic Ocean and its rugged terrain offer sporting activities such as hiking, fishing, and sailing.

GENERAL INFORMATION

Year founded:	1906
Undergraduate enrollment, full-time:	800
Graduate enrollment, full-time:	20
Faculty, full-time:	75
Number of international students:	35
Male/female ratio (%)	40:60
Residence spaces available:	350
Residence space guaranteed for 1st-year students:	No
Student media website:	www.nsac.ns.ca/su/

UNDERGRADUATE ADMISSIONS

Office of the Registrar
P.O. Box 550 Station Main
Truro, NS   B2N 5E3
PH: 902.893.6722   FAX: 902.895.5529
WEBSITE: www.nsac.ns.ca

Minimum high school average:	60
Applications, 2000-2001:	N/A
Rolling admissions:	Yes
International fall application deadline:	Apr 1
Application fee:	$25
Domestic fall application deadline:	Aug 1
Application fee:	$25
Electronic application accepted:	Yes
Admissions notification by:	N/A
Required with application:	HS Transcripts

UNDERGRADUATE FINANCES

Undergraduate tuition:		
International students:	$11,000	(US $9900)
Canadian students:	$5500	(US $4950)
Estimated annual health insurance:	$650	(US $585)
Estimated annual books & supplies:	$1000	(US $900)
Financial aid available for international students:	No	
Application deadline:	N/A	
Scholarships available for international students:	Yes	
Application deadline:	Varies	
Annual room/board cost for students in residence:	$5800-6800	(US $5200-6100)
Residence space guaranteed for first-year students:	No	
Average monthly rent for students living off campus:		
1 bedroom: $300+, 2 bedroom: $400+		

UNDERGRADUATE INSTRUCTIONAL PROGRAM

Most popular majors: Animal Science, Aquaculture, Agri-Business
Percentages by program: 90% Science, 5% Business, 5% Engineering/Computer Science
Special study options: Internships, study abroad, language programs (ESL)

Science and Mathematics

Agriculture Sciences, Animal Science, Aquaculture, Biological Sciences/Life Sciences, Biology, Botany, Ecology, Entomology, Environmental Sciences, Fisheries Sciences & Management, Forestry Sciences, Genetics/Plant & Animal, Horticulture Science, Mathematics, Marine/Aquatic Biology, Microbiology/Bacteriology, Natural Resources Management & Protective Services, Oceanography, Physics, Physiology/Human & Animal, Plant Sciences, Statistics, Zoology

Computer Science and Engineering

(Bioengineering Engineering, Chemical Engineering, Civil Engineering, Electrical Engineering, Industrial Engineering, Mechanical Engineering, Metallurgical Engineering & Mining Engineering)*

Professional Studies

Landscape Architecture

Business and Economics

Agricultural Business & Engineering, Agriculture & Resource Economics, Aquaculture Operations & Production Management, Business Administration & Management/Commerce

Health Professions & Related Sciences

Pre-Veterinary Medicine

*Through Dalhousie University

GRADUATE ADMISSIONS

Research & Graduate Studies
Nova Scotia Agricultural College
Truro, NS B2N 5E3
WEBSITE: **www.nsac.ns.ca/rgs/graduate/**

International fall application deadline:	Jan 1
Application fee:	$50
Domestic fall application deadline:	Mar 1
Application fee:	$50
Electronic application accepted:	Yes
Required with application:	Transcripts
Graduate student housing:	Available off campus at Atlantic Agri-Tech Park

GRADUATE FINANCES

Graduate tuition:		
International students:	$11,000	(US $9900)
Canadian students:	$5500	(US $4950)
Financial aid available for international students:	N/A	
Application deadline:	N/A	
Scholarships available for international students:	Yes	
Application deadline:	N/A	

GRADUATE INSTRUCTIONAL PROGRAM

Science and Mathematics

Mathematics, Physics, Statistics

Computer Science and Engineering

Agricultural Sciences, Agricultural Waste Management, Environmental Management

NOVA SCOTIA COLLEGE OF ART & DESIGN

Halifax, Nova Scotia

SCHOOL CATEGORY: Specialized   **TOTAL ENROLLMENT: 1000**   **SETTING: Urban**   **CITY POPULATION: 350,000**

The Nova Scotia College of Art and Design (NSCAD) is a principal Canadian center of excellence in the visual arts. The school is located in beautiful historic buildings on the waterfront of downtown Halifax.

The College offers four-year undergraduate programs leading to the Bachelor of Fine Arts, the Bachelor of Design, and the Bachelor of Arts in Visual Arts. The College also offers two graduate-degree programs: a Masters of Fine Arts degree and a Master of Arts degree in Art Education. The Foundation Year is required first-year program designed to give students a solid grounding in fundamental techniques and an understanding of artistic traditions. All students are assigned advisers.

NSCAD does not offer its own residence spaces to students. However housing is available through Dalhousie University. Reasonably priced off-campus housing is available nearby. Students are eligible for exchanges with various Canadian and American art colleges.

Halifax is known as one of Canada's foremost centers of higher learning as well as one of the largest ports on the Atlantic Coast. The city and port have enjoyed a colorful history since their founding 250 years ago as a British military center. With its gleaming waterfront, beautiful parks, and unique blend of modern and historic architecture, Halifax is a fascinating medium sized city.

GENERAL INFORMATION

Year founded:	1887
Undergraduate enrollment, full-time:	850
Graduate enrollment, full-time:	13
Faculty, full-time:	42
Number of international students:	37
Male/female ratio (%)	35:65
Residence spaces available:	No
Residence space guaranteed for 1st-year students:	No
Student media website:	www.nscad.ns.ca/student_union

UNDERGRADUATE ADMISSIONS

Office of Student Academic Services
5163 Duke Street
Halifax, NS B3J 3J6
PH: **902.494.8129**   FAX: **902.494.2987**
URL: **www.nscad.ns.ca**

Minimum high school average:	70
Rolling Admissions:	No
Fall application deadline:	Apr 1-May 15
Application fee:	$35
Electronic application accepted:	No
Admissions notification by:	N/A
Required with application:	HS transcript, essay, recommendations, portfolio required for some program

UNDERGRADUATE FINANCES

Undergraduate tuition:		
International students:	$12,000	(US $10,800)
Canadian students:	$5700	(US $5130)
Estimated annual health insurance:	$400	(US $360)
Estimated annual books & supplies:	$1900	(US $1710)
Financial aid available for international student:	Yes, once enrolled	
Application deadline:	N/A	
Scholarships available for international students:	Yes	
Application deadline:	Early Sept & Jan	
Annual room/board cost for students in residence:	N/A	
Average monthly rent for students living off campus:		
1 bedroom $400-650; 2 bedroom: $500-750		
Federal School Code: G10123		

UNDERGRADUATE INSTRUCTIONAL PROGRAM

Most popular majors: Design, Fine Arts, Graphic Design, Photography
Percentages by program: 100% Arts
Special study options: Internships, study abroad, special summer programs, distance learning programs (limited)

Arts/Fine Arts

Art, Art History, Ceramic Arts & Ceramics, Environmental Design, Fine/Studio Arts, Graphic Design, Jewelry Design & Metalsmithing, Media Arts, Photography, Textiles

BA International Graphic Design: Graphic Design (with Universidad de las Americas, Pueblo Mexico)

GRADUATE ADMISSIONS

MA/MFA Admissions
NSCAD
Halifax, NS B3J 3J6
WEBSITE: **www.nscad.ns.ca/graduate/**

International & Domestic fall		
application deadline:	Jan 31	
Application fee:	$35	(US $25)
Electronic application accepted:	No	
Required with application:	College transcript, Personal statement, Portfolio, Recommendations,	
Graduate student housing:	N/A	

GRADUATE FINANCES

Graduate tuition:		
International students:	$12,000	(US $10,800)
Canadian students:	$5700	(US $5130)
Financial aid & Scholarships available		
for international students:	N/A	
Application deadline:	N/A	

GRADUATE INSTRUCTIONAL PROGRAM

Arts: Education
MFA: Design; Environmental Planning, Digital Communications Design, Communications Design, Crafts, Ceramics, Jewelry Design, Metalsmithing, Textiles

ST. FRANCIS XAVIER UNIVERSITY

Antigonish, Nova Scotia

SCHOOL CATEGORY: Bachelor's/Liberal Arts | **TOTAL ENROLLMENT: 5000** | **SETTING: Suburban** | **CITY POPULATION: 6000**

St. Francis Xavier University (StFX) is a leading national university with a longstanding tradition of academic excellence, service to society and innovation in teaching. StFX is ranked as one of the leading undergraduate universities in Canada.

StFX offers over 30 programs at the undergraduate and graduate levels through departments in the faculties of Arts and Science. StFX offers students a low student to faculty ratio, small class sizes and a friendly, supportive environment to pursue learning.

The StFX scholarship program recognizes superior scholastic achievement by entering students and those who are currently enrolled at the university. In recent years approximately 20 percent of students have been scholarship holders.

StFX has a long and illustrious history. One of the driving forces behind the institution's legacy and tradition has been the loyalty of its alumni, nearly 50,000 worldwide, and the strength of their support.

The historic StFX campus is located in the town of Antigonish, the Highland Heart of Nova Scotia, along the northeastern shore of the province. Home to warm sandy beaches and scenic nature trails, northeastern Nova Scotia is an ideal area for year-round outdoor activity or the quiet enjoyment of nature.

GENERAL INFORMATION

Year founded:	1853
Undergraduate enrollment, full-time:	4200
Graduate enrollment, full-time:	100
Faculty, full-time:	190
Number of international students:	215
Male/female ratio (%)	50:50
Residence spaces available:	1800
Residence space guaranteed for 1st-year students:	Yes
Student media website:	www.stfxu.ca/xw/

UNDERGRADUATE ADMISSIONS

Department of Admissions
P.O. Box 5000
Antigonish, NS B2G 2W5
PH: 902.863.3300
WEBSITE: **www.stfx.ca**

Minimum high school average:	70
Applications, 2000-2001:	N/A
Rolling admissions:	Yes
Fall application deadline:	Mar 1
Application fee:	$40
Electronic application accepted:	Yes
Admissions notification by:	N/A
Required with application:	HS Transcripts, essay, recommendations

UNDERGRADUATE FINANCES

Undergraduate tuition:		
International students:	$10,875	(US $9800)
Canadian students:	$5975	(US $5400)
Estimated annual health insurance:	N/A	
Estimated annual books & supplies:	$1200	(US $1080)
Financial aid & Scholarships available for		
international students:	N/A	
Application deadline:	Mar 1	
Annual room/board cost for students in residence:	$6500	(US $5850)
Average monthly rent for students living off campus:		
1 bedroom: $350-450; 2 bedroom: $500-600		
Federal School Code: G06681		

UNDERGRADUATE INSTRUCTIONAL PROGRAM

Most popular majors: Business, Biology, Celtic Studies, Education
Percentages by program: 34% Sciences, 33% Liberal Arts, 12% Business, 12% Engineering/Computer
Special study options: N/A

Liberal Arts and Sciences, General Studies, and Humanities

Anthropology, Catholic Resources, Celtic Studies, English Language & Literature, French Language & Literature, History, Music, Philosophy, Political Science, Psychology, Religion/ Religious Studies, Sociology, Spanish Language & Literature, Women's Studies

Science and Mathematics

Aquatic Resources, Biology, Chemistry, Geology, Mathematics, Physics, Statistics

Computer Science and Engineering

Computer & Information Sciences, Engineering Science

Professional Studies

Education, Human Kinetics/Kinesiology

Business and Economics

Accounting, Aquaculture Operations & Production Management, Business Administration & Management/Commerce, Economics, Management Information Systems & Business Data Processing, Marketing Management & Research, Operations Management & Supervision

Health Professions and Related Sciences

Nursing, Nutrition

GRADUATE ADMISSIONS

Department of Graduate Studies
St. Francis Xavier University
Antigonish, NS B2G 2W5
WEBSITE: **www.stfx.ca/stfxismore/programs/graduate**

Fall application deadline:	N/A
Application fee:	N/A
Required with application:	N/A
Graduate student housing:	West Street apts. for upper level students

GRADUATE FINANCES

Graduate tuition:

International students:	$10,925	(US $9835)
Canadian students:	$6025	(US $5425)
Financial aid & Scholarships available for		
international students:	N/A	
Application deadline:	N/A	

GRADUATE INSTRUCTIONAL PROGRAM

Liberal Arts and Sciences, General Studies, and Humanities
Celtic Studies

Science and Mathematics
Biology, Chemistry, Earth Science, Physics

Professional Studies
Education

SAINT MARY'S UNIVERSITY

Halifax, Nova Scotia

SCHOOL CATEGORY: Bachelor's/General   **TOTAL ENROLLMENT: 8000**   **SETTING: Urban**   **CITY POPULATION: 350,000**

Saint Mary's University is one of Canada's oldest universities, celebrating it's 200th anniversary in 2002, and a has a reputation for excellence in teaching and research. Saint Mary's has an urban location near downtown Halifax. The beautiful tree-lined campus is found in the South End of the city.

Saint Mary's offers over 50 programs primarily at the undergraduate and graduate level. Business is the most popular program at St.Mary's and the Frank Sobey Faculty of Commerce is one of the leading business schools in Eastern Canada. Excellent pre-professional programs are offered in law, medicine, dentistry and architecture. A wide selection of programs provide a co-op education option, allowing students to mix academics with practical skills.

Residence spaces for first year students are available on a first-come, first-served basis. Athletics play a big part in campus life here. The school has excellent athletic facilities and strong team spirit in support of the Huskies. There is a wide variety of student organizations on campus and ample opportunities for participating and making new friends.

The campus is only minutes from shopping areas, restaurants and live entertainment spots. Halifax is a vibrant, cosmopolitan, coastal city with the second largest harbor in the world and a rich and varied history. Halifax is the Atlantic region's center for business, education and research.

GENERAL INFORMATION

Year founded:	1802
Undergraduate enrollment, full-time:	7000
Graduate enrollment, full-time:	300
Faculty, full-time:	300
Number of international students:	1000
Male/female ratio (%)	48:52
Residence spaces available:	1000
Residence space guaranteed for 1st-year students:	N/A
Student media website:	www.stmarys.ca/students/journal

UNDERGRADUATE ADMISSIONS

923 Robie Street
Halifax, NS   B3H 3C3
PH: **902.420.5415**   FAX: **902.496.8100**
WEBSITE: **www.stmarys.ca**

Minimum high school average:	70
Applications, 2000-2001:	N/A
Rolling admissions:	N/A
Fall application deadline:	Apr 1
Application fee:	$40
Electronic application accepted:	N/A
Admissions notification by:	N/A
Required with application:	HS transcripts, essay, recommendations

UNDERGRADUATE FINANCES

Undergraduate tuition:		
International students:	$11,000	(US $9900)
Canadian students:	$5700	(US $5130)
Estimated annual health insurance:	$590	(US $530)
Estimated annual books & supplies:	$1000	(US $900)
Financial aid & Scholarships available for		
international students:	Yes	
Application deadline:	May 1	
Annual room/board cost for students in residence:	$4500	(US $4050)

Average monthly rent for students living off campus:
1 bedroom: $450-800, 2 bedroom: $500-1000
Federal School Code: G08364

UNDERGRADUATE INSTRUCTIONAL PROGRAM

Most popular majors: Atlantic Canada Studies, Environmental Sciences, Forensic Sciences
Percentages by program: N/A
Special study options: N/A

Liberal Arts and Sciences, General Studies, and Humanities

Anthropology, Art, Asian Studies, Canadian Studies, Celtic/Irish Studies, Classics, English Language & Literature, French Language & Literature, German Language & Literature, Film Studies, History, International Relations & Affairs, Linguistics, Philosophy, Psychology, Political Science, Religious Studies, Sociology, Spanish Language & Literature, Women's Studies

Science and Mathematics

Astronomy, Biology, Environmental Sciences, Forensic Science, Geography, Mathematics

Computer Science and Engineering

Computer & Information Sciences, Engineering Science

Professional Studies

Criminal Justice Studies

Business and Economics

Business Administration & Management/Commerce, Economics, Entrepreneurship, Finance, Human Resource Management, Industrial Relations, Management Information Systems, Marketing Management & Research

GRADUATE ADMISSIONS

Office of Graduate Studies & Research
Saint Mary's University
Halifax, NS B3H 3C3
WEBSITE: **www.stmarys.ca/academic/ogsr**
PH: **902.420.5406**   FAX: **902.420.5104**

Fall application deadline:	May 31 (MBA on rolling basis)
Application fee:	$50
Required with application:	Transcript, 2 letters of recommendations
Graduate student housing:	Apartment-style and family housing

GRADUATE FINANCES

Graduate tuition:

International students:	$12,600	(US $11,340)
Canadian students:	$7200	(US $6552)

Financial aid & Scholarships available for

International students:	N/A
Application deadline:	N/A

GRADUATE INSTRUCTIONAL PROGRAM

Liberal Arts and Sciences, General Studies, and Humanities

Applied Psychology, Atlantic Canada Studies, Astronomy, Criminology, History, International Development Studies, Philosophy, Women's Studies

Science and Mathematics

Astronomy

Business and Economics

Business Administration & Management/Commerce

UNIVERSITÉ SAINTE-ANNE

Pointe-de-l'Eglise, Nova Scotia

SCHOOL CATEGORY: Bachelor's   **TOTAL ENROLLMENT: 400**   **SETTING: Urban**   **CITY POPULATION: 10,000**

The Université Sainte-Anne is a small French-language university located on the shores of Baie Sainte-Marie. Since the school's founding in 1890, it has played a central role in the development of the Acadian culture.

The program of instruction in French consists of various programs in the arts, business administration, science, and education. The school also offers a two year pre-veterinary preparatory program for entry into the Atlantic Veterinary School at the University of Prince Edward Island.

The school is very well known for its French-immersion programs. Offered at various times throughout the year and varying in length from intensive four-week sessions to longer 100-day programs, these sessions are an excellent way to acquire fluency in the French language quickly.

Students at the Université Sainte-Anne are treated to a unique Acadian cultural curriculum of music, literature, and various performing arts in addition to their language instruction. Accommodations are on site, and an abundance of outdoor activities are available in the area. If learning a new language and culture are part of your plans, the Université Sainte-Anne is worth a closer examination.

GENERAL INFORMATION

Year founded:	1890
Undergraduate enrollment, full-time:	400
Graduate enrollment, full-time:	N/A
Faculty, full-time:	N/A
Number of international students:	N/A
Male/female ratio (%)	30:70
Residence spaces available:	365
Residence space guaranteed for 1st-year students:	Yes

UNDERGRADUATE ADMISSIONS

Pointe-de-l'Eglise, NS   B0W 1M0
PH: 902.769.2114   FAX: 902.769.2930
WEBSITE: www.usainteanne.ca

Fall application deadline:	Mar 25
Application fee:	$30
Electronic application accepted:	N/A
Admissions notification by:	N/A
Required with application:	HS transcript

UNDERGRADUATE FINANCES

Undergraduate tuition:		
International students:	$9250	(US $8325)
Canadian students:	$5450	(US $4900)
Estimated annual health insurance:	$500	(US $450)
Estimated annual books & supplies:	$1000	(US $900)
Financial aid & Scholarships available for		
international students:	N/A	
Application deadline:	N/A	
Annual room/board cost for students in residence:	$6000	(US $5400)
Average monthly rent for students living off campus:		
1 bedroom: $350-450, 2 bedroom: $550 +		

UNDERGRADUATE INSTRUCTIONAL PROGRAM

Most popular majors: Arts, French, Education
Percentages by program: N/A
Special study options: Co-op programs, internships, study abroad, language programs, special summer programs, distance learning programs

Liberal Arts and Sciences, General Studies, and Humanities

Acadian Studies, Canadian Studies, Drama/Theater, English Language & Literature, French Language & Literature, History

Science and Mathematics

Biochemistry, Mathematics, Physics

Professional Studies

Education

Business and Economics

Business Administration & Management/Commerce

Health Professions and Related Sciences

Pre-Veterinary Medicine

UNIVERSITY OF KING'S COLLEGE

Halifax, Nova Scotia

SCHOOL CATEGORY: Bachelor's/Liberal Arts   **TOTAL ENROLLMENT: 1000**   **SETTING: Urban**   **CITY POPULATION: 350,000**

The University of King's College, founded in 1789, is one of the oldest universities in Canada. King's, a small liberal arts college, is affiliated with Dalhousie University. Students share Dalhousie's facilities and services while enjoying the unique community of a smaller school.

The college offers programs in arts, science, and journalism. A unique aspect of the curriculum is the Foundation Year Program, which takes an interdisciplinary approach to the exploration of Western culture.

Most first-year students live in residence. The university's location in a residential area of Halifax ensures that there are a variety of conveniently located houses and apartments available for renting off campus. The King's College community spirit is very strong, and students also have access to Dalhousie's more than 150 campus clubs and extensive sporting activities.

Halifax is the commercial, technological, and educational center of Atlantic Canada. Founded in the 1700s as a military base, the city retains a historic central core that is easy to explore on foot. With its gleaming waterfront, beautiful parks, and lively cultural scene, Halifax is a fascinating medium- sized city.

GENERAL INFORMATION

Year founded:	1789
Undergraduate enrollment, full-time:	1000
Graduate enrollment, full-time:	N/A
Faculty, full-time:	40
Number of international students:	N/A
Male/female ratio (%):	45:55
Residence spaces available:	246
Residence space guaranteed for 1st-year students:	Yes
Student media website:	www.novanewsnet.ukings.ns.ca/

UNDERGRADUATE ADMISSIONS

Registrar's Office
1236 Henry Street
Halifax, NS   B3H 3J5
PH: **902..422.1271**   FAX: **902.423.3357**
WEBSITE: **www.ukings.ns.ca**

Minimum high school average:	70
Applications, 2000-2001:	N/A
Rolling admissions:	N/A
Fall application deadline:	Jun 1
Application fee:	$35
Electronic application accepted:	N/A
Admissions notification by:	N/A
Required with application:	HS transcript
Recommended:	SAT/ACT

UNDERGRADUATE FINANCES

Undergraduate tuition:		
International students:	$12,000	(US $10,800)
Canadian students:	$6000	(US $5400)
Estimated annual health insurance:	$500	(US $450)
Estimated annual books & supplies:	$900	(US $810)
Financial aid & Scholarships available for		
international students:	N/A	
Application deadline:	N/A	
Annual room/board cost for students in residence:	$7500	(US $6750)
Average monthly rent for students living off campus:		
1 bedroom: $300-350, 2 bedroom: $300-500		

UNDERGRADUATE INSTRUCTIONAL PROGRAM

Most popular majors: Journalism, Liberal Arts
Percentages by program: N/A
Special study options: Through Dalhousie University

Liberal Arts and Sciences, General Studies, and Humanities*

Classics & Classical Languages & Literature, Comparative Religion, Contemporary Studies, English, French, German, History, International Development Studies, Linguistics, Philosophy, Political Science, Psychology, Russian & Slavic Area Studies, Sociology & Social Anthropology, Spanish Language & Literature, Theater, Women's Studies

Science and Mathematics*

Biochemistry, Biology, Chemistry, Earth & Planetary Science, Marine/Aquatic Science, Mathematics, Microbiology, Neurobiology, Physics, Statistics

Computer Science and Engineering*

Computer & Information Sciences

Professional Studies

Journalism

Business and Economics*

Economics

*In Conjunction with Dalhousie University

PRINCE EDWARD

UNIVERSITY OF PRINCE EDWARD ISLAND

Charlottetown, Prince Edward Island

SCHOOL CATEGORY: Bachelor's/General   **TOTAL ENROLLMENT: 4000**   **SETTING: Suburban**   **CITY POPULATION: 60,000**

The University of Prince Edward Island is a small, primarily undergraduate university that combines teaching excellence with research innovation. The school is steeped in the traditions of more than 200 years of higher education on Prince Edward Island.

Although the tree-lined, historic core of the campus proudly traces its roots back to 1804, most facilities are either recently built or recently expanded and renovated. The Duffy Science Centre has been completely redesigned. The National Research Council Institute for Nutrisciences and Health brings a remarkable new science platform, to be joined by a $32 million expansion of the Atlantic Veterinary College.

UPEI provides a rich blend of academic programs in Arts, Science, Business, Education, Nursing and Veterinary Medicine to over 4000 students.

Residence space is limited and is available on a first-come, first-served basis. A gleaming new apartment-style residence has transformed the south face of campus. The university's location in a residential area of Charlottetown ensures that there are a variety of conveniently located houses and apartments available for renting off campus. The school offers a full range of athletic facilities.

Prince Edward Island offers many recreational opportunities and cultural events. Students can choose to go hiking, skiing, fishing, windsurfing, kayaking, golfing, or snowboarding, among the many outdoor opportunities. PEI is justly famous for its many miles of sandy beaches, as well as for its laid-back lifestyle.

A great university should be transformative: for students, for the power of knowledge, for communities, and for the future. That's the principle behind everything at the University of Prince Edward Island.

GENERAL INFORMATION

Year founded:	1969
Undergraduate enrollment, full-time:	3383
Graduate enrollment, full-time:	96
Faculty, full-time:	200
Number of international students:	230
Male/female ratio (%)	40:60
Residence spaces available:	400
Residence space guaranteed for 1st-year students:	No
Student media website:	www.upeisu.com/

UNDERGRADUATE ADMISSION

Registrar's Office
550 University Avenue
Charlottetown, PEI C1A 4P3
PH: 902.894.2801   FAX: 902.566.0420
WEBSITE: www.upei.ca

Minimum high school average:	70
Applications, 2005:	N/A
Rolling admissions:	No
International fall application deadline:	Apr 1
Application fee:	$75
Domestic fall application deadline:	Aug 13
Application fee:	$75
Electronic application accepted:	No
Admissions notification by:	N/A
Required with application:	HS transcripts

UNDERGRADUATE FINANCES

Undergraduate tuition:		
International students:	$8430	(US $7587)
Canadian students:	$4620	(US $4158)
Estimated annual health insurance:	$647	(US $582)
Estimated annual books & supplies:	$1000	(US $900)
Financial aid available for international students:	No	
Application deadline:	N/A	
Scholarships available for international students:	Yes (limited)	
Application deadline:	Mar 1	
Annual room/board cost for students in residence:	$7800	(US $7020)
Average monthly rent for students living off campus:		
1 bedroom: $375+, 2 bedroom: $600+		
Federal School Code: G09367		

UNDERGRADUATE INSTRUCTIONAL PROGRAM

Most popular majors: Arts, Science, Business, Nursing, Veterinary Medicine
Percentages by program: N/A
Special study options: Co-op programs, internships, study abroad, language programs, special summer programs, distance learning programs (limited)

Liberal Arts and Sciences, General Studies, and Humanities

Asian Studies, Canadian Studies, Classics & Classical Languages & Literature, English Language & Literature, Fine Arts, History, Modern Languages, Music, Philosophy, Political Science, Psychology, Religion/Religious Studies, Sociology, Theatre, Women's Studies

Science and Mathematics

Animal Science, Biology, Chemistry, Fishing & Fisheries Sciences/Management, Mathematics, Physics, Statistics

Computer Science and Engineering

Computer & Information Sciences, Engineering Science

Professional Studies

Clothing & Textiles, Criminal Justice Studies, Education, Journalism, Tourism

Business and Economics

Business Administration & Management/Commerce, Economics

Health Professions and Related Sciences

Nutritional Sciences, Nursing, Pre-Veterinary Science

GRADUATE ADMISSIONS

Office of Graduate Studies and Research
Atlantic Veterinary College
550 University Avenue
Charlottetown, PEI   C1A 4P3
PH: **902.566.0542**   FAX: **902.566.0846**
E-MAIL: **McIver@upei.ca**

International fall application deadline:	Oct 1
Application fee:	$75
Domestic fall application deadline:	Jan 1
Application fee:	$75
Required with application:	College transcript, references, GRE
Graduate student housing:	Single residences at Blanchard Hall

GRADUATE FINANCES

Graduate tuition:		
International students:	$6843	(US $6159)
Domestic students:	$3033	(US $2730)
Financial aid & Scholarships available for		
International students:	Yes	
Application deadline:	N/A	

GRADUATE INSTRUCTIONAL PROGRAM

Health Professions and Related Sciences
Veterinary Medicine

Master of Arts
Master of Education
Master of Science (Biology, Chemistry)
Doctor of Philosophy

NEW BRUNSWICK

MOUNT ALLISON UNIVERSITY

Sackville, New Brunswick

SCHOOL CATEGORY: Bachelor's/Liberal Arts   **TOTAL ENROLLMENT: 2100**   **SETTING: Rural**   **CITY POPULATION: 5000**

Mount Allison University is a small, primarily undergraduate liberal arts university located in Sackville, a small town in southeastern New Brunswick with a population of 5,000, less than half an hour's drive from Moncton and two and a half hours' drive from Halifax.

Founded in 1839, the school has a long tradition of excellence. The well-kept campus has a combination of historic and modern facilities that lend it a unique charm.

Because of the school's small size, students enjoy close interactions with faculty. Mount Allison's compact scholarly community is designed to foster excellence in teaching and mentoring. Admission is competitive. The university looks for applicants who possess a strong academic record, leadership skills, and a high level of commitment. Scholarships are available; approximately 30 percent of international applicants are offered entrance scholarships.

Mount Allison is primarily a residential university. Overall, more than 60 percent of students and over 85 percent of first-year students choose to live in residence. Good housing is available in Sackville for anyone who desires to live off campus. Extracurricular life is active at Mount Allison, with over 100 clubs and societies. Athletic activities are abundant at both intercollegiate and recreational levels. The school has an active alumni network, and its graduates are well prepared for the outside world.

GENERAL INFORMATION

Year founded:	1939
Undergraduate enrollment, full-time:	2100
Graduate enrollment, full-time:	10
Faculty, full-time:	140
Number of international students:	160
Male/female ratio (%):	40:60
Residence spaces available:	1100
Residence space guaranteed for 1st-year students:	Yes
Student media website:	www.argosy.mta.ca/

UNDERGRADUATE ADMISSIONS

Student Administrative Services
65 York Street
Sackville, NB   E4L 1E4
PH: 506.363.2269   FAX: 506.363.2272
WEBSITE: www.mta.ca/

Minimum high school average:	75
Applications, 2005:	N/A
Rolling admissions:	Yes
International fall application deadline:	Apr 1
Application fee:	$50 online/$60 paper
Domestic fall application deadline:	Apr 1
Application fee:	$40
Electronic application accepted:	Yes
Admissions notification by:	N/A
Required with application:	HS transcript
Recommended:	Essay (Interviews depending upon program)

UNDERGRADUATE FINANCES

Undergraduate tuition:		
International students:	$12,200	(US $10,980)
Canadian students:	$6100	(US $5490)
Estimated annual health insurance:	$400	(US $360)
Estimated annual books & supplies:	$1200	(US $1080)
Financial aid available for international students:	Yes	
Application deadline:	With application Apr 14	
Scholarships available for international students:	Yes	
Application deadline:	Mar 15	
Annual room/board cost for students in residence:	$6930	(US $6237)
Average monthly rent for students living off campus:		
1 bedroom: $250-450, 2 bedroom: $400-600		
Federal School Code: G09503		

UNDERGRADUATE INSTRUCTIONAL PROGRAM

Most popular majors: Biology, Business, English, Psychology, International Relations
Percentages by program: BA 54%, BSc 28%, B Comm. 10%
Special study options: Internships, study abroad, language programs, special summer programs, distance learning programs

Liberal Arts and Sciences, General Studies, and Humanities

American Studies, Anthropology, Art History, Canadian Studies, Classics & Classical Languages & Literature, Drama/Theater, English Language & Literature, Fine/Studio Arts, French Language & Literature, German Language & Literature, Greek Language & Literature, History, International Relations, Japanese Language & Literature, Latin American Studies, Latin Language & Literature, Modern Languages, Music, Philosophy, Political Science, Psychology, Religion/Religious Studies, Sociology, Theology/Theological Studies

Science and Mathematics

Biochemistry, Biology, Biopsychology, Chemistry, Cognitive Science, Environmental Sciences, Mathematics, Physics

Computer Science and Engineering

Computer & Information Sciences

Professional Studies

Pre: Architecture, Education, Law, Teaching, Journalism, Home Economics

Business and Economics

Accounting, Business Administration & Management/Commerce, Economics, International Economics & Business, Marketing Management & Research

Health Professions and Related Sciences

Pre: Dentistry, Medicine, Optometry, Occupational Therapy, Pharmacy, Physiotherapy, Chiropractic Medicine, Veterinary Medicine

GRADUATE ADMISSIONS

Department of Biology/Biology Building
Department of Chemistry/Barclay Building
Mount Allison University
Sackville, NB   E4L 1E4

Fall application deadline:	N/A
Application fee:	N/A
Required with application:	College transcript & departmental requirements
Graduate student housing:	N/A

GRADUATE FINANCES

International Graduate tuition:	$12,200	(US $10,980)
Financial aid & Scholarships available for international students:	N/A	

GRADUATE INSTRUCTIONAL PROGRAM

Science and Mathematics

Biology, Chemistry

ST. THOMAS UNIVERSITY

Fredericton, New Brunswick

SCHOOL CATEGORY: Bachelor's/Liberal Arts   **TOTAL ENROLLMENT: 3000**   **SETTING: Suburban**   **CITY POPULATION: 80,000**

St. Thomas University is a small liberal arts institution with a long tradition of excellence. The university takes pride in its Catholic heritage as well as its concern for people, ideas, and values.

St. Thomas shares a campus with the University of New Brunswick in Fredericton. The two universities share many facilities, including the library, student union building, and athletic facilities.

St. Thomas offers over 25 undergraduate programs in Arts and Science, Business and Economics, and Professional Studies. There is also an innovative first-year program called the Aquinas Program. Students in this program participate in a small-group interdisciplinary learning experience that explores one central theme or issue.

The school enjoys a friendly, informal atmosphere. There are 700 residence spaces available in male-only, female-only and co-ed settings. St. Thomas offers students a variety of athletic, recreational and cultural activities.

Fredericton, the capital city of New Brunswick, overlooks the majestic Saint John River Valley. Fredericton has a great deal to offer, from parks, hiking, and biking trails to theaters, music festivals, galleries, and museums.

GENERAL INFORMATION

Year Founded:	1910
Undergraduate enrollment, full-time:	2800
Graduate enrollment, full time:	N/A
Faculty, full-time:	120
Number of international Students:	100
Male/Female ratio (%):	30:70
Residence spaces available:	700
Residence space guaranteed for 1st yr students:	Yes

UNDERGRADUATE ADMISSIONS

Office of the Registrar
Admissions Office
P.O. Box 4589
Fredericton, NB   E3B 5G3
PH: 506.452.0532   FAX: 506.452.0617
WEBSITE: **www.stu.ca**

Minimum high school average:	70%
Applications, 2000-01:	N/A
Rolling admissions:	Yes
International fall application deadline:	N/A
Application fee:	$35
Domestic Fall application deadline	Jul 31
Application fee:	$35
Electronic application accepted:	Yes
Admissions notification by:	N/A
Required with application:	HS transcript (essay, interview by dept)
Recommended:	SAT

UNDERGRADUATE FINANCES

Undergraduate tuition:

International students:	$8500	(US $7650)
Canadian students:	$4300	(US $3870)
Estimated annual health insurance:	Included in tuition	
Estimated annual books & supplies:	$1000	(US $900)
Financial aid & Scholarships available for		
international students:	Yes	
Application deadline:	Mar 1	
Annual room/board cost for students in residence:	$5600-7900	(US $5040-7110)
Average monthly rent for students living off campus:	N/A	
Federal School Code:	G06682	

UNDERGRADUATE INSTRUCTIONAL PROGRAM

Most popular majors: Criminal Justice Studies, English, History, Psychology
Percentages by program: 90% Liberal Arts
Special study options: Co-op, internships, study abroad, language programs, special summer programs, distance learning programs

Liberal Arts and Sciences, General Studies, and Humanities

Anthropology, Catholic Studies, English Language & Literature, French Language & Literature, Gender Studies, Gerontology, History, Human Rights, Native Studies, Philosophy, Political Science, Psychology, Religion/Religious Studies, Russian Languages & Literature, Romance Language, Sociology, Social Work, Spanish Language & Literature

Science and Mathematics

Biotechnology Research, Mathematics

Professional Studies

Criminal Justice Studies, Education, Journalism

Business and Economics

Business Administration & Management/Commerce, Economics

UNIVERSITÉ DE MONCTON

Moncton, New Brunswick

SCHOOL CATEGORY: Bachelor's/General   **TOTAL ENROLLMENT: 6000**   **SETTING: Urban**   **CITY POPULATION: 115,000**

The Université de Moncton is Canada's largest unilingual French university outside of Quebec. The university has three campuses located throughout the province, in Moncton, Edmundston, and Shippagan. The Moncton campus, founded in 1963, is the principal campus.

The university offers over 120 programs at the undergraduate level and more than 30 graduate and professional programs. Education is one of the most popular programs offered.

Residences and recreational facilities vary by campus. Residence spaces are allocated on a first-come, first-served basis. The school boasts a very strong community spirit.

New Brunswick's ruggedly beautiful landscape ranges from the Bay of Fundy to gently rolling farms and Acadian villages tucked into quiet coves. The province has developed a diversified economy in recent years and has a growing high-tech presence. Maine shares a border with the province on the south, and getting to New England is an easy drive.

GENERAL INFORMATION

Year founded:	1963
Undergraduate enrollment, full-time:	4800
Graduate enrollment, full-time:	400
Faculty, full-time:	N/A
Number of international students:	N/A
Male/female ratio (%)	40:60
Residence spaces available:	320

UNDERGRADUATE ADMISSIONS

Campus de Moncton
165, rue Massey
Moncton, NB   E1A 3E9
PH: 506.858.4000   FAX: 506.858.4379
WEBSITE: www.umoncton.ca

Camous d'Edmundston
165, boulevard Hebert
Edmundston, NB   E3V 2S8
PH: 506.737.5050 FAX: 506.737.5373

Campus de Shippagan
218, boulevard J.D. - Gauthier
Shippagan, NB   E8S 1P6
PH: 506.336.3400 FAX: 506.336.3434

International fall application deadline:	Feb 1
Application fee:	$39
Domestic fall application deadline:	Apr 1
Application fee:	$39
Required with application:	HS transcript

UNDERGRADUATE FINANCES

Undergraduate tuition:		
International students:	$8000	(US $7200)
Canadian students:	$5060	(US $4554)
Estimated annual health insurance:	$500	(US $450)
Financial aid & Scholarships available for		
international students:	Yes	
Application deadline:	Feb 1	
Annual room/board cost for students in residence:	$4500	(US $4050)
Average monthly rent for students living off campus:		
1 bedroom: $350-450, 2 bedroom: $550 +		
Federal School Code: G09119		

UNDERGRADUATE INSTRUCTIONAL PROGRAM

Most popular majors: Arts, Commerce, Kinesiology, Nursing
Percentages by program: N/A
Special study options: Co-op programs, internships, study abroad, language programs, special summer programs

Liberal Arts and Sciences, General Studies, and Humanities

Ceramic Arts & Ceramics, Communications, Drama/Theater Arts, English Language & Literature, History, Linguistics, Music, Philosophy, Political Science, Psychology, Public Administration, Social Work, Sociology, Translation, Visual & Performing Arts

Science and Mathematics

Agricultural Sciences, Biochemistry, Biology, Chemistry, Food Science, Forestry Sciences, Geography, Mathematics, Physics

Computer Science and Engineering

Civil Engineering, Computer & Information Sciences, Electrical Engineering, Mechanical Engineering

Professional Studies

Education, Family & Community Studies, Human Kinetics/Kinesiology, Leisure & Recreational Activities

Business and Economics

Accounting, Business Administration & Management/Commerce, Economics, Entrepreneurship, Finance, International Business, Management Information Systems, Marketing Management & Research, Operations Management & Supervision

Health Professions and Related Sciences

Diagnostic & Treatment Services, Nursing, Nutritional Sciences

GRADUATE ADMISSIONS

Faculte des etudes superieures et de la recherche
Université de Moncton
Moncton, NB   E1A 3E9
PH: **506.858.4310**   FAX: **506.858.4279**
WEBSITE: **www.umoncton.ca**

Fall application deadline:	Feb 1
Application fee:	$39
Required with application:	College transcript, essay, recommendations, portfolio required for some programs

GRADUATE FINANCES

Graduate tuition:

International students:	$7600	(US $6840)
Canadian students:	$4500	(US $4050)

Financial aid & Scholarships available for
international students:	Yes
Application deadline:	Feb 1

GRADUATE INSTRUCTIONAL PROGRAM

Liberal Arts and Sciences, General Studies, and Humanities
French Language & Literature, Philosophy, Psychology, Public Administration, Social Work, Sociology

Science and Mathematics
Biochemistry, Biology, Chemistry, Environmental Sciences, Forestry Sciences, Physics

Computer Science and Engineering
Civil Engineering, Mechanical Engineering

Professional Studies
Education, Family & Community Studies, Law

Business and Economics
Business Administration & Management/Commerce, Economics

Health Professions and Related Sciences
Nutritional Sciences, Nursing

UNIVERSITY OF NEW BRUNSWICK

Fredericton/Saint John, New Brunswick

SCHOOL CATEGORY: Master's   **TOTAL ENROLLMENT: 13,000**   **SETTING: Urban**   **CITY POPULATION: 80,000/125,000**

The University of New Brunswick (UNB) is a medium-sized institution with one campus in Fredericton and a second in Saint John. Both Fredericton and Saint John are situated on the Saint John River. Located in the provincial capital of New Brunswick, the Fredericton campus offers a larger selection of courses than the smaller Saint John campus. The Saint John campus has more of an urban atmosphere, as it is located in the commercial center of New Brunswick.

The University of New Brunswick offers over 70 undergraduate and 50 graduate degree programs on its campuses. UNB has a proud history as a leader in Canadian education since it was established in 1785 by British Loyalists. Among the most popular programs at the school today are engineering, liberal arts and marine biology.

Residence space is limited at both campuses, but a variety of conveniently located houses and apartments are readily available for renting off campus. Students will find a wide variety of opportunities to participate in recreational, social, and cultural activities at both campuses.

New Brunswick is an ideal location for students who wish to explore Atlantic Canada and the eastern United States. New Brunswick offers picturesque beaches, great skiing, and many other recreational activities.

GENERAL INFORMATION

Year founded:	1785
Undergraduate enrollment, full-time:	10,000
Graduate enrollment, full-time:	1000
Faculty, full-time:	720
Number of international students:	N/A
Male/female ratio (%)	50:50
Residence spaces available:	2100
Residence space guaranteed for 1st-year students:	1500
Student media website:	www.unb.ca/bruns

UNDERGRADUATE ADMISSIONS

Fredericton Campus
P.O. Box 4400, Station A
Fredericton, NB   E3B 5A3
PH: 506.453.4666   FAX: 506.453.4599
WEBSITE: www.unb.ca

Saint John Campus
Tucker Park, P.O. Box 5050
Saint John, NB   E2L 4L5
PH: 506.648.5500   FAX:506.648.5528

Minimum high school average:	70
Applications, 2000-2001:	N/A
Fall application deadline:	Mar 31
Application fee:	$35
Electronic application accepted:	N/A
Required with application:	HS transcript
Recommended:	SAT/ACT

UNDERGRADUATE FINANCES

Undergraduate tuition:		
International students:	$10,500	(US $9450)
Canadian students:	$5500	(US $4950)
Estimated annual health insurance:	$600	(US $540)
Estimated annual books & supplies:	$1000	(US $900)
Financial aid & Scholarships available for		
international students:	N/A	
Annual room/board cost for students in residence:	$6000	(US $5400)
Average monthly rent for students living off campus:		
1 bedroom: $300-350, 2 bedroom: $300-500		
Federal School Code: G06685		

UNDERGRADUATE INSTRUCTIONAL PROGRAM

Most popular majors: Engineering, Liberal Arts, Marine Biology
Percentages by program: N/A
Special study options: Co-op programs, internships, study abroad, language programs, special summer programs, distance learning programs

Liberal Arts and Sciences, General Studies, and Humanities

American Studies, Anthropology, Asian Studies, Classics & Classical Languages & Literature, English Language & Literature, French Language & Literature, Fine Arts, German Language & Literature, Greek Language & Literature, History, Humanities/Humanistic Studies, International Relations & Affairs, Latin, Linguistics, Multimedia Studies, Philosophy, Political Science, Psychology, Russian & Slavic Area Studies, Sociology, Spanish Language & Literature, Visual Arts, Women's Studies

Science and Mathematics

Biology, Biochemistry, Chemistry, Environmental Sciences, Forestry Sciences, Geology, Geophysics & Seismology, Marine/Aquatic Biology,* Mathematics, Microbiology, Physics, Statistics, Wilderness Studies, Wood Product Sciences

Computer Science and Engineering

Chemical Engineering, Civil Engineering, Computer & Information Sciences, Computer & Electrical Engineering, Forestry Sciences, Geological Engineering, Geophysics & Seismology, Marine Engineering,* Mechanical Engineering

Professional Studies

Education, Kinesiology/Human Kinetics, Hospitality/Administration Management,* Law, Tourism

Business and Economics

Accounting, Business Administration, Computers in Wilderness Management, Economics, Environmental Management, Finance, Human Resource Management, Industrial Relations, International Development, Marketing Management & Research, Operations Management & Supervision

Health Professions and Related Sciences

Health Sciences, Neuroscience, Nursing, Nuclear Medicine,* Radiation Therapy,* Radiography,* Respiratory Therapy *

*Saint John Campus Only

GRADUATE ADMISSIONS

School of Graduate Studies
University of New Brunswick
P.O. Box 4400
Fredericton, NB E3B 5A3
PH: **506.458.7153** FAX: **506.453.4813 (F)**
506.648.5528 (SJ)
WEBSITE: **www.unb.ca/gradschl/**

Fall application deadline:	Feb 1
Application fee:	$25/$100 (MBA)
Required with application:	College transcript, essay, recommendations, GRE might be required
Graduate student housing:	Single student accommodations

GRADUATE FINANCES

Graduate tuition:		
international students:	$9500	(US $8550)
Canadian students:	$5500	(US $4950)
Financial aid & Scholarships available for		
International students:	N/A	
Application deadline:	N/A	

GRADUATE INSTRUCTIONAL PROGRAM

Liberal Arts and Sciences, General Studies, and Humanities

Anthropology, Classics, English Language & Literature, French Language & Literature, German Language & Literature, History, North American Studies, Philosophy, Psychology, Sociology

Science and Mathematics

Biology, Forestry Sciences, Geology (Mapping/Charting), Mathematics, Physics, Statistics

Computer Science and Engineering

Chemical Engineering, Civil Engineering, Computer & Information Science, Engineering Science, Forestry Engineering, Geophysics & Seismology, Mechanical Engineering, Water Resources Engineering

Professional Studies

Education, Kinesiology/Human Kinetics, Sports & Recreation Administration/Management

Business and Economics

Business Administration, Economics, Land Information Management

Health Professions and Related Sciences

Nursing

QUEBEC

BISHOP'S UNIVERSITY

Lennoxville, Quebec

SCHOOL CATEGORY: Bachelor's/Liberal Arts　**TOTAL ENROLLMENT: 2600**　**SETTING: Suburban**　**CITY POPULATION: 140,000**

Bishop's University is a small residential university offering undergraduate students a quality education in the liberal arts and sciences. Bishop's is located in Lennoxville, population 5000, in the Eastern Townships of southern Quebec. The scenic campus is over 100 years old and provides a rich setting for academic, cultural and social activities.

The school has many strong academic programs, including business administration and education. Programs at Bishop's stress the interrelationships between disciplines. The school attracts a cosmopolitan mix of students, with over half the student body coming from outside of Quebec. Bishop's has one of the highest percentages of American students of any university in Canada.

Sherbrooke, with a population of 140,000, is only five minutes away. The area is home to many impressive ski resorts and lakes. The U.S. border and the states of Vermont, New Hampshire, and Maine are all within a short drive of Bishop's.

Bishop's has much to offer, with tradition, academic excellence, and small size combining to create an informal academic and social atmosphere that has made it a popular choice for American students.

GENERAL INFORMATION

Year founded:	1843
Undergraduate enrollment, full-time:	2200
Graduate enrollment, full-time:	N/A
Faculty, full-time:	107
Number of international students:	120
Male/female ratio (%)	44:56
Residence spaces available:	515
Residence space guaranteed for 1st-year students:	No
Student media website:	N/A

UNDERGRADUATE ADMISSIONS

Office of Admissions
P.O. Box 5000
Lennoxville, QC　J1M 1Z7
PH: 819.822.9600 ext. 2681　FAX: 819.822.9661
WEBSITE: www.ubishops.ca

Minimum high school average:	75
Rolling admissions:	No
Fall application deadline:	Mar 1
Application fee:	$55
Electronic application accepted:	Yes
Admissions notification by:	1 month after application
Required with application:	HS transcript
Recommended:	ACT, SAT, essay

UNDERGRADUATE FINANCES

Undergraduate tuition:
International students:	$11,000-12,000	(US $9900-10,800)
Canadian students:	$2095-4430	(US $1900-4000)
Estimated annual health insurance:	$600	(US $540)
Estimated annual books & supplies:	$1000	(US $900)
Financial aid available for international students:	Yes	
Application deadline:	Mar 1	
Annual room/board cost for students in residence:	$6000-7000	(US $5400-6300)

Average monthly rent for students living off campus:
1 bedroom: $500, 2 bedroom: $650+
Federal School Code: G08365

UNDERGRADUATE INSTRUCTIONAL PROGRAM

Most popular majors: Biology, Business, Education, English
Percentages by program: 23% Business, 16% Science, 15% Social Science
Special study options: Study abroad, language programs, special summer programs

Liberal Arts and Sciences, General Studies, and Humanities

Anthropology, Classics & Classical Languages & Literature, Drama/Theater Arts, English Language & Literature, Fine/Studio Arts, French Language & Literature, Greek Language & Literature, History, Music, Philosophy, Playwriting & Screenwriting, Political Science, Psychology, Religion/Religious Studies, Sociology, Visual & Performing Arts, Women's Studies

Science and Mathematics

Biology, Biochemistry, Biophysics, Chemistry, Geography, Mathematics, Physics

Computer Science and Engineering

Computer & Information Sciences

Professional Studies

Education

Business and Economics

Accounting, Business Administration & Management/Commerce, Economics, Finance, Human Resource Management, International Business, Management Information Systems & Business Data Processing, Marketing Management & Research, Organizational Behavior Studies

CONCORDIA UNIVERSITY

Montreal, Quebec

SCHOOL CATEGORY: MASTER'S **TOTAL ENROLLMENT: 31,000** **SETTING: Urban** **CITY POPULATION: 3,000,000**

Concordia is one of Canada's largest urban universities. Situated in the predominantly French city of Montreal, Concordia offers an interdisciplinary approach to learning and emphasizes programs with practical applications.

The modern school was founded in 1974 and evolved from institutions tracing their roots back more than a century. Concordia is set on two campuses, one downtown and one 15 minutes away by free shuttle in a residential area.

Business, journalism, communication studies, computer science, fine arts, and film are just a few of Concordia's nearly 250 programs with strong reputations. Concordia's Simone de Beauvoir Institute enjoys an international reputation as a pioneer in Women's Studies. Admission is competitive.

Residence spaces are very limited at Concordia, but its downtown location makes off-campus housing easily available at reasonable rates. Montreal, one of North America's oldest cities, enjoys a thriving entertainment and cultural scene. Quebec's Laurentian Mountains, as well as those of nearby New England, offer plenty of potential for outdoor recreation.

GENERAL INFORMATION

Year founded:	1974
Undergraduate enrollment, full-time:	16,365
Graduate enrollment, full-time:	3,795
Faculty, full-time:	831
Number of international students:	3515
Male/female ratio (%):	49:51
Residence spaces available:	147
Residence space guaranteed for 1st-year students:	No
Student media website:	www.theconcordian.com

UNDERGRADUATE ADMISSIONS

Admissions Application Centre
Concordia University, P.O. Box 2900
Montreal, QU   H3G 2S2
PH: 514.848.2424   FAX: 514.848.2621
WEBSITE: www.concordia.ca

Minimum high school average:	70
Applications, 2005-2006:	Received 19000; Accepted 12500; Enrolled 7700
Rolling admissions:	Yes
International fall application deadline:	Feb 1
Application fee:	$50
Domestic fall application deadline:	Mar 1
Application fee:	$50
Electronic application accepted:	Yes
Admissions notification by:	June 1
Required with application:	HS transcript, (essay, recommendations, interview, portfolio) per department
Recommended:	SAT I/II

UNDERGRADUATE FINANCES

Undergraduate tuition:		
International students:	$10,068-14,000	(US $9060-12,600)
Canadian students:	$4650	(US $4185)
Estimated annual health insurance:	$480	(US $432)
Estimated annual books & supplies:	$1500	(US $1350)
Financial aid available for international students:	Yes	
Application deadline:	N/A	
Scholarships available for international students:	Yes	
Application deadline:	Various	
Annual room/board cost for students in residence:	$4300-5300	(US $3870-4770)
Average monthly rent for students living off campus:		
1 bedroom: $500, 2 bedroom: $650+		
Federal School Code: G08365		

UNDERGRADUATE INSTRUCTIONAL PROGRAM

Most popular majors: Accounting, Computer Science, Marketing, Political Science, Communication, Journalism
Percentages by program: 39% Liberal Arts, 17% Business, 17% Engineering/Computer Science, 9% Fine Arts, 8% Science
Special study options: Co-op programs, internships, study abroad, language programs

Liberal Arts and Sciences, General Studies, and Humanities

Anthropology, Art Education, Art History, Asian Studies, Ceramic Arts & Ceramics, Cinema/Film, Classics, Communications, Dance, Design & Applied Arts, Divinity/Ministry, Drama/Theater Arts, English Language & Literature, Fibres, Fine/Studio Arts, French Language & Literature, German Language & Literature, History, Humanities/Humanistic Studies, Intermedia, Italian Language & Literature, Judaic Studies, Linguistics, Music, Painting/Drawing, Philosophy, Playwriting, Photography, Political Science, Psychology, Religion/Religious Studies, Sculpture, Social Work, Sociology, Spanish Language & Literature, Studio Art, Theological Studies, Urban Planning Studies, Visual & Performing Arts, Western Society, Women's Studies

Science and Mathematics

Biology, Biochemistry, Biophysics, Cell & Molecular Biology, Chemistry, Ecology, Environmental Sciences, Exercise Science, Geography, Mathematics, Neuroscience, Physics, Statistics

Computer Science and Engineering

Building Engineering, Civil Engineering, Computer & Information Sciences, Computer Engineering, Electrical Engineering, Industrial Engineering, Mechanical Engineering, Software Engineering

Professional Studies

Journalism

Business and Economics

Accounting, Business Administration, Economics, Finance, Human Resource Management, International Business, Management, Management Information Systems & Business Data Processing, Marketing Supply Chain, Operations Management & Supervision

GRADUATE ADMISSIONS

School of Graduate Studies
2145 Mackay Street
Montreal, QU H3G 1MB
PH: **514.848.2424 ext 3800** FAX: **514.848.2812**
WEBSITE: **www.graduatestudies.concordia.ca/**

Fall Application Deadline:	Feb 15
Application fee:	$50
Required with application:	GRE, college transcript, essay, recommendations, portfolio required for some programs
Graduate student housing:	No

GRADUATE FINANCES

Graduate tuition:

International students:	$10,000-14,000	(US $9000-12,600)
Canadian students:	$4650	(US $4185)
Financial aid & Scholarships available for		
international students:	N/A	
Application deadline:	N/A	

GRADUATE INSTRUCTIONAL PROGRAM

Liberal Arts and Sciences, General Studies, and Humanities

Anthropology, Art, Art History, Child Studies, Communications, Education, English Language & Literature, Film Studies, Fine Arts, French Language & Literature, History, Humanities/Humanistic Studies, Judaic Studies, Media Studies, Music, Philosophy, Psychology, Public Policy, Religion/Religious Studies, Sociology, Theological Studies, Translation

Science and Mathematics

Biology, Biotechnology, Computer & Information Sciences, Exercise Science, Physics, Geography, Mathematics, Statistics

Computer Science and Engineering

Aerospace Engineering, Civil Engineering, Computer Sciences, Computer Engineering, Electrical Engineering, Industrial Engineering, Information Systems Security, Mechanical Engineering

Professional Studies

Art Education, Education, Journalism, Sport Administration

Business and Economics

Accounting, Business Administration, E-Business, Economics, Entrepreneurship, Human Resources Management, International Aviation, Investment Management, Management Accounting

MᶜGILL UNIVERSITY

Montreal, Quebec

SCHOOL CATEGORY: Doctoral/Research   **TOTAL ENROLLMENT: 30,000**   **SETTING: Urban**   **CITY POPULATION: 3,000,000**

McGill University enjoys an outstanding international reputation for academic excellence and research achievement. It is one of Canada's largest universities, and its vibrant main campus is located in the heart of Montreal, one of Canada's leading commercial centers. Montreal is home to over 3 million people from both French- and English-speaking communities and is functionally bilingual (French and English).

McGill was founded in 1821. Its main campus includes 70 buildings on 80 wooded acres a the foot of the Mount Royal Park in downtown Montreal. The building style is a mix of historic and modern. In 1906 the MacDonald campus was added at the western tip of the island of Montreal, half an hour away. McGill has 22 faculties and professional schools offering undergraduate and graduate programs in over 300 disciplines. The school offers a full range of professional programs in areas ranging from architecture to urban planning. All tenured professors are required to teach at the undergraduate level, ensuring that students have access to the very latest thinking in their fields. Admission to McGill is highly competitive, with 25 percent of applicants enrolling. Approximately 15 percent of the students are from outside Canada, resulting in a stimulating and open cosmopolitan atmosphere.

The majority of students choose to live off campus, and accommodations are widely available at reasonable rates. First-year students from the U.S. are guaranteed a residence spot either on or off campus. Residences range from modern apartments to ivy-covered heritage buildings. McGill maintains an online database of available student housing.

Montreal is a bustling, vibrant city that revels in the arts, featuring world-class jazz and comedy festivals as well as a major symphony and ballet company. The school has a large and active international alumni network. The university's reputation for quality make a McGill degree highly portable.

GENERAL INFORMATION

Year founded:	1821
Undergraduate enrollment, full-time:	19,000
Graduate enrollment, full-time:	6000
Faculty, full-time:	1509
Number of international students:	5000
Male/female ratio (%)	43:51
Residence spaces available:	2200
Residence space guaranteed for 1st-year students:	Yes
Student media website:	www.mcgill.ca/public/reporter

UNDERGRADUATE ADMISSIONS

Admissions Office
845 Sherbrooke Street
James Administration Building
Montreal, QU   H3A 2T5
PH: **514.398.3910**   FAX: **514.398.4193**
WEBSITE: **www.mcgill.ca**

Minimum high school average:	80
Rolling admissions:	No
International fall application deadline:	Jan 15
Application fee:	$80 (paper), $50 (electronic)
Domestic fall application deadline:	Feb 1
Application fee:	$80 (paper), $50 (electronic)
Electronic application accepted:	Yes
Admissions notification by:	June 1
Required with application:	HS transcript, SAT I/II, ACT

UNDERGRADUATE FINANCES

Undergraduate tuition:		
International students:	$12,000-15,000	(US $10,800-13,500)
Canadian students:	$3000-6000	(US $2700-5400)
Estimated annual health insurance:	$700	(US $630)
Estimated annual books & supplies:	$1000	(US $900)
Financial aid & Scholarships available for		
international students:	Yes	
Application deadline:	Jan 15	
Annual room/board cost for students in residence:	$6800-8000	(US $6100-7200)
Average monthly rent for students living off campus:		
1 bedroom: $500, 2 bedroom: $650+		
Federal School Code: G06677		

UNDERGRADUATE INSTRUCTIONAL PROGRAM

Most popular majors: English, Mechanical Engineering, Political Science, Psychology
Percentages by program: N/A
Special study options: Co-op programs, internships, study abroad, language programs, special summer programs, distance learning programs

Liberal Arts and Sciences, General Studies, and Humanities

African Studies, Anthropology, Art, Art History, Asian Studies, Canadian Studies, Classics & Classical Languages & Literature, Communications, Comparative Literature, East Asian Studies, English Language & Literature, Fine/Studio Arts, French Language & Literature, German Language & Literature, Gerontology, History, Humanities/Humanistic Studies, International Relations & Affairs, Islamic Studies, Italian Studies, Latin American Studies, Latin Language & Literature, Linguistics, Middle Eastern Languages & Literature, Music, Philosophy, Political Science, Psychology, Religion/Religious Studies, Sociology, South Asian Studies, Spanish Language & Literature, Women's Studies

Science and Mathematics

Agriculture Sciences, Animal Science, Applied Mathematics, Archaeology, Atmospheric Sciences & Meteorology, Astronomy/Astrophysics, Biological Sciences/Life Sciences, Biology, Biophysics, Biotechnology Research, Botany, Chemistry, Earth & Planetary Science, Food Sciences, Genetics/Plant & Animal, Geochemistry, Geography, Geophysics & Seismology, Mathematics, Microbiology, Molecular Biology, Natural Resources Management & Protective Services, Oceanography, Parasitology, Physics, Physiology: Human & Animal, plant Sciences, Soil Science, Statistics, Wildlife Biology, Zoology

Computer Science and Engineering

Aeronautical Engineering, Aerospace Engineering, Bioengineering & Biomedical Engineering, Chemical Engineering, Civil Engineering, Computer & Information Sciences, Computer Engineering, Construction Engineering & Technology, Electrical/Electronics & Communication Engineering, Engineering/Industrial Management, Engineering Physics, Engineering

Science, Environmental/Environmental Health Engineering, Mechanical Engineering, Metallurgical Engineering, Mining & Mineral Engineering, Software Engineering

Professional Studies

Architecture, City/Urban, Community & Regional Planning, Domestic Environments/Housing, Development Studies, Criminal Justice Studies, Human Kinetics/Kinesiology, Library & Information Studies, EDUCATION: arboriginal studies, business & industrial trainer development, counseling psychology, curriculum studies, ESL, FSL, human relation, inclusion (special education), kindergarten & elementary education, literacy studies, middle school education, music education, french (elementary & secondary), psychology & education of the gifted, (general, science & vocational education)

Business and Economics

Accounting, Actuarial Science, Agricultural business & Engineering, Aquaculture Operations, & Production Management, Business Administration & Management/Commerce, Economics, Entrepreneurship, Human Resources Management, International Business, Labor/Personnel Relations & Studies, Management Science, Management Information Systems & Business Data Processing, Marketing Management & Research, Operations Management & Supervision, Organizational Behavior Studies, Public relations & Organizational Communications

Health Professions and Related Sciences

Child Psychiatry, Dietetics, Epidemiology & Biostatistics, Nursing, Neuroscience, Nutritional Sciences, Occupational Therapy, Physical Therapy, Rehabilitation Science

GRADUATE ADMISSIONS

Graduate Studies and Research
845 Sherbrooke Street West
James Administration Building
Montreal, QU   H3A 2T5
PH: 514.348.3990   FAX: 514.348.1626
WEBSITE: www.mcgill.ca/fsgr

International fall application deadline:	Jan 1
Application fee:	$50
Domestic fall application deadline:	Mar 1
Application fee:	$50
Required with application:	GRE, college transcript, essays, recommendations, portfolio required for some programs

GRADUATE FINANCES

Graduate tuition:		
International students:	$9000	(US $8100)
Canadian students:	$3000-6000	(US $2700-5400)
Financial aid & Scholarships available for		
international students:	Yes	
Application deadline:	Varies	
Graduate student housing:	No on-campus housing for students over 21	

GRADUATE INSTRUCTIONAL PROGRAM

Liberal Arts and Sciences, General Studies, and Humanities

Anthropology, Art History, Asian Studies, Classics & Classical Languages & Literature, Communications, East asian Studies, English Language & Literature, French Language & Literature, German Language & Literature, History, Islamic Studies, Italian Language & Literature, Jewish/Judaic Studies, Latin American Studies, Linguistics, Medieval & Renaissance Studies, Middle Eastern Language & Literature, Music, Philosophy, Political Science, Psychology, Religion/Religious Studies, Russian & Slavic Area Studies, Social Work, Sociology

Science and Mathematics

Agriculture Sciences, Atmospheric Sciences & Meteorology, Biochemistry, Biology, Chemistry, Earth & Planetary Science, Ecology, Food Science & Agricultural Chemistry, Geography, Mathematics, Microbiology, Natural Resource Sciences, Oceanography, Physiology/Human & Animal, Plant Sciences, Statistics

Computer Science and Engineering

Agricultural Engineering, Bioengineering & Biomedical Engineering, Chemical Engineering, Civil Engineering, Computer & Information Sciences, Computer Engineering, Electrical/Electronics & Communication Engineering, Mechanical Engineering, Mining & Metallurgical Engineering

Professional Studies

City/Urban/Community & Regional Planning, Counseling, Library Science, Law, Physical Education Teaching & Coaching

Business and Economics

Agricultural Economics, Economics

Health Professions and Related Sciences

Anatomy & Cell Biology, Communication Sciences & Disorders, Chiropractic, Counseling Psychology, Dentistry, Diagnostic & Treatment Services, Dietetics & Human Nutrition, Environmental Health, Epidemiology, Health Services Administration, Medicine, Nursing, Occupational Therapy, Optometry, Pharmacy, Physical therapy, Public Health, Speech–Language Pathology & Audiology, Veterinary Medicine

UNIVERSITÉ DE MONTREAL

Montreal, Quebec

SCHOOL CATEGORY: Doctoral/Research   **TOTAL ENROLLMENT: 36,000**   **SETTING: Urban**   **CITY POPULATION: 3,000,000**

The Université de Montreal is the largest unilingual French university in Canada and one of the largest French universities in the world. Its large campus spreads across almost two miles of the side of Mount Royal in the city center.

The school's history dates back to 1878. Its famous alumni include the former Canadian prime minister Pierre Trudeau and numerous premiers of Quebec.

The university offers over 250 programs at the undergraduate, graduate, and professional levels. Health science studies and research are a strong focus, with programs in medicine, dentistry, pharmacy, veterinary science, optometry, nursing, physical therapy, and drug development. Two affiliated schools, the École des Hautes Études Commerciale for business studies and the École Polytechnique de Montréal for engineering and technology studies, share the main campus.

Residence space is limited, but off-campus housing is easily found nearby. The school has excellent athletic facilities, a legacy of the 1976 Olympics which were hosted in part at the school.

Montreal offers all of the attractions of a large city while retaining the safety and affordable living of a small town. It is a vibrant, multicultural city that hosts world-class jazz and comedy festivals as well as other major cultural and sporting events. Montreal's century-old origins are preserved and displayed in the historic architecture of Old Montreal. The Laurentian Mountains and those of the Eastern Townships are nearby and offer a year-round playground for outdoor enthusiasts.

GENERAL INFORMATION

Year founded:	1878
Undergraduate enrollment, full-time:	20,000
Graduate enrollment, full-time:	8000
Faculty, full-time:	N/A
Number of international students:	400
Male/female ratio (%)	45:55
Residence spaces available:	1200
Residence space guaranteed for 1st-year students:	No
Student media website:	www.faccum.uc.ca

UNDERGRADUATE ADMISSIONS

C.P. 6128, succursale Centre-Ville
Montreal, QU H3C 3J7
PH: 514.343.6111   FAX: 514.343.2098
WEBSITE: www.umontreal.ca

Fall application deadline:	Mar 1
Application fee:	$30
Required with application:	HS transcript

UNDERGRADUATE FINANCES

Undergraduate tuition:		
International students:	$11,500	(US $10,350)
Canadian students:	$1850-4000	(US $1670-3600)
Estimated annual health insurance:	$600	(US $540)
Estimated annual books & supplies:	$800	(US $720)
Financial Aid & Scholarship available for		
international students:	Mar 1	
Application deadline:	Yes	
Annual room cost for students in residence:	$4000-6000	(US $3600-5400)

Average monthly rent for students living off campus:
1 bedroom: $350-450, 2 bedroom: $550+
Federal School Code: G08366

UNDERGRADUATE INSTRUCTIONAL PROGRAM

Most popular majors: Business Administration, Science
Percentages by program: N/A
Special study options: Co-op programs, internships, study abroad, language programs, special summer programs, distance learning programs

Liberal Arts and Sciences, General Studies, and Humanities

Anthropology, Art, Art History, Asian Studies, Classics & Classical Languages & Literature, Communications, Comparative Literature, Design & Applied Arts, English Language & Literature, Film/Cinema, French Language & Literature, German Language & Literature, History, Linguistics, Music, Philosophy, Political Science, Psychology, Public Administration, Religion/Religious Studies, Social Work, Sociology, Spanish Language & Literature, Theology, Translation, Urban Affairs, Visual & Performing Arts

Science and Mathematics

Biological Sciences/Life Sciences, Biochemistry, Biology, Chemistry, Ecology, Environmental Sciences, Geography, Mathematics, Microbiology, Physics, Statistics

Computer Science and Engineering

Chemical Engineering, Civil Engineering, Computer & Information Sciences, Computer Engineering, Electrical Engineering, Geological Engineering, Mechanical Engineering

Professional Studies

Architecture, Child Growth, Care & Development Studies, Counseling, Criminal Justice, Education, Human Kinetics/Kinesiology, Library Science, Landscape Architecture

Business and Economics

Accounting, Business Administration & Management/Commerce, Economics, Finance, Human Resources Management, International Business, Labour/Personnel Relations & Studies, Management Studies, Management Information Systems, Marketing Management & Research, Operations Management and Supervision

Health Professions and Related Sciences

Health Services Administration, Nursing, Nutritional Sciences, Occupational Therapy, Physical Therapy, Physiology, Speech-Language Pathology & Audiology

GRADUATE ADMISSIONS

Faculte des estudes superieures
Université de Montreal
C.P. 6128, Succursale Centre-Ville
Montreal, QU H3C 3J7
PH: **514.343.6537**   FAX: **514.343.2252**
WEBSITE: **www.umontreal.ca/english/index.htm**

Fall application deadline:	Mar 1
Application fee:	$30
Required with application:	College transcript, essay, recommendations portfolio required for some programs
Graduate student housing:	N/A

GRADUATE FINANCES

Graduate tuition:

International students:	$9000-11,000	(US $8100-9900)
Canadian students:	$2500-4000	(US $2250-3600)
Financial aid & Scholarships available for		
international students:	Yes	
Application deadline:	Mar 1	

GRADUATE INSTRUCTIONAL PROGRAM

Liberal Arts and Sciences, General Studies, and Humanities

Anthropology, Art, Art History, Classics & Classical Languages & Literature, Communications, Comparative Literature, English Language & Literature, Film/Cinema, French Language & Literature, German, History, Linguistics, Medieval & Renaissance, Music, Philosophy, Political Science, Psychology, Religion/Religious Studies, Russian & Slavic Area Studies, Social Work, Sociology, Spanish Language & Literature, Theology/Theological Studies, Translation, Urban Affairs/Studies

Science and Mathematics

Biochemistry, Biological/Life Sciences, Chemistry, Geography, Mathematics, Molecular Biology, Physics, Physiology, Statistics, Toxicology

Computer Science and Engineering

Aerospace Engineering, Bioengineering & Biomedical Engineering, Chemical Engineering, Civil Engineering, Computer & Information Sciences, Electrical Engineering, Engineering Physics, Mechanical Engineering, Metallurgical Engineering, Mining & Mineral Engineering

Professional Studies

Child Growth & Development Studies, Counseling, Criminal Justice Studies, Education, Law

Business and Economics

Business Administration & Management/Commerce, Economics, Entrepreneurship, Finance, Human Resources Management, International Business, Labour/Personnel Relations & Studies, Management Science, Management Information Systems, Marketing, Operations Management

Health Professions and Related Sciences

Counseling Psychology, Dentistry, Environmental Health, Health Services Administration, Medicine, Nursing, Nutritional Sciences, Speech-Language Pathology & Audiology, Veterinary Medicine

UNIVERSITÉ DE SHERBROOKE

Sherbrooke, Montreal

SCHOOL CATEGORY: Doctoral/Research   **TOTAL ENROLLMENT: 16,500**   **SETTING: Urban**   **CITY POPULATION: 140,000**

The Université de Sherbrooke is a medium-sized unilingual French university located in the Eastern Townships of Quebec, an hour and a half south of Montreal. The university has an attractive modern campus on the outskirts of Sherbrooke.

Sherbrooke offers over 100 different programs at the undergraduate, graduate, and professional levels, including medicine. The university is known for its spirit of innovation. It boasts one of the most active internship programs in Canada, with over 900 industry partners offering over 4,000 paid internships to students every year. The school is proud of its role in technology transfer and holds numerous patents.

Residence space is limited, but affordable housing is easily found close to campus. The school's athletic facilities are excellent. Several major lakes and ski resorts in the area allow for year-round outdoor recreational opportunities. Mont Bellevue is just ten minutes away. With the Canada-U.S. border nearby, Vermont, New Hampshire, and Maine are all within a short drive of Sherbrooke.

GENERAL INFORMATION

Year founded:	1954
Undergraduate enrollment, full-time:	9800
Graduate enrollment, full-time:	3000
Faculty, full-time:	N/A
Number of international students:	N/A
Male/female ratio (%)	50:50
Residence spaces available:	1200
Residence space guaranteed for 1st-year students:	No
Student media website:	www.usherb.ca/liaison

UNDERGRADUATE ADMISSIONS

Registraire
2500, boulevard de l'Université
Sherbrooke, QU J1K 2R1
PH: 819.821.7000
WEBSITE: **www.usherb.ca**

Fall application deadline:	Mar 1
Application fee:	$30
Electronic application accepted:	Yes
Required with application:	HS transcript

UNDERGRADUATE FINANCES

Undergraduate tuition:		
International students:	$10,500	(US $9450)
Canadian students:	$2200	(US $1980)
Estimated annual health insurance:	$525	(US $475)
Estimated annual books & supplies:	$800	(US $720)
Financial aid & Scholarships available for		
international students:	Yes	
Application deadline:	Mar 1	
Annual room/board cost for students in residence:	$3900	(US $3500)
Average monthly rent for students living off campus:		
1 bedroom: $300-450, 2 bedroom: $350-550		
Federal School Code: G08742		

UNDERGRADUATE INSTRUCTIONAL PROGRAM

Most popular majors: Business, Education, Humanities, Sciences
Percentages by program: N/A
Special study options: Co-op programs, internships, study abroad

Liberal Arts and Sciences, General Studies, and Humanities

Communications, English Language & Literature, French Language & Literature, History, Music, Philosophy, Political Science, Psychology, Social Work, Spanish Language & Literature, Theology/Theological Studies, Translations, Visual & Performing Arts

Science and Mathematics

Biochemistry, Biology, Biotechnology Research, Chemistry, Ecology, Geography, Mathematics, Microbiology, Physics, Statistics

Computer Science and Engineering

Computer & Information Science

Professional Studies

Child Growth Care & Development Studies, Counseling, Education, Human Kinetics/Kinesiology, Physical Education

Business and Economics

Accounting, Business Administration & Management/Commerce, Economics, Finance, International Business, Management Science, Management Information Systems & Business Data Processing, Marketing, Organizational Behavior Studies

Health Professions and Related Sciences

Nursing

GRADUATE ADMISSIONS

Vice-rectorat a la recherche
Université de Sherbrooke
2500, boul. de l'Universite
Sherbrooke, QU   J1K 2R1
PH: **819.821.7700**   FAX: **819.821.6970**
WEBSITE: **www.usherbrooke.ca**

Fall application deadline:	Mar 1
Application fee:	$30
Required with application:	College transcript, essay, recommendations, portfolio required for some programs

GRADUATE FINANCES

Graduate tuition:		
International students:	$10,500	(US $9450)
Canadian students:	$2200	(US $1980)
Financial aid & Scholarships available for		
international students:	Yes	
Application deadline:	Mar 1	

GRADUATE INSTRUCTIONAL PROGRAM

Liberal Arts and Sciences, General Studies, and Humanities

Canadian Studies, French Language & Literature, Gerontology, History, Philosophy, Political Science, Religion/Religious Studies, Social Work, Theology/Theological Studies

Science and Mathematics

Biochemistry, Biology, Chemistry, Environmental Studies, Mathematics, Physics

Computer Science and Engineering

Aerospace Engineering, Chemical Engineering, Civil Engineering, Civil Engineering, Computer & Information Sciences, Computer Engineering, Electrical/ Electronics & Communication Engineering, Mechanical Engineering

Professional Studies

Child Growth/Care & Development Studies, Counseling, Education, Law

Business and Economics

Accounting, Business Administration & Management/Commerce, Economics, International Business, Management Information Systems & Business Data Processing, Marketing Management & Research, Organizational Behavior Studies

Health Professions and Related Sciences

Medicine

UNIVERSITÉ DU QUÉBEC

Montreal, Quebec, Rouyn-Noranda, Hull, Chicoutimi, Rimouski, Trois Rivieres

SCHOOL CATEGORY: Master's   **TOTAL ENROLLMENT: 30,000**   **SETTING: Urban**   **CITY POPULATION: 3,000,000**

The Université du Québec is a diversified French-language university system with campuses located throughout the province of Quebec. The university has six general campuses located in Montreal, Trois-Rivières, Hull, Chicoutimi, Rouyn-Noranda, and Rimouski. The system also has four specialized colleges: Institut Nationale de la Recherche Scientifique, a scientific research institute; École Nationale d'Administration Publique, a public policy institute; Tele-Université, offering distance-learning programs—all in the greater Quebec city area—and École de Technologie Superieure, a high-technology institute located in Montreal.

Enrollment ranges from under 1,000 full-time students in Rouyn-Noranda to over 18,000 students in Montreal. Total full-time system enrollment is over 30,000 students.

Over 200 programs are offered at the undergraduate, graduate and professional levels. The Trois-Rivières and Montreal campuses both offer excellent French-language training programs for non-French speakers. Students should visit the individual school Web sites for additional details. Residence accommodations and facilities vary by campus.

The province of Quebec is Canada's largest and is also the biggest French-speaking territory in the world, many times larger in area than France. Its landscape varies from quiet agricultural villages along the U.S. border to the vast regions of lakes, forest, and tundra in the north. There are two major cities: cosmopolitan Montreal and the provincial capital of Quebec City. The province is a vibrant place from end to end, and those interested in a taste of Europe close to home will find a lot to enjoy here.

GENERAL INFORMATION

Year founded:	1969
Undergraduate enrollment, full-time:	30,000
Graduate enrollment, full-time:	4000
Faculty, full-time:	N/A
Number of international students:	N/A
Male/female ratio (%)	40:60
Residence spaces available:	N/A
Residence space guaranteed for 1st-year students:	No

UNDERGRADUATE ADMISSIONS

475, rue de l'Eglise
Quebec, QC G1K 9H7
PH: **418.657.3551**
FAX: **418.657.2132**
WEBSITE: **www.uquebec.ca**

C.P. 1250, Succursale B
Hull, QC J8X 3X7
PH: **819.595.3900**
FAX: **819.595.3924**
WEBSITE: **www.uqah.uquebec.ca**

C.P. 8888, Succursale Centre Ville
Montreal, QC H3C 3P8
PH: **514.987.3000**
FAX: **514.987.3095**
WEBSITE: **www.uquam.ca**

555, boulevard de l'Universite Est
Chicoutimi, QC G7H 2B1
PH: **418.545.5011**
FAX: **418.545.5012**
WEBSITE: **www.uqac.uquebec.ca**

445, boulevard de l'Universite
Rouyn-Noranda, QC J9X 5E4
PH: **819.762.0971**
FAX: **819.797.4727**
WEBSITE: **www.uquat.uquebec.ca**

C.P. 3300, Succursale Bureau-chef
Rimouski, QC G5L 3A1
PH: **418.723.1986**
FAX: **418.724.1525**
WEBSITE: **www.uquar.qc.ca**

Fall application deadline:	Mar 1
Application fee:	$30
Required with application:	HS transcript

UNDERGRADUATE FINANCES

Undergraduate tuition:		
International students:	$10,000-11,000	(US $9000-10,000)
Canadian students:	$1850-4700	(US $1700-4200)
Estimated annual health insurance:	$600	(US $540)
Estimated annual books & supplies:	$800	(US $720)
Financial aid & Scholarships available for		
international students:	Yes	
Application deadline:	Mar 1	
Annual room/board cost for students in residence:	N/A	

Average monthly rent for students living off campus:
1 bedroom: $350-450, 2 bedroom: $550+
Federal School Code: G22097

UNDERGRADUATE INSTRUCTIONAL PROGRAM

Most popular majors: N/A
Percentages by program: N/A
Special study options: Co-op programs, internships, study abroad, language programs, special summer programs, distance learning programs

Liberal Arts and Sciences, General Studies, and Humanities

Art, Art History, Asian Studies, Communications, Design & Applied Arts, Drama/Theater, English Language & Literature, Film/Cinema, French Language & Literature, Gerontology, History, Linguistics, Music, Philosophy, Political Science, Psychology, Public Administration, Religion/Religious Studies, Social Work, Sociology, Spanish Language & Literature, Theology, Translation, Visual & Performing Arts, Women's Studies

Science and Mathematics

Biological Sciences/Life Sciences, Biotechnology Research, Chemistry, Ecology, Forestry Sciences, Geography, Geology, Mathematics, Molecular Biology, Statistics, Toxicology

Computer Science and Engineering

Civil Engineering, Computer & Information Sciences, Computer Engineering, Electrical Engineering, Geological Engineering, Mechanical Engineering, Metallurgical Engineering

Professional Studies

Child Growth, Care & Development Studies, Counseling, Education, Fashion, Hospitality/Administration Management, Journalism, Leisure & Recreational Activities

Business and Economics

Accounting, Business Administration & Management/Commerce, Economics, Finance, Human Resources Management, International Business, Labour/Personnel Relations and Studies, Management Studies, Management Information Systems, Marketing Management & Research, Operations Management and Supervision, Organizational Behavior Studies, Public Relations & Organizational Communications

Health Professions and Related Sciences

Nursing

GRADUATE ADMISSIONS

Direction des etudes de cycle superieurs et de la recherche
Université du Québec
475, rue de l'Eglise
Québec, QC G1K 9H7
PH: **418.657.4118**   FAX: **418.657.2132**

Fall application deadline:	Mar 1
Application fee:	$30
Required with application:	College transcript, essay, recommendations portfolio required for some programs
Graduate student housing:	N/A

GRADUATE FINANCES

Graduate tuition:

International students:	$9000-10,000	(US $8100-9,000)
Canadian students:	$2500-4000	(US $2250-3600)
Financial aid & Scholarships available for		
international students:	Yes	
Application deadline:	Mar 1	

GRADUATE INSTRUCTIONAL PROGRAM

Liberal Arts and Sciences, General Studies, and Humanities

Art, Art History, Drama/Theater, History, Linguistics, Philosophy, Political Science, Public Administration, Religion/Religious Studies, Social Work, Sociology, Theology/Theological Studies

Science and Mathematics

Atmospheric Sciences & Meteorology, Biological/Life Sciences, Biotechnology Research, Chemistry, Environmental Sciences, Forestry Sciences, Geography, Mathematics, Microbiology, Physics, Statistics

Computer Science and Engineering

Civil Engineering, Computer & Information Sciences, Computer Engineering, Electrical Engineering, Mechanical Engineering

Professional Studies

Counseling, Education

Business and Economics

Accounting, Business Administration & Management/Commerce, Economics, Entrepreneurship, Finance, Human Resources Management, International Business, Labour/Personnel Relations & Studies, Management Science, Management Information Systems, Marketing, Operations Management, Organizational Studies, Public Relations & Organizational Communications

Health Professions and Related Sciences

Nursing

UNIVERSITÉ LAVAL

Laval, Quebec

SCHOOL CATEGORY: Doctoral/Research   **TOTAL ENROLLMENT: 35,000**   **SETTING: Urban**   **CITY POPULATION: 200,000**

Université Laval is a large, comprehensive, French-language university located in Quebec City. It was the first French university in North America and traces its roots back more than 300 years. Laval has played a dominant role in the formation of Canada and of Quebec's elite, counting many prime ministers, writers, business leaders, and artists among its alumni. The university enjoys worldwide recognition for academic excellence and research. The large, wooded campus is located in a residential section of the city.

Laval offers more than 350 programs at the undergraduate, graduate and professional levels. The school is particularly well known for its teaching of French as a second language; it offers courses of various length for non-French speakers. Laval has large faculties of agriculture, food science, and forestry and is strong in all areas of high technology.

The more-than-2,000 residence spaces on campus are allocated on a first-come, first-served basis. Affordable off-campus housing is also easily available nearby. The school has excellent athletic facilities and a large number of clubs and societies that promote learning beyond the classroom.

Quebec City has narrow, cobblestoned streets and eighteenth-century buildings that lend a European air to this provincial capital. The imposing Château Frontenac dominates the city's skyline. Within the historic area are many shops and restaurants. World-class skiing and outdoor recreational activities are found in the nearby Parc du Mont Ste-Anne. The city hosts a wonderful Winter Carnival and numerous cultural events throughout the year.

GENERAL INFORMATION

Year founded:	1663
Undergraduate enrollment, full-time:	20,000
Graduate enrollment, full-time:	5000
Faculty, full-time:	N/A
Number of international students:	N/A
Male/female ratio (%)	45:55
Residence spaces available:	2300
Residence space guaranteed for 1st-year students:	No
Student media website:	N/A

UNDERGRADUATE ADMISSIONS

C.P.2208, succursale Terminus
Ste-Foy, QU G1K 7P4
PH: 418.656.2131   FAX: 418.656.2809
WEBSITE: www.ulaval.ca

Fall application deadline:	Mar 1
Application fee:	$30

UNDERGRADUATE FINANCES

Undergraduate tuition:		
International students:	$11,500	(US $10,350)
Canadian students:	$1850-4000	(US $1670-3600)
Estimated annual health insurance:	$600	(US $540)
Estimated annual books & supplies:	$800	(US $720)
Financial aid & Scholarships available for		
international students:	Yes	
Application deadline:	Mar 1	
Annual room cost for students in residence:	$2400	(US $2160)
Average monthly rent for students living off campus:		
1 bedroom: $350-450, 2 bedroom: $550+		
Federal School Code: G06837		

UNDERGRADUATE INSTRUCTIONAL PROGRAM

Most popular majors: Arts, Forestry, Liberal Arts
Percentages by program: N/A
Special study options: Co-op programs, internships, study abroad, language programs, special summer programs, distance learning programs.

Liberal Arts and Sciences, General Studies, and Humanities

Anthropology, Art History, Communications, Drama/Theater Arts, English Language & Literature, Film/Cinema, French Language & Literature, German Language & Literature, Gerontology, History, Linguistics, Music, Philosophy, Political Science, Religion/Religious Studies, Russian & Slavic Area Studies, Russian Languages & Literature, Social Work, Sociology, Spanish Language & Literature, Theology/Theological Studies, Translation, Visual & Performing Arts, Women's Studies

Science and Mathematics

Agriculture Sciences, Biology, Biochemistry, Biotechnology Research, Chemistry, Forestry Sciences, Geography, Mathematics, Microbiology, Oceanography, Physics, Statistics

Computer Science and Engineering

Chemical Engineering, Civil Engineering, Computer & Information Sciences, Computer Engineering, Electrical/Electronics & Communication Engineering, Geological Engineering, Mechanical Engineering, Metallurgical Engineering, Mining & Mineral Engineering

Professional Studies

Archaeology, Architecture, Child Growth, Care & Development Studies, Counseling, Education, Journalism

Business and Economics

Accounting, Business Administration & Management/Commerce, Economics, Labour/Personnel Relations & Studies, Public Relations & Organizational Communications

Health Professions and Related Sciences

Nursing, Pharmacology, Physical Therapy

GRADUATE ADMISSIONS

Faculte des estudes superieures
Université Laval
Pavillon Jean-Charles-Bonenfant, bureau 3445
Ste-Foy, QU G1K 7P4
PH: 418.656.5318   FAX: 418.656.3691

Fall application deadline:	Mar 1
Application fee:	$30
Required with application:	College transcript, essay, recommendations, portfolio required for some programs
Graduate student housing:	Yes

GRADUATE FINANCES

Graduate tuition:

International students:	$9000-11,000	(US $8100-9900)
Canadian students:	$2500-4000	(US $2250-3600)

Financial aid & Scholarships available for

international students:	Yes
Application deadline:	Mar 1

GRADUATE INSTRUCTIONAL PROGRAM

Liberal Arts and Sciences, General Studies, and Humanities

Archaeology, Anthropology, Art History, Communications, English Language & Literature, French Language & Literature, History, International Relations, Linguistics, Music, Philosophy, Political Science, Public Administration, Religion/Religious Studies, Social Work, Sociology, Theology/Theological Studies, Translation, Visual & Performing Arts

Science and Mathematics

Agriculture Sciences, Biology, Botany, Chemistry, Forestry Sciences, Geography, Mathematics, Microbiology, Neuroscience, Physics, Physiology, Statistics

Computer Science and Engineering

Aerospace Engineering, Chemical Engineering, Civil Engineering, Computer & Information Sciences, Computer Engineering, Electrical/ Electronics & Communication Engineering, Mechanical Engineering, Mining & Mineral Engineering

Professional Studies

Architecture, Child Growth, Care, & Development Studies, City/ Urban/ Community & Regional Planning, Counseling, Education

Business and Economics

Business Administration & Management/Commerce, Economics, Labour/Personnel Relations & Studies

Health Professions and Related Sciences

Dentistry, Medicine, Nutritional Sciences, Nursing, Pharmacy, Physiology

ONTARIO

BRESCIA UNIVERSITY COLLEGE

London, Ontario

SCHOOL CATEGORY: Bachelor's/Liberal Arts   **TOTAL ENROLLMENT: 1000**   **SETTING: Suburban**   **CITY POPULATION: 330,000**

Brescia University College is Canada's only university-level women's college. Founded in 1919 as a Catholic liberal arts college, Brescia is affiliated with the University of Western Ontario. Brescia is located on beautiful grounds next to the Western campus. Brescia students enjoy the activity and resources of a large university plus the sense of community found in a smaller institution.

Some of Brescia's most highly regarded programs are in the fields of nutrition, sociology, community development, religious studies and English. Brescia students can take courses at Western and are awarded a degree from The University of Western Ontario upon completion.

Residence is guaranteed to all first year students. Students have full access to the wide range of facilities and campus services offered at Western, including over 100 different student clubs.

London, with a population of over 300,000, is Canada's tenth-largest city and is situated midway between Toronto and Detroit, roughly two hours' drive from each. The city offers all the urban amenities—shopping, dining, theaters, clubs, art galleries, and parks—but also has a comfortable "college town" feel. Throughout the year there are many festivals in the area, including the world-famous Stratford Theatre Shakespeare festival.

GENERAL INFORMATION

Year founded:	1919
Undergraduate enrollment, full-time:	900
Graduate enrollment, full-time:	N/A
Faculty, full-time:	60
Number of international students:	N/A
Male/female ratio (%):	0:100
Residence spaces available:	167
Residence space guaranteed for 1st-year students:	Yes
Student media website:	N/A

UNDERGRADUATE ADMISSIONS

Office of the Registrar
London, ON N6G 1H2
PH: 519.432.8353 ext. 266   FAX: 519.679.6489
WEBSITE: www.uwo.ca/brescia/

Minimum high school average:	65
Rolling admissions:	Yes
International fall application deadline:	Jun 1
Application fee:	$105
Domestic fall application deadline:	Mar 1 (for scholarship consideration)
Application fee:	$105
Electronic application accepted:	No
Admissions notification by:	N/A
Required with application:	HS transcript, SAT

UNDERGRADUATE FINANCES

Undergraduate tuition:		
International students:	$12,600	(US $11,300)
Canadian students:	$4200	(US $3800)
Estimated annual health insurance:	$700	(US $630)
Estimated annual books & supplies:	$1000	(US $900)
Financial aid available for international students:	Yes	
Application deadline:	Mar 31	
Scholarships available for international students:	Yes	
Application deadline:	N/A	
Annual room/board cost for students in residence:	$6500	(US $5850)
Average monthly rent for students living off campus:		
1 bedroom: $350+, 2 bedroom: $450+		

UNDERGRADUATE INSTRUCTIONAL PROGRAM

Most popular majors: Arts, Social Science, Business, Nutritional Sciences
Percentages by program: 70% Liberal Arts, 20% Science, 8% Business, 2% Health Professions
Special study options: Internships, study abroad, language programs, special summer programs, distance learning programs

Liberal Arts and Sciences, General Studies, and Humanities

Anthropology, English Language & Literature, Fine/Studio Arts, French Language & Literature, German Language & Literature, History, Philosophy, Political Science, Psychology, Religion/Religious Studies, Sociology, Spanish Language & Literature

Science and Mathematics

Chemistry, Food Science & Technology, Geography, Mathematics

Professional Studies

Family & Community Studies, Human Ecology

Business and Economics

Business Administration & Management/Commerce, Economics

Health Professions and Related Sciences

Nutritional Sciences

BROCK UNIVERSITY

St. Catharines, Ontario

SCHOOL CATEGORY: Bachelor's/General   **TOTAL ENROLLMENT: 15,000**   **SETTING: Urban**   **CITY POPULATION: 140,000**

Brock University is a medium-sized comprehensive school characterized by a friendly atmosphere and attention to the individual. Located in St. Catharine's on the Niagara Peninsula, the school sits on a beautiful campus where students are surrounded by unique architecture, well-kept grounds, and modern sculptures. The school was founded in 1964.

Brock's six faculties offer more than 100 undergraduate majors. The school emphasizes the seminar system and small-group learning. Brock has close ties to local industries, as seen in its unique programs such as the bachelor's program in viticulture, developed in partnership with local wine producers.

Residence spaces are guaranteed to first-year students with averages over 75 percent. Brock students are active in sports and other recreational activities. The school has excellent athletic facilities.

Located about an hour's drive from both Toronto and Buffalo, Brock students can enjoy the features of both cities and countries. The Niagara Peninsula is a well-known tourist area featuring excellent theater, restaurants, museums, and historic sites.

GENERAL INFORMATION

Year founded:	1964
Undergraduate enrollment, full-time:	13,000
Graduate enrollment, full-time:	500
Faculty, full-time:	366
Number of international students:	801
Male/female ratio (%)	40:60
Residence spaces available:	1638
Residence space guaranteed for 1st-year students:	Yes (with 75% average)
Student media website:	www.brockpress.com

UNDERGRADUATE ADMISSIONS

Recruitment & Liasion Office
500 Glenridge Avenue
St. Catharines, ON L2S 3A1
PH: **905.688. 5550** EXT.**4293**   FAX: **902.688.4283**
WEBSITE: **www.brocku.ca**

Minimum high school average:	70
Applications, 2000-2001:	N/A
Rolling admissions:	Yes
Fall application deadline:	Mar 1
Application fee:	$105
Electronic application accepted:	Yes
Admissions notification by:	Mar 1
Required with application:	HS transcript
Recommended:	SAT

UNDERGRADUATE FINANCES

Undergraduate tuition:		
International students:	$12,000	(US $10,800)
Canadian students:	$4200	(US $3800)
Estimated annual health insurance:	$700	(US $630)
Estimated annual books & supplies:	$1000	(US $900)
Financial aid available for international students:	No	
Application deadline:	N/A	
Scholarships available for international students:	Yes	
Application deadline:	Mar	
Annual room/board cost for students in residence:	$7000-9000	(US $6300-8100)
Average monthly rent for students living off campus:		
1 bedroom: $300-600, 2 bedroom: $450-700		
Federal School Code: G09252		

UNDERGRADUATE INSTRUCTIONAL PROGRAM

Most popular majors: Accounting, Business, Health Sciences, Physical Eduction Teaching & Coaching
Percentages by program: N/A
Special study options: Co-op programs, internships, study abroad, language programs, special summer programs

Liberal Arts and Sciences, General Studies, and Humanities

Applied Language Studies, Canadian Studies, Classics & Classical Languages & Literature, Communications, Contemporary Cultural Studies, Comparative Literature, Drama/Theater Arts, English Language & Literature, French Language & Literature, German Language & Literature, History, Humanities/Humanistic Studies, International Relations & Affairs, Italian Language & Literature, Music, Philosophy, Political Science, Spanish Language & Literature, Visual & Performing Arts, Women's Studies

Science and Mathematics

Biochemistry, Biological Sciences/Life Sciences, Biology, Biotechnology Research, Chemistry, Earth & Planetary Science, Environmental Sciences, Geography, Mathematics, Oenology & Viticulture, Physical Geography, Physics

Computer Science and Engineering

Computer & Information Sciences, Computer Engineering, Environmental/Environmental Health Engineering

Professional Studies

Adult Education, Child Growth/Care & Development Studies, Criminal Justice Studies, Education (enterprise, native teacher), Leisure & Recreation Activities, Physical Education Kinesiology & Sports Management, Tourism

Business and Economics

Accounting, Business Administration & Management/Commerce, Entrepreneurship, Finance, Human Resource Management, International Business, Public Administration, Quantitative Analysis

Health Professions and Related Sciences

Health Sciences, Neuroscience, Nursing, Public Health

GRADUATE ADMISSIONS

Office of Graduate Admissions
Brock University
500 Glenridge Avenue
St. Catharines, ON   L2S 3A1
PH: 905.688.5550 EXT. **3239**   FAX:**905.684.2277**
WEBSITE: **www.brocku.ca/gradstudies/**

International fall application deadline:	Mar 1
Application fee:	$35
Domestic fall application deadline:	Mar 1
Application fee:	$50
Required with application:	GRE (for physics & psychology), college transcript, essay, recommendations, required for some programs
Graduate student housing:	Single student accommodations

GRADUATE FINANCES

Graduate tuition:

International students:	$11,000	(US $9900)
Canadian students:	$4600-7000	(US $4100-6300)
Financial aid & Scholarships available for		
international students:	Yes	
Application deadline:	Mar 1	

GRADUATE INSTRUCTIONAL PROGRAM

Liberal Arts and Sciences, General Studies, and Humanities
Philosophy, Politics, Popular Culture, Psychology

Science and Mathematics
Accounting, Biological/Life Sciences, Biotechnology Research, Chemistry, Earth & Planetary Sciences, Physics

Professional Studies
Child Growth Care & Development, Education

Business and Economics
Accounting

Health Professions and Related Sciences
Health Sciences

CARLETON UNIVERSITY

Ottawa, Ontario

SCHOOL CATEGORY: Master's	TOTAL ENROLLMENT: 20,000	SETTING: Urban	CITY POPULATION: 1,000,000

Carleton University is a medium-sized comprehensive university located in the Canadian capital of Ottawa, a friendly, clean, and safe city of approximately one million people. Carleton students benefit from the university's close links to government departments, research laboratories and the capital's diplomatic and business community. Ottawa, often referred to as Silicon Valley North, boasts a fast-growing concentration of high-tech companies.

The school offers undergraduate programs in over 60 areas and graduate programs in over 50 areas. Carleton has earned an excellent reputation in the fields of public affairs and management as well as in high technology, computer science and engineering. Journalism and the liberal arts areas are also areas of strength. Carleton has forged many partnerships with business and industry and with other educational institutions. Many graduate programs are jointly offered with the University of Ottawa, allowing the sharing of resources and expertise. Job prospects for graduates are very good; local high-tech companies such as Nortel Networks and JDS Uniphase heavily recruit students.

First-year students with an average of 75 percent or better are given priority in residence accommodation selection. First-year students live in double rooms and are given a choice of all-female, all-male, or coed accommodations. Outdoor enthusiasts will find plenty to enjoy in the surrounding countryside; excellent skiing, hiking, and water-sport areas abound. Ottawa has a thriving cultural scene which includes the National Gallery of Canada and the Canadian Museum of Civilization.

With its wealth of advantages, Carleton provides a vibrant living and learning environment for college students.

GENERAL INFORMATION

Year founded:	1942
Undergraduate enrollment, full-time:	17,000
Graduate enrollment, full-time:	2000
Faculty, full-time:	620
Number of international students:	N/A
Male/female ratio (%)	44:56
Residence spaces available:	1700
Residence space guaranteed for 1st-year students:	Yes (with 75% HS average)
Student media website:	www.thecharlatan.on.ca

UNDERGRADUATE ADMISSIONS

Office of Admissions
315 Robertson Hall
Ottawa, ON K1S 5B6
PH: 613.520.3663   FAX: 613.520.3847
WEBSITE: www.carleton.ca

Minimum high school average:	80
Applications, 2000-2001:	N/A
Rolling admissions:	Yes
Fall application deadline:	Apr 1
Application fee:	$105
Electronic application accepted:	Yes
Admissions notification by:	N/A
Required with application:	HS transcript
Recommended:	SAT

UNDERGRADUATE FINANCES

Undergraduate tuition:		
International students:	$12,000	(US $10,800)
Canadian students:	$4200	(US $3780)
Estimated annual health insurance:	$700	(US $630)
Estimated annual books & supplies:	$1000	(US $900)
Financial aid available for international students:	No	
Application deadline:	N/A	
Scholarships available for international students:	Yes	
Application deadline:	May 1	
Annual room/board cost for students in residence:	$6500-8500	(US 5850-7650)

Average monthly rent for students living off campus:
1 bedroom: $550-850, 2 bedroom: $700-1000
Federal School Code: G08368

UNDERGRADUATE INSTRUCTIONAL PROGRAM

Most popular majors: Business, Computer Science, Engineering, Journalism
Percentages by program: N/A
Special study options: Co-op programs, internships, study abroad, language programs, special summer programs, distance learning programs

Liberal Arts and Sciences, General Studies, and Humanities

Anthropology, Art, Art History, Canadian Studies, Classics & Classical Languages & Literature, English Language & Literature, European Studies, Film/Cinema, French Language & Literature, International Studies, History, Humanities/Humanistic Studies, Linguistics, Music, Philosophy, Political Science, Psychology, Religion/Religious Studies, Russian & Slavic Area Studies, Russian Languages & Literature, Social Work, Sociology, Women's Studies, Writing

Science and Mathematics

Applied Physics, Biochemistry, Biological/Life Sciences, Biology, Biophysics, Biotechnology Research, Chemistry, Earth & Planetary Science, Environmental Sciences, Geography, Geology, Geophysics & Seismology, Mathematics, Microbiology, Physics

Computer Science and Engineering

Aerospace Engineering, Civil Engineering, Computer & Information Sciences, Computer Engineering, Electrical/ Electronics & Communication Engineering, Engineering Physics, Environmental/ Environmental Health Engineering, Engineering Science, Mechanical Engineering, Software Engineering

Professional Studies

Child Growth, Criminal Justice Studies, Journalism

Business and Economics

Accounting, Business Operations Analysis, Business Administration & Management/Commerce, Economics, Finance, Human Resources Management, Information Sciences & Systems, International Business, Labor/Personnel Relations & Studies, Management Science, Management Information Systems & Business Data Processing, Marketing Management & Research, Operations Management & Supervision

Health Professions and Related Sciences

Neuroscience

GRADUATE ADMISSIONS

Faculty of Graduate Studies and Research
1516 Dunton Tower/ 1125 Colonel By Drive
Ottawa, ON K1S 5B6
PH: **613.520.2525**   FAX: **613.520.4049**
WEBSITE: **www.gs.carleton.ca**

Fall application deadline:	Mar 1–Jul 1
Application fee:	N/A
Electronic application accepted:	Yes, depending upon program
Required with application:	College transcript, honours bachelor's degree
Graduate student housing:	Available with single rooms in single gender or co-ed living, no married/family housing

GRADUATE FINANCES

Graduate tuition:

International students:	$8300-9000	(US $7500-8100)
Canadian students:	$4000-5500	(US $3600-4950)

Financial aid & Scholarships available for

for international students:	Yes
Application deadline:	Mar 1

GRADUATE INSTRUCTIONAL PROGRAM

Liberal Arts and Sciences, General Studies, and Humanities

Anthropology, Applied Language Studies, Art History, Canadian Studies, Cognitive Studies, Communications, Comparative Literature, Cultural Mediations, English Language & Literature, European Studies, Film/Cinema, French Language & Literature, History, International Relations & Affairs, Linguistics, Philosophy, Political Science, Psychology, Religion/Religious Studies, Russian & Slavic Area Studies, Russian Languages & Literature, Social Work, Sociology

Science and Mathematics

Biology, Chemistry, Geography, Geosciences, Environmental Sciences, Science, Mathematics, Physics, Statistics

Computer Science and Engineering

Aerospace Engineering, Computer Science, Civil Engineering, Electrical/Electronics & Communications Engineering, Environmental/Environmental Health Engineering, Materials Engineering, Mechanical Engineering, Software Engineering, Telecommunications Technology Management

Professional Studies

Law

Business and Economics

Economics, Information Sciences & Systems, Public Administration

Health Professions and Related Sciences

Neuroscience

HURON UNIVERSITY COLLEGE

London, Ontario

SCHOOL CATEGORY: Bachelor's/Liberal Arts   **TOTAL ENROLLMENT: 1100**   **SETTING: Suburban**   **CITY POPULATION: 330,000**

Huron University College is a small residential liberal arts college academically affiliated with the University of Western Ontario. Huron students have full access to the courses, facilities and sports at Western. Students enjoy personal attention and small classes. Ninety percent of first-year classes have less than fifty students.

Residence is guaranteed to all first-year students. Huron offers residence accommodations for 329 students in single and double rooms. Co-ed and single-sex residences are available. Off-campus housing is also widely available in London.

London, Canada's tenth largest city, with a population of over 300,000, is situated midway between Toronto and Detroit, roughly 2 hours' drive from each. The city offers all the urban amenities—shopping, dining, theaters, clubs, art galleries, and parks. It also has a comfortable "college town" feel. Throughout the year there are many festivals in the area, including the world-famous Stratford Theatre Shakespeare festival.

GENERAL INFORMATION

Year founded:	1863
Undergraduate enrollment, full-time:	1100
Graduate enrollment, full-time:	N/A
Faculty, full-time:	43
Number of international students:	90
Male/female ratio (%)	50:50
Residence spaces available:	332
Residence space guaranteed for 1st-year students:	Yes
Student media website:	N/A

UNDERGRADUATE ADMISSIONS

Office of the Registrar
1349 Western Road
London, ON   N6G 1H3
PH: **519.438.7224 ext.203**   FAX: **519.438.3938**
WEBSITE: **www.huronuc.on.ca**

Minimum high school average:	75
Rolling admissions:	No
International fall application deadline:	N/A
Application fee:	$105
Domestic fall application deadline:	Mar 1
Application fee:	$105
Electronic application accepted:	Yes
Admissions notification by:	N/A
Required with application:	HS transcript, SAT

UNDERGRADUATE FINANCES

Undergraduate tuition:		
International students:	$12,600	(US $11,300)
Canadian students:	$4200	(US $3800)
Estimated annual health insurance:	$700	(US $630)
Estimated annual books & supplies:	$1000	(US $900)
Financial aid & Scholarships available for		
international students:	Yes	
Application deadline:	Mar 1	
Annual room/board cost for students in residence:	$7000-7500	(US $6300-6750)
Average monthly rent for students living off campus:		
1 bedroom: $400-600, 2 bedroom: $500-800		

UNDERGRADUATE INSTRUCTIONAL PROGRAM

Most popular majors: Economics, English, Political Science, History
Percentages by program: 95% Liberal Arts, 1% Health Professions
Special study options: Co-op programs, internships, study abroad, language programs

Liberal Arts and Sciences, General Studies, and Humanities

Anthropology, Classics & Classical Languages & Literature, Comparative Literature, English Language & Literature, Film/Cinema, French Language & Literature, German Language & Literature, History, International Relations & Affairs, Philosophy, Political Science, Psychology, Russian & Slavic Area Studies, Religion/Religious Studies, Sociology, Spanish Language & Literature, Theology/Theological Studies, Visual & Performing Arts, Women's Studies

Science and Mathematics

Geography, Mathematics

Business and Economics

Business Administration & Management/Commerce, Economics

Professional Studies

Human Kinetics/Kinesiology, Physical Education Teaching & Coaching

GRADUATE ADMISSIONS

Huron University College
Faculty of Theology
London, ON   N6G 1H3
Ph: 519.438.7224 ext. 289
E-Mail: srice@julian.uwo.ca

GRADUATE INSTRUCTIONAL PROGRAM

Divinity/Ministry, Theology/Theological Studies

KING'S COLLEGE

London, Ontario

SCHOOL CATEGORY: Bachelor's/Liberal Arts　**TOTAL ENROLLMENT: 3000**　**SETTING: Suburban**　**CITY POPULATION: 330,000**

King's College is a Catholic liberal arts university affiliated with the University of Western Ontario. Located next to Western's campus in London, Ontario, King's offers students all the advantages of belonging to a small college while having full access to a larger university's facilities.

King's offers degree programs in arts and social science, administrative and commercial studies, childhood and family relations, health sciences, kinesiology, media, and social work. Class sizes are small, and the faculty/student ratio is low.

Residence is guaranteed to all first-year students. Off-campus housing is also widely available in London. Students enjoy the use of all services and facilities of the University of Western Ontario. Through Western students also have access to excellent cultural and athletic activities.

London, Canada's tenth largest city, with a population of over 300,000, is situated midway between Toronto and Detroit, roughly two hours' drive from each. The city offers all the urban amenities—shopping, dining, theaters, clubs, art galleries, and parks. It also has a comfortable "college town" feel. Throughout the year there are many festivals in the area, including the world-famous Stratford Theatre Shakespeare festival.

GENERAL INFORMATION

Year founded:	1954
Undergraduate enrollment, full-time:	3000
Graduate enrollment, full-time:	N/A
Faculty, full-time:	65
Number of international students:	115
Male/female ratio (%)	45:55
Residence spaces available:	375
Residence space guaranteed for 1st-year students:	Yes
Student media website:	N/A

UNDERGRADUATE ADMISSIONS

Office of the Registrar
288 Epworth Avenue
London, ON   N6A 2M3
PH: **519.433.3491**   FAX: **519.433.2227**
WEBSITE: **www.uwo.ca/kings**

Minimum high school average:	75
Rolling admissions:	Yes
International fall application deadline:	Mar 1
Application fee:	$105
Domestic fall application deadline:	Jun 1
Application fee:	$105
Electronic application accepted:	No
Admissions notification by:	N/A
Required with application:	HS transcript, SAT
Recommended:	Essay

UNDERGRADUATE FINANCES

Undergraduate tuition:		
International students:	$12600	(US $11,300)
Canadian students:	$4200	(US $3800)
Estimated annual health insurance:	$703	(US $630)
Estimated annual books & supplies:	$1000	(US $900)
Financial aid available for international students:	Yes	
Application deadline:	ASAP	
Scholarships available for international students:	Yes	
Application deadline:	Automatically considered	
Annual room/board cost for students in residence:	$7000	(US $6300)
Average monthly rent for students living off campus:		
1 bedroom: $350+, 2 bedroom: $500+		

UNDERGRADUATE INSTRUCTIONAL PROGRAM

Most popular majors: Childhood & Family Relations, Arts & Social Sciences, Commerce, Media
Percentages by program: 60% Liberal Arts, 17% Business
Special study options: Internships, study abroad, language programs, special summer programs, distance learning programs

Liberal Arts and Sciences, General Studies, and Humanities

English Language & Literature, French Language & Literature, History, Philosophy, Political Science, Psychology, Religion/Religious Studies, Social Work, Sociology, Writing

Computer Science and Engineering

Computer & Information Sciences, Management Information Systems

Professional Studies

Child Growth/ Care & Development Studies, Family & Community Studies, Human Kinetics/Kinesiology, Radio & Television Broadcasting

Business and Economics

Accounting, Business Administration and Management/ Commerce, Economics, Finance, Human Resources Management, Marketing Management & Research, Operations Management & Supervision

Health Professions and Related Sciences

Health Sciences

LAKEHEAD UNIVERSITY

Thunder Bay, Ontario

SCHOOL CATEGORY: Bachelor's/General   **TOTAL ENROLLMENT: 7000**   **SETTING: Suburban**   **CITY POPULATION: 117,000**

Established in 1965, medium-sized Lakehead University is dedicated to achieving excellence in teaching, research, and scholarship. With a campus backyard that includes the Canadian Shield and Lake Superior, Lakehead is situated on approximately 300 acres of wooded land overlooking the city of Thunder Bay. Thunder Bay, with a population of about 125,000, is located on the northern shore of Lake Superior, the world's largest lake.

Lakehead has tailored much of its curriculum to reflect the natural resources and environment of its boreal forest region. Programs such as biology, forestry, geography, geology, outdoor recreation, and parks and tourism take advantage of a natural laboratory in and around the university. Lakehead also has the Northern Ontario School of Medicine, west campus – Canada's first medical school in 30 years. It has also opened a new campus in Orillia in Southern Ontario, approximately 40 miles from Toronto.

Opened in 2004, Lakehead's Advanced Technology and Academic Centre (ATAC) is considered one of the most technologically advanced teaching and learning facilities. It has 16 smart classrooms, video and teleconferencing facilities, a virtual reality lab, and a robotics facility. Special classes often connect with lectures in other countries.

Residence spaces are guaranteed to first-year students who register on time, and are a mix of coed, male-only, and female-only. The size and location of the university promote an intimate, socially active campus life experience. The school has excellent athletics facilities with the recent addition of The Hangar, a 60-000-square foot facility which houses an indoor running track, multi-purpose indoor field, aerobic/yoga studio, weight room and fitness center, climbing wall, student lounge, and a sports medicine clinic.

The northwestern Ontario region offers a wide variety of recreational opportunities for students. Within 15 minutes of the campus are three local ski resorts for both alpine and Nordic skiing, and recreational activities such as sailing, fishing, rock climbing, kayaking, and swimming are readily available.

GENERAL INFORMATION

Year Founded:	1965
Undergraduate enrollment, full-time:	5702
Graduate enrollment, full-time:	385
Faculty, full-time:	285
Number of International Students:	140
Male/Female ratio (%):	43:57
Resident Spaces available:	1281
Residence space guaranteed for 1st-year students:	No
Student media website:	www.lusu.lakeheadu.ca/outpost

UNDERGRADUATE ADMISSIONS

Department of International Activities
955 Oliver Road, Thunder Bay, ON P7B 5E1
PH: 807.343.8133 FAX: 807.343.7829
WEBSITE: www.lakeheadu.ca

Minimum high school average:	70
Applications, 2000-01:	N/A
International fall application deadline:	Mar 1
Application fee:	$105
Domestic fall applications deadline:	Dec-Mar
Application fee:	$105
Rolling admissions:	Yes
Electronic application accepted:	Yes
Admissions notification by:	N/A
Required with application:	HS transcript, (SAT & ACT required for some programs)

UNDERGRADUATE FINANCES

Undergraduate tuition:		
International students:	$9400	(US $8460)
Canadian students:	$4200	(US $3780)
Estimated annual health insurance:	$125	(US $110)
Estimated annual books & supplies:	$1000	(US $900)
Financial aid & Scholarships available for		
International students:	No	
Application deadline:	N/A	
Annual room/board cost for students in residence:	$6700-7700	(US $6000-7000)

Average monthly rent for students living off campus:
One bedroom $350-600; Two bedroom: $550-700
Federal School Code: G08913

UNDERGRADUATE INSTRUCTIONAL PROGRAM

Most popular majors: Business, Engineering, Kinesiology, Nursing, Outdoor Recreation
Percentages by program: 33% Liberal Arts, 19% Health Professions, 16% Science, 10% Engineering/Computer Science, 8% Business
Special study options: Co-op, internships, study abroad, language programs, special summer programs, distance learning programs

Liberal Arts and Sciences, General Studies, and Humanities

Anthropology, Art, English Language & Literature, History, Interdisciplinary Studies, Humanities/Humanistic Studies, Language & Literature, Music, Northern Studies, Philosophy, Political Science, Psychology, Religion/Religious Studies, Social Work, Sociology, Visual & Performing Arts, Women's Studies

Science and Mathematics

Biological/Life Sciences, Biology, Chemistry, Environmental Sciences, General Science, Geoarchaeology, Geography, Geology, Mathematics, Physics, Water Resource Science

Computer Science and Engineering

Chemical Engineering, Civil Engineering, Computer & Information Sciences, Electrical/ Electronics & Communication Engineering, Mechanical Engineering, Software Engineering

Professional Studies

Education, Human Kinetics/Kinesiology, Library & Information Sciences, Leisure & Recreational Activities, Tourism

Business and Economics

Business Administration & Management/Commerce, Economics, Public Administration

Health Professions & Related Sciences

Nursing

GRADUATE ADMISSIONS

Office of Graduate Studies
Lakehead University
955 Oliver Road
Thunder Bay, ON   P7B 5E1
PH: **807.343.8785**   FAX: **807.346.7749**
E-MAIL: **graduate.studies@lakeheadu.ca**

Fall application deadline:	Feb 1 (For financial assistance consideration)
Application fee:	$100
Required with application:	College transcript, recommendations
Graduate student housing:	Townhouses for upper year students with 3 & 4 bedrooms, single rooms

GRADUATE FINANCES

Graduate tuition:

International students:	$10,000-15,000	(US $9000-13,500)
Canadian students:	$5200-9000	(US $4700-8100)
Financial aid & Scholarships available for		
international students:	Yes	
Application deadline:	Mar 1	

GRADUATE INSTRUCTIONAL PROGRAM

Liberal Arts and Sciences, General Studies, and Humanities
Canadian Philosophy, Clinical Psychology, English Language & Literature, Experimental Psychology, Gerontology, History, Social Work, Sociology, Women's Studies

Science and Mathematics
Biology, Chemistry, Environmental Studies, Forestry Sciences, Geology, Mathematics, Physics

Business and Economics
Economics, Management

Computer Science and Engineering
Control Engineering

Professional Studies
Sport & Fitness Administration/Management/Coaching, Education, Human Kinetics/Kinesiology

LAURENTIAN UNIVERSITY

Sudbury, Ontario

SCHOOL CATEGORY: Bachelor's/General   **TOTAL ENROLLMENT: 8100**   **SETTING: Suburban**   **CITY POPULATION: 100,000**

Laurentian University is a young, primarily undergraduate bilingual institution. The campus is located on 750 acres of scenic countryside a short distance from downtown Sudbury. Sudbury is one of the leading mining centers in the world and today the city is emerging as a thriving center for high-technology industries. Adjacent to the main campus is the affiliated University of Sudbury, a small undergraduate liberal arts institution. Other affiliated colleges include: Algoma, Huntington and Thorneloe.

Laurentian offers a broad variety of three- and four-year programs in the arts, social sciences and humanities, science, and professional schools. Laurentian has maintained a friendly, accessible atmosphere, with small class sizes that allow students ready interaction with professors.

The university has residence accommodations for over 1,200 students. First-year students who submit their applications on time are guaranteed a space in residence. Laurentian offers a variety of extracurricular activities and has excellent athletic facilities. For outdoor enthusiasts, recreational opportunities, including skiing, hiking, and canoeing, abound in and around Sudbury.

GENERAL INFORMATION

Year founded:	1960
Undergraduate enrollment, full-time:	6074
Graduate enrollment, full-time:	234
Faculty, full-time:	370
Number of international students:	500
Male/female ratio (%)	41:59
Residence spaces available:	1270
Residence space guaranteed for 1st-year students:	Yes
Student media website:	www.sga.laurentian.ca

UNDERGRADUATE ADMISSIONS

Office of Admissions
935 Ramsey Lake Road
Sudbury, ON   P3E 2C6
PH: **705.675.1151**   FAX: **705.675.4847**
WEBSITE: **www.laurentian.ca**

Minimum high school average:	70
Applications, 2005:	N/A
Rolling admissions:	Yes
International fall application deadline:	Mar 31
Application fee:	$55
Domestic fall application deadline:	Dec 15
Application fee:	$85
Electronic application accepted:	Yes
Admissions notification by:	Jun 1
Required with application:	HS transcript, SAT I (1100 min.), ACT
Recommendation:	Essay, recommendations, interview

UNDERGRADUATE FINANCES

Undergraduate tuition:		
International students:	$10,087	(US $9078)
Canadian students:	$4515	(US $4063)
Estimated annual health insurance:	$300-600	(US $270-540)
Estimated annual books & supplies:	$800	(US $720)
Financial aid available for international students:	No	
Application deadline:	N/A	
Scholarships available for international students:	Yes, after 1st year	
Application deadline:	Jun 1	
Annual room/board cost for students in residence:	$4500-4900	(US $4050-4410)
Average monthly rent for students living off campus:		
1 bedroom: $400-500, 2 bedroom: $500-700		
Federal School Code: G09180		

UNDERGRADUATE INSTRUCTIONAL PROGRAM

Most popular majors: Business, Environmental Studies, Human Kinetics, Nursing
Percentages by program: 22% Liberal Arts, 22% Science, 12% Business, 6% Engineering/Computer Science
Special study options: Co-op programs, internships, language programs, distance learning programs

Liberal Arts and Sciences, General Studies, and Humanities

Anthropology, Classics & Classical Languages & Literature, English Language & Literature, French Language & Literature, Ethics Studies, Modern Languages & Literatures, German Language & Literature, Gerontology, History, Humanities/Humanistic Studies, Liberal Science, Native Studies, Philosophy, Political Science, Psychology, Religion/Religious Studies, Social Work, Sociology, Spanish Language & Literature, Translation, Visual & Performing Arts, Women's Studies

Science and Mathematics

Biology, Biochemistry, Chemistry, Environmental Science, Geography, Geology, Mathematics, Microbiology, Physics

Computer Science and Engineering

Electrical/Electronics & Communication Engineering, Engineering Science

Professional Studies

Criminal Justice Studies, Human Kinetics/Kinesiology

Business and Economics

Business Administration & Management/Commerce, Economics, Labour/Personnel Relations & Studies, Sport & Fitness Administration/Management

Health Professions and Related Sciences

Nursing

GRADUATE ADMISSIONS

School of Graduate Studies
JD Parket Building/ L-314
Sudbury, ON   P3E 2C6
PH: **705.675.1151 ext 3423**   FAX: **705.671.3840**
WEBSITE: **www.laurentian.ca/admin/grad_study**

Fall application deadline:	Mar 1
Application fee:	$50
Electronic application accepted:	Yes
Required with application:	GRE, college transcript, essay, recommendations, (GRE & GMAT per department)
Graduate student housing:	1 BR apartments available for mature/married students

GRADUATE FINANCES

Graduate tuition:		
International students:	$8300-13,250	(US $7455-11,925)
Canadian students:	$6600	(US $5940)
Financial aid & Scholarships available for		
international students:	Yes	
Application Deadline:	Early application preferred	

GRADUATE INSTRUCTIONAL PROGRAM

Liberal Arts and Sciences, General Studies, and Humanities
English, History, Humanities/Humanistic Studies, Social Work, Sociology

Science and Mathematics
Biology, Botany, Chemistry, Geology, Microbiology, Physiology, Physics, Zoology

Computer Science and Engineering
Mineral & Mineral Engineering

Business and Economics
Business Administration & Management/Commerce

McMASTER UNIVERSITY

Hamilton, Ontario

SCHOOL CATEGORY: Doctoral/Research   **TOTAL ENROLLMENT: 25,000**   **SETTING: Suburban**   **CITY POPULATION: 500,000**

McMaster University is one of the top teaching and research institutions in Canada. The university's attractive main campus combines traditional and modern construction and is located next to the Royal Botanical Gardens at the western end of Lake Ontario in a residential section of Hamilton.

McMaster, offers 135 undergraduate and 65 graduate degree programs. McMaster is known as a pioneering institution in many areas. McMaster was the first medical school in the world to train doctors using the problem-based learning method, which has subsequently been adopted by other leading medical schools including Harvard. Many of the school's programs are interdisciplinary. McMaster is a leader in telecommunications, manufacturing, materials, and health research. The school operates 18 research centers and institutes. Admission to McMaster is competitive.

On-campus men's, women's, and coeducational residences are available for about 2,800 students. Residence spaces are guaranteed to students applying with a 75% or higher average. The recreation and intramural programs offer more than 30 different sports, in which over 5,000 students participate. The athletic facilities include an Olympic-sized pool, track and field facilities, and fully equipped gyms.

Less than an hour from Toronto, Hamilton is a part of southern Ontario's Golden Horseshoe region surrounding Lake Ontario. Historically known for its heavy industry and steel mills, it is also a cultural and recreational center. Niagara Falls and Buffalo, New York, are less than an hour's drive away. The area also offers abundant recreational activities.

GENERAL INFORMATION

Year founded:	1887
Undergraduate enrollment, full-time:	18,921
Graduate enrollment, full-time:	2300
Faculty, full-time:	1152
Number of international students:	950
Male/female ratio (%)	46:54
Residence spaces available:	2800
Residence space guaranteed for 1st-year students:	Yes (with 75% average)
Student media website:	www.thesil.ca

UNDERGRADUATE ADMISSIONS

Office of Admissions
1280 Main Street West
Hamilton, ON   L8S 4L8
PH: 905.525.9140   FAX: 905.546.5212
WEBSITE: www.mcmaster.ca

Minimum high school average:	72-80%
Applications, 2000-2001:	N/A
Rolling admissions:	No
International fall application deadline:	May 1
Application fee:	$145
Domestic fall application deadline:	Jul 15
Application fee:	$145
Electronic application accepted:	Yes
Admissions notification by:	Apr 23/May 30
Required with application:	HS transcript; essay for some programs

UNDERGRADUATE FINANCES

Undergraduate tuition:		
International students:	$13,000-18,000	(US $11,700-16,500)
Canadian students:	$5000-6000	(US $4500-5500)
Estimated annual health insurance:	$703	(US $630)
Financial aid available for international students:	No	
Application deadline:	N/A	
Scholarships available for international students:	Yes	
Application deadline:	N/A	
Annual room/board cost for students in		
residence:	$4900-8000	(US $4400-7200)
Average monthly rent for students living off campus:		
1 bedroom: $400-500, 2 bedroom: $550-650		
Federal School Code: G06853		

UNDERGRADUATE INSTRUCTIONAL PROGRAM

Most popular majors: Commerce, Kinesiology, Nursing, Engineering
Percentages by program: 39% Liberal Arts, 19% Science, 18% Engineering/Computer Science, 12% Business, 12% Health Professions
Special study options: Co-op programs, internships, study abroad, language programs, special summer programs, distance learning programs

Liberal Arts and Sciences, General Studies, and Humanities

Anthropology, Archaeology, Art, Art History, Classics & Classical Languages & Literature, Communications, Comparative Literature, Drama/Theater Arts, English Language & Literature, Fine/Studio Arts, French Language & Literature, German Language & Literature, Hispanic Studies, Gerontology, History, Humanities/Humanistic Studies, Italian Language & Literature, Japanese Language & Literature, Linguistics, Modern Languages, Multimedia, Music, Native Studies, Peace Studies, Philosophy, Political Science, Psychology, Religion/Religious Studies, Social Work, Sociology, Women's Studies

Science and Mathematics

Applied Mathematics, Astronomy/Astrophysics, Biological Sciences/Life Sciences, Biology, Biochemistry, Chemistry, Environmental Science, Geography, Geophysics & Seismology, Mathematics, Physical Science, Physics, Statistics

Computer Science and Engineering

Chemical Engineering, Civil Engineering, Computer & Information Sciences, Computer Engineering, Electrical/Electronics & Communication Engineering, Engineering Physics, Engineering Science, Geological Engineering, Industrial/Manufacturing Engineering, Materials Engineering, Materials Science, Mechanical Engineering, Software Engineering

Business and Economics

Business Administration & Management/Commerce, Economics, Business, Labor/Personnel Relations & Studies

Professional Studies

Human Kinetics/Kinesiology

Health Professions and Related Sciences

Health Studies, Life Sciences, Medical & Health Physics, Neurosciences, Nursing

GRADUATE ADMISSIONS

School of Graduate Studies
McMaster University
Togo Salmon Hall Room 111
Hamilton, ON   L8S 4M2
PH: **905.525.9140**   FAX: **905.529.0689**
WEBSITE: **www.mcmaster.ca/graduate/**

International fall application deadline:	N/A
Application fee:	$75
Domestic fall application deadline:	Feb
Application fee:	$50
Electronic application accepted:	No
Required with application:	Transcripts, letters of recommendations, essay (per department)
Graduate student housing:	Single residences in Bates Residence/ apartments with 4 & 6 bedrooms

GRADUATE FINANCES

Graduate tuition:		
International students:	$13,000-25,000	(US $11,700-22,500)
Canadian students:	$5000-8000	(US $4500-7200)
Financial aid & Scholarships available for		
international students:	Yes	
Application deadline:	Varies	

GRADUATE INSTRUCTIONAL PROGRAM

Liberal Arts and Sciences, General Studies, and Humanities

Anthropology, Classics & Classical Languages & Literature, English Language & Literature, French Language & Literature, History, Music, Philosophy, Political Science, Psychology, Social Work, Sociology

Science and Mathematics

Astronomy, Biochemistry, Biology, Geography, Geology, Mathematics, Statistics

Computer Science and Engineering

Chemical Engineering, Civil Engineering, Computer & Information Sciences, Computer Engineering, Electrical/ Electronics & Communication Engineering, Engineering Physics, Materials Science, Materials Engineering, Mechanical Engineering

Professional Studies

Human Kinetics/Kinesiology

Business and Economics

Labour/Personnel Relations & Studies

Health Professions

Health Sciences, Nursing, Medicine, Occupational Therapy, Physiotherapy, Rehabilitation Science

NIPISSING UNIVERSITY

North Bay, Ontario

SCHOOL CATEGORY: Bachelor's/Liberal Arts   **TOTAL ENROLLMENT: 4000**   **SETTING: Suburban**   **CITY POPULATION: 56,000**

Nipissing University, located in the rugged northern Ontario city of North Bay, is a small liberal arts university. The campus is located to the north of the city and is shared with Canadore College. The campus is situated in a beautiful wooded area, with many hiking and running trails.

Nipissing offers a variety of programs in the arts, sciences, business and education. The Faculty of Education represents over a third of the schools' overall enrollment. The university is noted for its Faculty of Education which is well-regarded for its ITeach program. The ITeach Laptop Learning Program involves the continuous use of laptop computers by all students and faculty. Research has demonstrated that expertise in the use of information technology in education is best acquired through ongoing "hands-on" exposure. Nipissing education students are known for their enthusiasm as well as the many clubs, groups and activities they partake in.

There are many year-round activities to enjoy, both on and off campus. From viewing the beautiful fall colors along Duchesney Falls in September to cross-country skiing and snowshoeing in winter, you'll have every opportunity to enjoy 12 miles of trails right on campus. Students can sign out cross-country skis and snowshoes free-of-charge from the Athletics Centre. Outdoor enthusiasts may also want to check out Jack Pine Hill, located just 10 minutes from Nipissing. This facility is well-known for its mountain biking in the summer and it's downhill skiing, snowboarding and tubing in the winter

At Nipissing students will find themselves in a high-quality academic environment that is student-focused and based on personal teaching practices, innovative approaches to learning, and a growing research culture.

GENERAL INFORMATION

Year founded:	1992
Undergraduate enrollment, full-time:	3071
Graduate enrollment, part-time:	349
Faculty, full-time:	200
Number of international students:	26
Male/female ratio (%)	28:72
Residence spaces available:	1007
Residence space guaranteed for 1st-year students:	Yes
Student media website:	www.nusu.com

UNDERGRADUATE ADMISSIONS

Office of the Registrar
100 College Drive/P.O. Box 5002
North Bay, ON   P1B 8L7
PH: **705.474.3461**   FAX: **705.495-1772**
WEBSITE: **www.nipissingu.ca**

Minimum high school average:	70
Applications, 2005-2006:	3000 Received; 1500 Accepted; 600 Enrolled
Rolling admissions:	Yes
Fall application deadline:	Apr 1
Application fee:	$145
Electronic application accepted:	Yes
Admissions notification by:	Jun 1
Required with application:	HS transcript

UNDERGRADUATE FINANCES

Undergraduate tuition:		
International students:	$9000	(US $8600)
Canadian students:	$4000	(US $3600)
Estimated annual health insurance:	$700	(US $490)
Estimated annual books & supplies:	$700	(US $350)
Financial aid available for international students:	No	
Application deadline:	N/A	
Scholarships available for international students:	No	
Application deadline:	N/A	
Annual room/board cost for students in residence:	$3600-4000	(US $3240-3600)
Average monthly rent for students living off campus:		
1 bedroom: $350-450, 2 bedroom: $500-600		
Federal School Code: G34653		

UNDERGRADUATE INSTRUCTIONAL PROGRAM

Most popular majors: Criminal Justice, Education, English, Environmental Studies, History, Psychology
Percentages by program: N/A
Special study options: Study abroad, distance learning programs

Liberal Arts and Sciences, General Studies, and Humanities

Anthropology, Classics & Classical Languages & Literature, English Language & Literature, French Language & Literature, Gender Equality: Social Justice, History, Humanities/Humanistic Studies, Native Studies, Philosophy, Psychology, Religion, Social Work, Sociology, Visual Arts

Science and Mathematics

Biology, Chemistry, Computer & Information Science, Environmental Science, Geography, General Science, Geology, Mathematics, Physical Geography, Physics

Professional Studies

Criminal Justice Studies, Education

Business and Economics

Business Administration & Management/Commerce, Economics, Human Resources Management, Information Sciences & Systems, Management Information Systems

Health

Nursing

ONTARIO COLLEGE OF ART & DESIGN

Toronto, Ontario

SCHOOL CATEGORY: Specialized   **TOTAL ENROLLMENT: 2400**   **SETTING: Urban**   **CITY POPULATION: 4,000,000**

The Ontario College of Art and Design (OCAD) is the largest university in Canada devoted exclusively to the education of professional artists and designers. Celebrating 125 years in 2001, the college, located in the heart of Toronto, is today an internationally recognized institution.

Students can choose from four-year programs with a concentration in either the Faculty of Arts or the Faculty of Design. The Foundation Year is a required first-year program designed to give students a solid grounding in fundamental techniques and an understanding of artistic traditions.

All students interested in attending the OCAD must participate in a portfolio review and interview, held each spring. Interviews are scheduled after applications have been received. A student's portfolio should contain 15 pieces of original artwork in a variety of media, and should represent a student's best work. The school does not provide residence accommodations, but these are easily available nearby.

The fifth largest city in North America, Toronto is one of the world's most cosmopolitan cities and is an exciting place to live. The city is home to hundreds of restaurants, theaters, art galleries, museums, clubs, and other cultural opportunities. Sports fans can choose to watch some of the area's many professional sports teams, including baseball's Blue Jays and hockey's Maple Leafs.

GENERAL INFORMATION

Year founded:	1876
Undergraduate enrollment, full-time:	1800
Graduate enrollment, full-time:	N/A
Faculty, full-time:	N/A
Number of international students:	N/A
Male/female ratio (%)	N/A
Residence spaces available:	No
Residence space guaranteed for 1st-year students:	No

UNDERGRADUATE ADMISSIONS

Admissions Department
100 McCaul Street
Toronto, ON   M5T 1W1
PH: **416.977.6000**
WEBSITE: **www.ocad.ca**

Minimum high school average:	70
Applications, 2000-2001:	N/A
Rolling admissions:	N/A
Fall application deadline:	Feb 3
Application fee:	$105
Electronic application accepted:	N/A
Required with application:	HS transcripts, portfolio, interview

UNDERGRADUATE FINANCES

Undergraduate tuition:		
International students:	$12,500	(US $11,250)
Canadian students:	$4200	(US $3800)
Estimated annual health insurance:	$528	(US $475)
Estimated annual books & supplies:	$2400	(US $2200)
Financial aid & Scholarships available for		
international students:	Yes	
Application deadline:	Feb 3	
Annual room/board cost for students in residence:	N/A	

Average monthly rent for students living off campus:
1 bedroom: $700-900, 2 bedroom: $1000-1200
Federal School Code: G20958

UNDERGRADUATE INSTRUCTIONAL PROGRAM

Most popular majors: Drawing & Painting, Graphic Design, Integrated Media
Percentages by program: 100% Arts
Special study options: Study abroad

Liberal Arts and Sciences, General Studies, and Humanities

Art, Art History, Ceramic Arts & Ceramics, Design & Applied Arts, Fine/Studio Arts, Integrated Media, Material & Art Design, Painting

ONTARIO UNIVERSITY OF TECHNOLOGY

Oshawa, Ontario

SCHOOL CATEGORY: Bachelor's   **TOTAL ENROLLMENT: 3000**   **SETTING: Suburban**   **CITY POPULATION: 150,000**

Canada's newest post-secondary institution, the University of Ontario Institute of Technology (UOIT), was created as a public, career-focused, research-intensive university emphasizing science and technology. UOIT opened in September 2003 and is located in Oshawa.

Ontario's fastest growing university, UOIT is also the province's first fully laptop-based university. Every student uses a current model IBM laptop to access course materials, conduct research, make presentations and communicate with faculty. Students are required to pay an additional fee for the lease of the laptop, software, and technical support.

UOIT offers a range of undergraduate programs with an oriented towards the practical application of Science and Technology. UOIT offers the only Nuclear Engineering program in Canada. The school also offers a specialization in video games. The automobile industry has always been Oshawa's lifeblood and the school has established close working ties with the area's automobile industry.

UOIT is located at a single campus on a 400 acre property, which it shares with Durham College. A $25-million engineering building is slated to open in the fall of 2006, followed by the new Automotive Center of Excellence in 2007. A multimillion-dollar renovation and expansion of the Campus Athletic Center will also be completed in 2007.

Residence space is guaranteed to all qualified first-year students. Rooms and suites in the Simcoe Village and South Village residences offer amenities and accommodation for over 1,300 students. With over 25 clubs the vibrant campus always has something to offer students.

Oshawa is a growing city on Lake Ontario located just 40 miles east of downtown Toronto. This close proximity to one of North America's most dynamic cities allows students to experience a wide range of cultural and entertainment options.

GENERAL INFORMATION

Year founded:	2003
Undergraduate enrollment, full-time:	3000
Faculty, full-time:	N/A
Number of international students:	150
Male/female ratio (%)	50:50
Residence spaces available:	1300
Residence space guaranteed for 1st-year students:	Yes
Student media website:	N/A

UNDERGRADUATE ADMISSIONS

Office of the Registrar
2000 Simcoe Street North
Oshawa, ON L1H 7K4
PH: 905.721.8668   FAX: 905.721.3178
WEBSITE: www.uoit.ca

Minimum high school average:	70
Applications, 2005-2006:	N/A
Rolling admissions:	No
International fall application deadline:	Feb 1
Application fee:	$105
Domestic fall application deadline:	Jan 11
Application fee:	$105
Electronic application accepted:	Yes
Admissions notification by:	May 30
Required with application:	HS transcript (plus required items dependent upon programs)

UNDERGRADUATE FINANCES

Undergraduate tuition:		
International students:	$12,000	(US $10,800)
Canadian students:	$4200	(US $3800)
Estimated annual health insurance:	$530	(US $480)
Estimated annual books & supplies:	$2500	(US $2250)
Financial aid available for international students:	No	
Application deadline:	N/A	
Scholarships available for international students:	Yes	
Application deadline:	Varies	
Annual room/board cost for students in residence:	$7500-8000	(US $6800-7200)
Average monthly rent for students living off campus:		
1 bedroom: $600, 2 bedroom: $800		

UNDERGRADUATE INSTRUCTIONAL PROGRAM

Most popular majors: Engineering, Education, Nursing
Special study options: Co-op programs

Liberal Arts and Sciences, General Studies, and Humanities
Education

Science and Mathematics
Biology, Biotechnology. Forensics, Math, Physics

Computer Science and Engineering
Automotive Engineering, Computer Science, Electrical Engineering, Mechanical Engineering, Nuclear Engineering, Software Engineering

Business and Economics
Accounting, Business, Commerce

Health Professions and Related Sciences
Health, Science, Nursing

Professional Studies
Criminal Justice

QUEEN'S UNIVERSITY

Kingston, Ontario

SCHOOL CATEGORY: Doctoral/Research   **TOTAL ENROLLMENT: 20,000**   **SETTING: Urban**   **CITY POPULATION: 125,000**

Founded over 160 years ago, Queen's University was one of the first universities established in Canada and has maintained its position as one of the country's leading schools. Strong academics, research, and tradition are its distinguishing characteristics.

The main campus, a ten-minute walk from downtown Kingston, is a mix of stately historic buildings and modern structures in a tree-lined setting. Kingston, a historic city of 125,000, occupies a strategic location on the shore of Lake Ontario, halfway between Canada's two largest cities, Toronto and Montreal, two hours' drive from each. Syracuse, in upstate New York, is also a two-hour drive from Kingston.

Queen's offers undergraduate, graduate, and professional degrees in 16 faculties and schools. It is host to 14 Centers of Excellence and to 23 research groups and institutes. Admission is very selective.

There is residence space for slightly more than 3,000 students, and all residence rooms are wired for high-speed Internet access. Off-campus housing is available nearby, and the city offers a friendly mix of shops, pubs, and cafés. Extracurricular activities and athletics are well established at Queen's. Forty interuniversity teams participate in competition, one of the highest numbers of teams of any school in North America.

The Kingston area is well known as a sailing haven and a gateway to the Thousand Islands tourist area. School spirit and pride are as strong as academic quality at this pioneering institution.

GENERAL INFORMATION

Year founded:	1841
Undergraduate enrollment, full-time:	14,000
Graduate enrollment, full-time:	2,500
Faculty, full-time:	850
Number of international students:	700
Male/female ratio (%):	40:60
Residence spaces available:	189
Residence space guaranteed for 1st-year students:	Yes
Student media website:	www.ams.queensu/ca/united

UNDERGRADUATE ADMISSIONS

Office of Admissions
99 University Avenue
Kingston, ON   K7L 3N6
PH: **613.533.2000** FAX: **613.533.6810**
WEBSITE: **www.queensu.ca**

Minimum high school average:	70
Rolling admissions:	Yes
Fall application deadline:	Mar 30
Application fee:	$105
Electronic application accepted:	Yes
Admissions notification by:	May 30
Required with application:	HS transcript, SAT I (1200 min.), SAT II (for engineering students)
Recommended:	Essay and recommendations per department

UNDERGRADUATE FINANCES

Undergraduate tuition:		
International students:	$15,000	(US $13,500)
Canadian students:	$4200	(US $3800)
Estimated annual health insurance:	$700	(US $630)
Estimated annual books & supplies:	$1000	(US $900)
Financial aid available for international students:	Yes	
Application deadline:	Jul 1	
Scholarships available for international students:	Yes	
Application deadline:	Varies	
Annual room/board cost for students in residence:	$7000-9000	(US $6300-8100)
Average monthly rent for students living off campus:		
1 bedroom: $475-750, 2 bedroom: $650-950		
Federal School Code: G06679		

UNDERGRADUATE INSTRUCTIONAL PROGRAM

Most popular majors: Life Sciences, Biology, Business, English
Percentages by program: 23% Science, 20% Liberal Arts, 15% Sciences, 12% Engineering/Computer Science, 5% Business, 3% Health Sciences
Special study options: Co-op programs, internships, study abroad, language programs, special summer programs, distance learning programs

Liberal Arts and Sciences, General Studies, and Humanities

Anthropology, Art, Art History, Art Conservation, Canadian Studies, Classics, Drama/Theater Arts, English Language & Literature, Film/Cinema, Fine/Studio Arts, French Language & Literature, German Language & Literature, Gerontology, History, Humanities/Humanistic Studies, International Relations & Affairs, Italian Language & Literature, Jewish Studies, Latin American Studies, Linguistics, Medieval & Renaissance Studies, Music, Philosophy, Political Science, Psychology, Religion/Religious Studies, Sociology, Spanish Language & Literature, Theology/Theological Studies, Women's Studies

Science and Mathematics

Applied Science, Astronomy/Astrophysics, Biochemistry, Biology, Chemistry, Environmental Sciences, Geography, Geology, Geophysics & Seismology, Mathematics, Microbiology, Physics, Statistics

Computer Science and Engineering

Biomedical Computing, Chemical Engineering, Civil Engineering, Computer & Information Sciences, Computer Engineering, Electrical/ Electronics & Communication Engineering, Engineering Chemistry, Engineering Physics, Engineering Science, Geological Engineering, Mechanical Engineering, Metallurgical Engineering, Mining & Mineral Engineering

Professional Studies

City/Urban/Community & Regional Planning, Education, Family & Community Studies, Physical Education Teaching & Coaching

Business and Economics

Business Administration & Management/Commerce, Computing & Information Science, Economics, Human Resource Management, Labor/Personnel Relations & Studies, Management, Marketing, Public Relations & Organizational Communications

Health Professions and Related Sciences

Health Sciences, Life Sciences, Neuroscience, Nursing, Occupational Therapy, Physical Therapy, Pre-Medicine

GRADUATE ADMISSIONS

School of Graduate Studies & Research
Queen's University
Fleming Hall, Stewart-Pollack Wing
Kingston, ON   K7L 3N6
PH: **613.533.6079** FAX: **613.533.6015**
WEBSITE: **www.queensu.ca/sgsr/**

Fall application deadline:	Mar 1
Application fee:	$70
Electronic application accepted:	N/A
Required with application:	College transcript, recommendations
Graduate student housing:	Co-ed, room only residences with private bathrooms in Harkness and Jean Royce Hall

GRADUATE FINANCES

Graduate tuition:		
International students:	$11,237	(US $10,113)
Canadian students:	$5797	(US $5217)
Financial aid & Scholarships available for		
international students:	Yes	
Application deadline:	Jan (Sept applications advised)	

GRADUATE INSTRUCTIONAL PROGRAM

Liberal Arts and Sciences, General Studies, and Humanities

Art, Art History, Classics & Classical Languages & Literature, English Language & Literature, French Language & Literature, German Language & Literature, Italian Language & Literature, Philosophy, Political Science, Psychology, Sociology, Spanish Language & Literature, Theology/Theological Studies,

Science and Mathematics

Astronomy/Astrophysics, Biochemistry, Biology, Chemistry, Geography, Mathematics, Physics, Statistics

Computer Science and Engineering

Chemical Engineering, Civil Engineering, Computer & Information Sciences, Computer Engineering, Electrical/Electronics & Communication Engineering, Engineering Chemistry, Engineering Physics, Engineering Science, Geological Engineering, Mechanical Engineering, Mining & Mineral Engineering

Professional Studies

City/Urban/Community & Regional Planning, Criminal Justice Studies, Education, Law, Physical Education Teaching & Coaching

Business and Economics

Business Administration & Management/Commerce, Computing & Information Science, Economics, Executive MBA, Information Sciences & Systems, Industrial Relations, Management Information Systems, MBA Science & Technology, Public Administration

Health Professions and Related Sciences

Anatomy & Cell Biology, Community Health & Epidemiology, Health Education, Microbiology & Immunology, Medicine, Nursing, Pathology, Pharmacology & Toxicology, Rehabilitation Science

REDEEMER UNIVERSITY COLLEGE

Ancaster, Ontario

SCHOOL CATEGORY: Bachelor's/Liberal Arts **TOTAL ENROLLMENT: 675** **SETTING: Suburban** **CITY POPULATION: 100,000**

Redeemer University College is a small, interdenominational, Christian, liberal arts and science university. The school was founded in 1982 and is located in the city of Ancaster about ten minutes from the larger city of Hamilton.

Programs are offered in more than 30 different areas. The school's small size ensures that students receive individual mentoring from faculty members. The 78-acre campus includes modern academic facilities, a student recreation center and athletic facilities. Redeemer is primarily a residential campus. All first- and second-year students under the age of 21 are required to live on campus in college residences.

Less than an hour from Toronto, Hamilton is part of southern Ontario's Golden Horseshoe region surrounding Lake Ontario.

Approximately 500,000 people live in Hamilton. Historically known for its heavy industry and steel mills, it is also a cultural and recreational center. The US cities of Niagara Falls and Buffalo, New York are also less than an hour away.

GENERAL INFORMATION

Year founded:	1982
Undergraduate enrollment, full-time:	625
Graduate enrollment, full-time:	N/A
Faculty, full-time:	33
Number of international students:	55
Male/female ratio (%):	40:60
Residence spaces available:	417
Residence space guaranteed for 1st-year students:	Yes
Student media website:	www.redeemer.on.ca

UNDERGRADUATE ADMISSIONS

Department of Admissions
777 Garner Road East
Ancaster, ON L9K 1J4
PH: **905.648.2131 ext. 4224**
WEBSITE: **www.redeemer.on.ca**

Minimum high school average:	65
Rolling admissions:	N/A
International fall application deadline:	May 31
Application fee:	N/A
Domestic fall application deadline:	May 31
Application fee:	N/A
Electronic application accepted:	No
Required with application:	HS transcript

UNDERGRADUATE FINANCES

Undergraduate tuition:	$11,082	(US $9975)
Estimated annual health insurance:	$500	(US $450)
Estimated annual books & supplies:	$1000	(US $900)
Financial aid available for international students:	Yes	
Application deadline:	Mar 31	
Scholarships available for international students:	Yes	
Application deadline:	Mar 1	
Annual room/board cost for students in residence:	$5116	(US $4604)
Average monthly rent for students living off campus:		
1 bedroom: $500-600, 2 bedroom: $600-800		
Federal School Code: G33485		

UNDERGRADUATE INSTRUCTIONAL PROGRAM

Most popular majors: English, Psychology, Business, History
Percentages by program: 74% Liberal Arts, 9% Science, 7% Business
Special study options: Co-op programs, internships, study abroad

Liberal Arts and Sciences, General Studies, and Humanities

Art, Classics & Classical Languages & Literature, Dutch Language & Literature, English Language & Literature, French Language & Literature, History, Music, Philosophy, Political Science, Psychology, Religion/Religious Studies, Social Work, Sociology, Visual & Performing Arts

Science and Mathematics

Biology, Chemistry, Environmental/Environmental Health, Geography, Mathematics, Physics

Computer Science and Engineering

Computer & Information Sciences

Professional Studies

Education, Human Kinetics/Kinesiology, Physical Education

Business and Economics

Business Administration & Management/Commerce, Economics

RYERSON UNIVERSITY

Toronto, Ontario

SCHOOL CATEGORY: Bachelor's/General   **TOTAL ENROLLMENT: 30,000**   **SETTING: Urban**   **CITY POPULATION: 4,000,000**

Ryerson University is a primarily undergraduate university, located in the center of Toronto. The campus includes a landscaped square, a reflecting pond that becomes a skating rink in winter, and several green spaces that provide a welcome oasis in Ryerson's urban setting.

Ryerson offers more than 80 degree programs. The school is focused on providing practical skills to undergraduates. Among the most popular majors are architecture, business, electrical engineering and journalism.

Student facilities include three residences for on-campus living. The Recreation and Athletics Center is well equipped and conveniently built underground. Off-campus housing is easily available nearby. The campus is minutes away from two subway stations and other forms of public transportation.

Ryerson is located near the heart of Canada's business and financial center, providing students with exciting learning opportunities. Sports fans can choose from the Blue Jays, Raptors, Maple Leafs, or the Toronto Argonauts of the Canadian Football League. The campus is within easy walking distance of hundreds of restaurants, theaters, clubs, and other cultural attractions.

GENERAL INFORMATION

Year founded:	1948
Undergraduate enrollment, full-time:	15,000
Graduate enrollment, full-time:	500
Faculty, full-time:	538
Number of international students:	380
Male/female ratio (%)	45:55
Residence spaces available:	840
Residence space guaranteed for 1st-year students:	Preferred
Student media website:	www.theeyeopener.com

UNDERGRADUATE ADMISSIONS

Office of Admissions
350 Victoria Street
Toronto, ON   M5B 2KS
PH: 416.979.5028   FAX: 416.979.5221
WEBSITE: www.ryerson.ca

Minimum high school average:	70
Applications, 2000-2001:	N/A
Rolling admissions:	No
International fall application deadline:	Mar 1
Application fee:	$105
Domestic fall application deadline:	Mar 1
Application fee:	$105
Electronic application accepted:	Yes
Admissions notification by:	N/A
Required with application:	HS Transcripts (SAT, ACT, essay, interview, recommendations per department)

UNDERGRADUATE FINANCES

Undergraduate tuition:		
International students:	$14,000	(US $12,600)
Canadian students:	$4800	(US $4300)
Estimated annual health insurance:	$528	(US $492)
Estimated annual books & supplies:	$1000	(US $900)
Financial aid available for international students:	Yes	
Application deadline:	N/A	
Scholarships available for international students:	Yes (up to 1500 for 1st yr)	
Application deadline:	N/A	
Annual room/board cost for students in residence:	$8000-10,000	(US $7200-9000)
Average monthly rent for students living off campus:		
1 bedroom: $600-900, 2 bedroom: $1000		
Federal School Code: G10720		

UNDERGRADUATE INSTRUCTIONAL PROGRAM

Most popular majors: Architectural Science, Business, Electrical/Electronics & Communication Engineering, Journalism
Percentages by program: N/A
Special study options: Co-op programs, internships, study abroad, language programs, special summer programs, distance learning programs.

Liberal Arts and Sciences, General Studies, and Humanities
Drama/Theater Arts, Film/Cinemas, New Media, Photography, Social Work, Sociology, Visual & Performing Arts

Science and Mathematics
Biology, Chemistry, Geography

Computer Science and Engineering
Aerospace Engineering, Chemical Engineering, Civil Engineering, Computer & Information Sciences, Computer Engineering, Electrical/ Electronics & Communication Engineering, Graphic Communications Management, Industrial/Manufacturing Engineering, Mechanical Engineering

Professional Studies
Architecture, Child Growth/ Care & Development Studies, City/Urban/Community & Regional Planning, Criminal Justice Studies, Disability Studies, Education, Fashion, Hospitality/Administration Management, Interior Design, Journalism, Radio & Television Broadcasting

Business and Economics
Business Administration & Management/Commerce, Information Sciences & Systems, International Economics, Public Relations & Organizational Communications, Retail Management

Health Professions and Related Sciences
Disability Studies, Health Services Administration, Midwifery, Nursing, Nutritional Sciences, Public Health

GRADUATE ADMISSIONS

School of Graduate Studies
87 Gerrad Street/ 87 Eric Palin Hall
Toronto, ON   M5B 2K3
ph: 416.979.5365   fax: 416.979.5153
website: www.ryerson.ca/gradstudies/

Fall application deadline:	Jan 15
Application fee:	$60
Electronic application accepted:	No
Required with application:	College transcript plus departmental requirements
Graduate student housing:	No designated graduate housing

GRADUATE FINANCES

Graduate tuition:		
International students:	$14,000	(US $12,600)
Canadian students:	$5500	(US $4950)
Financial aid & Scholarships available for		
international students:	N/A	
Application deadline:	N/A	

GRADUATE INSTRUCTIONAL PROGRAM

Liberal Arts and Sciences, General Studies, and Humanities
Communications

Science and Mathematics
Mathematics (joint program with U of T)

Computer Science and Engineering
Chemical Engineering, Civil Engineering, Electrical/ Electronics & Communication Engineering, Mechanical Engineering

Business and Economics
Management Science

ST. JEROME'S UNIVERSITY

Waterloo, Ontario

SCHOOL CATEGORY: Bachelor's/Liberal Arts   **TOTAL ENROLLMENT: 800**   **SETTING: Suburban**   **CITY POPULATION: 300,000**

St. Jerome's University is a small Roman Catholic liberal arts institution affiliated with the University of Waterloo. The school is centrally located on the 900-acre campus of the University of Waterloo. Students enjoy the advantages of a small, vigorous academic community while also having access to all the resources of a larger school. The city of Waterloo is located in southwestern Ontario, about 90 miles from both Toronto and Buffalo and within two hours' drive of Detroit.

Students can pursue either a Bachelor of Arts or a Bachelor of Mathematics degree and graduate with a well-respected University of Waterloo degree. Class sizes are kept small and faculty are readily available to assist students.

St. Jerome's has a well-established, century-old spirit of free intellectual inquiry; lively discussions and detailed examination of ideas are prized. Admission to St. Jerome's is competitive.

St. Jerome's has two residences available for 280 students; 200 of these are reserved for first-year students. The University of Waterloo has excellent athletic facilities. Waterloo and its twin city of Kitchener have a combined population of close to 300,000. The area is home to numerous colleges and universities and is very student-friendly. Waterloo is a clean, safe city that offers excellent entertainment, dining, and shopping opportunities.

GENERAL INFORMATION

Year founded:	1960
Undergraduate enrollment, full-time:	800
Graduate enrollment, full-time:	N/A
Faculty, full-time:	66
Number of international students:	N/A
Male/female ratio (%)	40:60
Residence spaces available:	280
Residence space guaranteed for 1st-year students:	200
Student media website:	N/A

UNDERGRADUATE ADMISSIONS

200 Westmont Road North
Waterloo, ON   N2L 3G3
PH: 519.884.8110   FAX: 519.884.5759
WEBSITE: **www.sju.ca**

Minimum high school average:	70
Rolling admissions:	N/A
Fall application deadline:	Aug 1
Application fee:	N/A
Electronic application accepted:	Yes
Admissions notification by:	N/A
Required with application:	HS transcripts

UNDERGRADUATE FINANCES

Undergraduate tuition:		
International students:	$17,000	(US $15,300)
Canadian students:	$5000	(US $4500)
Estimated annual health insurance:	$600	(US $540)
Estimated annual books & supplies:	$1000	(US $900)
Financial aid & Scholarships available for		
international students:	N/A	
Application deadline:	N/A	
Annual room/board cost for students in residence:	$7000	(US $6300)
Average monthly rent for students living off campus:		
1 bedroom: $300-350, 2 bedroom: $300-500		

UNDERGRADUATE INSTRUCTIONAL PROGRAM

Most popular majors: Psychology, Religious Studies
Percentages by program: N/A
Special study options: N/A

Liberal Arts and Sciences, General Studies, and Humanities

English Language & Literature, French Language & Literature, History, Italian Language & Literature, Philosophy, Psychology, Religion/Religious Studies, Sociology

Science and Mathematics

Mathematics

Professional Studies

Family & Community Studies

TRENT UNIVERSITY

Peterborough, Ontario

SCHOOL CATEGORY: Bachelor's/Liberal Arts   **TOTAL ENROLLMENT: 6300**   **SETTING: Suburban**   **CITY POPULATION: 100,000**

Trent University, founded in 1963, is a small liberal arts university located in the city of Peterborough, less than two hours' drive from Toronto. Trent's campus features dramatic architecture in a natural setting on the banks of the Otanabee River. The university is based on a residential college system and is committed to providing strong student support.

Academically, Trent is renowned for its emphasis on small-group teaching and interdisciplinary studies. The interdisciplinary approach exposes students to courses in a wide variety of subject areas, encouraging them to develop a broad base of academic knowledge. Trent offers undergraduate programs in over 30 areas. Eighty percent of classes at Trent have less than 25 students.

Residence spaces, which are guaranteed to first-year students who register on time, are a mix of co-ed, male-only, and female-only. Over 50 percent of college residences are single rooms. The college system and the small size of the university promote an intimate, socially active campus life experience. Peterborough is close to many lakes, beaches, conservation areas, and hiking and ski trails for outdoor sports enthusiasts.

At Trent, students will find a friendly, welcoming environment with a strong sense of community.

GENERAL INFORMATION

Year founded:	1963
Undergraduate enrollment, full-time:	3908
Graduate enrollment:	150
Faculty, full-time:	323
Number of international students:	515
Male/female ratio (%):	31:69
Residence spaces available:	1250
Residence space guaranteed for 1st-year students:	Yes
Student media website:	www.trentarthur.info

UNDERGRADUATE ADMISSIONS

Registrar's Office
P.O. Box 4800, Station Main
Peterborough, ON   K9J 7B8
PH: 705.748.1629   FAX: 705.748.1011
WEBSITE: www.trentu.ca

Minimum high school average:	3.0 GPA
Applications, 2005:	14,000
Rolling admissions:	N/A
International fall application deadline:	Jul 15
Application fee:	$50
Domestic fall application deadline:	Jun 1
Application fee:	$50
Electronic application accepted:	N/A
Admissions notification by:	N/A
Required with application:	HS Transcripts, SAT

UNDERGRADUATE FINANCES

Undergraduate tuition:		
International students:	$12,000	(US $10,800)
Canadian students:	$4500	(US $4050)
Estimated annual health insurance:	$700	(US $630)
Estimated annual books & supplies:	$1000	(US $900)
Financial aid & Scholarships available for		
international students:	N/A	
Application deadline:	N/A	
Annual room/board cost for students in residence:	$5800-9200	(US $5220-8280)
Average monthly rent for students living off campus:		
1 bedroom: $425-600, 2 bedroom: $600-725		
Federal School Code: G09505		

UNDERGRADUATE INSTRUCTIONAL PROGRAM

Most popular majors: Business Administration, Biology/Biochemistry, Economics, Environmental Resource Studies, Psychology
Percentages by program: N/A
Special study options: Study abroad, exchange programs

Liberal Arts and Sciences, General Studies, and Humanities

Anthropology, Canadian Studies, Comparative Development Studies, Cultural Studies, Classics & Classical Languages & Literature, English Language & Literature, French Language & Literature, German Language & Literature, History, Museum Studies, Native Studies, Philosophy, Political Science, Psychology, Sociology, Spanish Language & Literature, Women's Studies

Science and Mathematics

Biochemistry, Biology, Chemical Physics, Chemistry, Environmental Sciences, Geography, Mathematics, Physics,

Computer Science and Engineering

Computer Sciences

Professional Studies

Education, Forensics

Business and Economics

Business Administration Economics, Native Management & Economic Development

Health Professions and Related Sciences

Nursing, Physiology

GRADUATE ADMISSIONS

Office of Research & Graduate Studies
Trent University/Otonabee College
Peterborough, ON   K9J 7B8
PH:**705.748.1011 ext.1245**   FAX: **705.748.1587**
WEBSITE: **www.trentu/gradstudies/**

Fall application deadline:	Mar 1
Application fee:	N/A
Required with application:	College transcript & departmental requirements
Graduate student housing:	Bradburn Apartments

GRADUATE FINANCES

Graduate tuition:

International students:	$12,000	(US $10,800)
Canadian students:	$5400	(US $4860)
Financial aid & Scholarships available for		
international students:	Yes	
Application deadline:	Mar 1	

GRADUATE INSTRUCTIONAL PROGRAM

Liberal Arts and Sciences, General Studies, and Humanities
Anthropology, Canadian Studies, History, Native Studies

Science and Mathematics
Modelling in Natural and Social Sciences, Watershed Ecosystems

UNIVERSITY OF GUELPH

Guelph, Ontario

SCHOOL CATEGORY: Master's   **TOTAL ENROLLMENT: 16,000**   **SETTING: Suburban**   **CITY POPULATION: 100,000**

The University of Guelph (U of G) is a medium-size, comprehensive university recognized for its high-quality programs. The school is located in the city of Guelph in southwestern Ontario. Officially founded in 1964, the University of Guelph is recognized as one of Canada's most research-intensive universities. The U of G is rich in tradition, with roots going back more than 120 years to the Ontario Agricultural College. The campus features an attractive mix of modern and traditional architecture. In addition to the campus in Guelph, the University has three regional campuses that offer diplomas in agriculture and applied training, outreach and research to the agricultural community.

More than 16,000 undergraduate and graduate students in six colleges benefit from a comprehensive and innovative curriculum that spans the arts, humanities, physical and natural sciences, and social sciences. These core disciplines are enhanced by Guelph's commitment to interdisciplinary programs, to a selected range of professional and applied programs and to its areas of special responsibility in agri-food and veterinary medicine. Admission is competitive.

Over the past several years, the University of Guelph has been investing heavily for the growth in university education in Ontario. Talented new faculty have been recruited and more than $250 million in new construction has been initiated or completed to accommodate a projected enrolment of 18,000 students by 2008. These new facilities include a townhouse-style student residence, a state-of-the-art classroom and teaching complex and a new science center.

The university has a very extensive and high-quality residence system. Residence space is guaranteed to first-year students who apply by the deadline date. The city of Guelph, with a population of 100,000, is a classic "just-big-enough" college town. It has a vibrant downtown section with great restaurants and clubs. The city of Toronto is an hour's drive away.

GENERAL INFORMATION

Year founded:	1964
Undergraduate enrollment, full-time:	14,987
Graduate enrollment, full-time:	2050
Faculty, full-time:	800
Number of international students:	700
Male/female ratio (%):	40:60
Residence spaces available:	5000
Residence space guaranteed for 1st-year students:	Yes
Student media website:	www.uoguelph.ca/ontarion/

UNDERGRADUATE ADMISSIONS

Admissions Services
University of Guelph
50 Stone Road East
Guelph, ON   N1G 2W1
PH: 519.821.2130
WEBSITE: **www.uoguelph.ca/admissions**

Minimum high school average:	75
Rolling admissions:	No
International fall application deadline:	Mar 1
Application fee:	$105
Domestic fall application deadline:	Apr 15
Application fee:	$105
Electronic application accepted:	Yes
Admissions notification by:	N/A
Required with application:	HS Transcripts, SAT I, ACT

UNDERGRADUATE FINANCES

Undergraduate tuition:		
International students:	$9730	(US $8757)
Canadian students:	$4200	(US $3800)
Estimated annual health insurance:	$700	
Estimated annual books & supplies:	$1000	(US $900)
Financial aid available for international students:	Yes	
Application deadline:	N/A	
Scholarships available for international students:	Yes	
Application deadline:	Mar 1	
Annual room/board cost for students in residence:	$5994	(US $5400)
Average monthly rent for students living off campus:		
1 bedroom: $450-650, 2 bedroom: $500-900		
Federal School Code: G06683		

UNDERGRADUATE INSTRUCTIONAL PROGRAM

Most popular majors: Biology, Business, Humanities, Physical Sciences
Percentages by program: 43% Engineering/Computer/General Science, 41% Liberal Arts, 15% Business
Special study options: Co-op programs, internships, study abroad, language programs, special summer programs, distance learning programs

Liberal Arts and Sciences, General Studies, and Humanities

Anthropology, Art History, Classics & Classical Languages & Literature, Communications, Drama/Theater Arts, English Language & Literature, European Studies, French Language & Literature, Gerontology, History, International Relations & Affairs, Linguistics, Music, Philosophy, Political Science, Psychology, Rural & Development Sociology, Sociology, Spanish Language & Literature, Studio Arts, Visual & Performing Arts, Women's Studies

Science and Mathematics

Agriculture Sciences, Animal Science, Agronomy, Biological Sciences/Life Sciences, Biology, Biophysics, Biotechnology, Botany, Chemistry, Chemical Physics, Earth & Planetary Science, Ecology, Environmental Geography, Environmental Sciences, Environmental Toxicology, Fishing & Fisheries Sciences & Management, Food Science, Forestry Sciences, Genetics, Geography, Geology, Geophysics & Seismology, Horticulture Science, Marine & Freshwater Biology, Marine/Aquatic Sciences, Mathematics, Microbiology, Molecular Biology & Genetics, Physical Science, Physics, Statistics, Plant Science, Theoretical Physics, Wild Life Biology, Zoology

Computer Science and Engineering

Bioengineering & Biomedical Engineering, Computer & Information Sciences, Engineering Systems & Computing, Environmental/Environmental Health Engineering, Water Resources Engineering

Professional Studies

Child Growth/Care & Development Studies, Criminal Justice Studies, Family & Community Studies, Hospitality Administration Management, Housing & Real Estate Management, Human Kinetics, Landscape Architecture, Tourism

Business and Economics

Agricultural Business & Engineering, Agroecosystem Management, Aquaculture Operations & Production Management, Business Administration & Management/Commerce, Economics, Environmental Economics & Policy, Environmental Monitoring & Analysis, Human Resources Management, Information Sciences & Systems, Labor/Personnel Relations & Studies, Management Science, Management Information Systems, Marketing Management & Research, Operations Management & Supervision, Organizational Behavior Studies, Public Management

Health Professions and Related Sciences

Nutritional Sciences, Pre-Medicine, Pre-Veterinary Medicine

GRADUATE ADMISSIONS

Office of Graduate Studies
University of Guelph
University Centre, Room 324B
Guelph, ON   N1G 2W1
PH: **519.824.4120**   FAX: **519.766.0143**
Website: **www.uoguelph.ca/GraduateStudies/calendar**

Fall application deadline:	N/A
Application fee:	$75
Required with application:	College transcript, recommendations, specific departmental requirements
Graduate student housing:	Various accommodations including graduate houses, couples & family housing

GRADUATE FINANCES

Graduate tuition:		
International students:	$8475	(US $7625)
Canadian students:	$5200	(US $4650)
Financial aid & Scholarships available for		
international students:	Yes	
Application deadline:	N/A	

GRADUATE INSTRUCTIONAL PROGRAM

Liberal Arts and Sciences, General Studies, and Humanities

Anthropology, Drama/Theater Arts, English Language & Literature, Fine Art, History, Humanities/Humanistic Studies, International Development Studies, Philosophy, Political Science, Psychology, Scottish Studies, Sociology

Science and Mathematics

Agriculture Sciences, Animal Science, Aquaculture, Applied Biological Sciences/Life Sciences, Biochemistry, Biology, Biophysics, Botany, Chemistry, Crop Science, Environmental Sciences, Food Science, Fishing & Fisheries Sciences & Management, Genetics/Plant & Animal, Geography, Horticulture Science, Land Resource Science, Mathematics, Microbiology/Bacteriology, Molecular Biology, Statistics, Zoology

Computer Science and Engineering

Computer & Information Sciences, Engineering Science, Environmental/Environmental Health Engineering

Professional Studies

City/Urban/Community & Regional Planning, Family & Community Studies, Hospitality Administration/Management, Landscape Architecture, Rural Extension Studies

Business and Economics

Business Administration & Management/Commerce, Economics, Natural Resources Management

Health Professions and Related Sciences

Pathobiology, Nutritional Sciences, Veterinary Medicine

UNIVERSITY OF OTTAWA

Ottawa, Ontario

SCHOOL CATEGORY: Doctoral/Research   **TOTAL ENROLLMENT: 30,000**   **SETTING: Urban**   **CITY POPULATION: 1,000,000**

The University of Ottawa is a bilingual school located in Canada's capital. As the capital, Ottawa has a cosmopolitan atmosphere, and it has also emerged as a high-technology powerhouse. The metropolitan area has a population of approximately one million. The campus is located downtown, next to the Rideau Canal.

The university's nine faculties offer over 140 undergraduate majors as well as a wide range of graduate and professional studies. Ottawa's location in the capital provides students with privileged access to the workings of the federal government and ample opportunities for political networking. The school has a strong reputation for its programs in political science and public policy. Saint Paul University is a bilingual, Catholic school that is federated with the University of Ottawa and offers degrees jointly with Ottawa.

Residence space on campus is limited, but off-campus housing is easy to find and is readily available nearby. The school has good athletic facilities, and many festivals, films, and public lectures make the campus a vibrant place. The nearby ByWard Market offers a bustling collection of restaurants, cafes, bistros, and nightclubs.

In addition to being a cultural center, Ottawa also has outstanding outdoor recreational activities. The Gatineau area north of the city has many lakes and streams for canoeing, kayaking and other water sports, as well as an abundance of hiking and mountain bike trails. In the winter, skiing is a popular sport.

With its distinctive bilingual character, its location in the Canadian capital city, and its strong academic credentials, the University of Ottawa has a strong appeal for international students.

GENERAL INFORMATION

Year founded:	1848
Undergraduate enrollment, full-time:	24,000
Graduate enrollment, full-time:	3000
Faculty, full-time:	1200
Number of international students:	575
Male/female ratio (%):	42:58
Residence spaces available:	2500 +
Residence space guaranteed for 1st-year students:	N/A
Student media website:	www.Ottawagazette.ca

UNDERGRADUATE ADMISSIONS

Office of the Registrar
550 Cumberland Street
P.O. Box 450, Station A
Ottawa, ON   K1N 6N5
PH: **519.823.1540**   FAX: **519.823.5236**
WEBSITE: **www.uottawa.ca**

Minimum high school average:	60
Applications, 2000-2001:	N/A
Rolling admissions:	N/A
International fall application deadline:	Apr 30
Application fee:	$105
Domestic fall application deadline:	Mar 1
Application fee:	$105
Electronic application accepted:	Yes
Admissions notification by:	N/A
Required with application:	HS transcripts, essay, recommendations

UNDERGRADUATE FINANCES

Undergraduate tuition:		
International students:	$13,000	(US $11,700)
Canadian students:	$4200	(US $3800)
Estimated annual health insurance:	$703	(US $630)
Estimated annual books & supplies:	$1000	(US $900)
Financial aid available for international students:	N/A	
Application deadline:	N/A	
Scholarships available for international students:	Yes	
Application deadline:	Varies	
Annual room/board cost for students in residence:	$5400-9000	(US $4900-8100)
Average monthly rent for students living off campus:		
1 bedroom: $650 +, 2 bedroom: $700+		
Federal School Code: G06686		

UNDERGRADUATE INSTRUCTIONAL PROGRAM

Most popular majors: Business, Communication, Engineering, Criminal Justice Studies
Percentages by program: N/A
Special study options: Co-op programs, internships, study abroad, language programs, special summer programs, distance learning programs

Liberal Arts and Sciences, General Studies, and Humanities

Canadian Studies, Classics & Classical Languages & Literature, Communications, Comparative Literature, Design & Applied Arts, Drama/Theater Arts, English Language & Literature, Fine/Studio Arts, French Language & Literature, German Language & Literature, History, Humanities/Humanistic Studies, International Relations & Affairs, Italian Language & Literature, Latin Language & Literature, Linguistics, Medieval & Renaissance Studies, Music, Philosophy, Political Science, Psychology, Religion/Religious Studies, Slavic Languages & Literature, Social Work, Sociology, Spanish Language & Literature, Translation, Visual & Performing Arts, Women's Studies, Writing

Science and Mathematics

Biochemistry, Biology, Chemistry, Environmental Sciences, Geography, Geology, Mathematics, Physics, Statistics

Computer Science and Engineering

Chemical Engineering, Civil Engineering, Computer & Information Sciences, Computer Engineering, Electrical/Electronics & Communication Engineering, Engineering Science, Environmental Engineering, Geological Engineering, Mechanical Engineering, Software Engineering

Professional Studies

Criminal Justice Studies, Education, Human Kinetics/Kinesiology, Law, Leisure & Recreational Activities

Business and Economics

Accounting, Business Administration & Management/Commerce, Economics, Entrepreneurship Management, Human Resources Management, Information Sciences & Systems, International Business, Management Information Systems, Marketing Management & Research, Operations Management & Supervision, Production-Management Science, Public Relations & Organizational Communications

Health Professions and Related Sciences

Biopharmaceutical Science, Nursing, Occupational Therapy, Physiotherapy

GRADUATE ADMISSIONS

Faculty of Graduate and Postdoctoral Studies
University of Ottawa
115 Seraphin Marion
P.O. Box 450, Station A
Ottawa, ON   K1N 6N5
PH: **613.562.5742**   FAX: **613.562.5992**
WEBSITE: **www.uottawa.ca/academic/grad-etudesup**

Fall application deadline:	Apr
Application fee:	$85
Electronic application accepted:	N/A
Required with application:	College transcript & departmental requirements
Graduate student housing:	Single rooms available

GRADUATE FINANCES

Graduate tuition:

International students:	$13,000	(US $11,700)
Canadian students:	$5500	(US $4950)
Financial aid & Scholarships available for		
international students:	Yes	
Application deadline:	N/A	

GRADUATE INSTRUCTIONAL PROGRAM

Liberal Arts and Sciences, General Studies, and Humanities

Canadian Studies, Classics & Classical Languages & Literature, Divinity/Ministry, English Language & Literature, French Language & Literature, History, Linguistics, Music, Pastoral Studies, Philosophy, Political Science, Psychology, Religion/Religious Studies, Social Work, Sociology, Spanish Language & Literature, Theology/Theological Studies, Translation, Women's Studies

Science and Mathematics

Biochemistry, Biology,* Biostatistics,* Environmental Sciences,* Chemistry,* Earth & Planetary Sciences,* Genetics/Plant & Animal, Geography, Mathematics,* Microbiology/Immunology, Physics,* Statistics*

Computer Science and Engineering

Chemical Engineering, Civil Engineering,* Computer & Information Sciences,* Electrical/ Electronics & Communication Engineering,* Engineering Management, Environmental Engineering, Mechanical Engineering,* Software Engineering*

Professional Studies

Criminal Justice Studies, Education, Human Kinetics/Kinesiology, Law, Religious Education

Business and Economics

Business Administration & Management/Commerce, Economics,* Information Science & Systems, International Business, Labour/Personnel Relations & Studies, Management Science, Management Information Systems & Business Data Processing, Marketing Management & Research, Operations Management & Supervision, Organizational Behavior Studies, Public Relations & Organizational Communications, Sport & Fitness Administration/Management

Health Professions and Related Sciences

Behavioral Neuroscience, Health Services Administration, Medicine, Neuroscience, Nursing, Speech Language Pathology & Audiology

*Joint Collaborative Programs with Carleton University

UNIVERSITY OF ST. MICHAEL'S COLLEGE

Toronto, Ontario

SCHOOL CATEGORY: Bachelor's/Liberal Arts   **TOTAL ENROLLMENT: 4000**   **SETTING: Urban**   **CITY POPULATION: 4,000,000**

St. Michael's provides an undergraduate and graduate education in arts and sciences. Some of St. Michael's most-distinguished programs are in Medieval studies, Theology, Philosophy and Celtic studies.

University of St. Michael's College has accommodation for approximately 800 students in all-women and all-men residences. Residence is guaranteed to all first year students. Off-campus housing is also widely available nearby. Students enjoy the use of all services and facilities of the University of Toronto.

Through the University of Toronto students also have access to excellent cultural and athletic activities. Canada's business centre, Toronto, is also rich in culture, sports and entertainment. Home to major theatres, movie complexes, international dining, the Blue Jays, Raptors and Maple Leafs, Toronto is truly a cosmopolitan city. The Royal Ontario Museum and The Ontario Art galleries are only blocks away from the downtown campus.

GENERAL INFORMATION

Year founded:	1852
Undergraduate enrollment, full-time:	4000
Graduate enrollment, full-time:	N/A
Faculty, full-time:	N/A
Number of international students:	N/A
Male/female ratio (%)	40:60
Residence spaces available:	800
Residence space guaranteed for 1st-year students:	Yes
Student media website:	www.the-mike.ca

UNDERGRADUATE ADMISSIONS

81 Saint Mary Street
Toronto, ON   M5S 1J4
PH: 416.926.1300   FAX: 416.926.7276
WEBSITE: www.utoronto.ca/stmikes/

Minimum high school average:	75
Applications, 2000-2001:	N/A
Rolling admissions:	N/A
Fall application deadline:	Mar 1
Application fee:	$105
Electronic application accepted:	N/A
Admissions notification by:	N/A
Required with application:	HS transcript
Recommended:	SAT/ACT

UNDERGRADUATE FINANCES

Undergraduate tuition:		
International students:	$17,000	(US $15,300)
Canadian students:	$4400	(US $3960)
Estimated annual health insurance:	$500	(US $450)
Estimated annual books & supplies:	$1000	(US $900)
Financial aid available for international students:	N/A	
Application deadline:	N/A	
Scholarships available for international students:	N/A	
Application deadline:	Mar 15	
Annual room/board cost for students in residence:	$8000-9000	(US $7200-8100)
Average monthly rent for students living off campus:		
1 bedroom: $700+, 2 bedroom: $800+		

UNDERGRADUATE INSTRUCTIONAL PROGRAM

Most popular majors: Celtic Studies, Medieval Studies
Percentages by program: N/A
Special study options: University of Toronto offerings

Liberal Arts and Sciences, General Studies, and Humanities

Classics, Celtic Studies, Christianity & Culture, Medieval Studies, Philosophy, Religion/Religious Studies, Theology & Ecology

UNIVERSITY OF TORONTO

Toronto, Ontario

SCHOOL CATEGORY: Doctoral/Research **TOTAL ENROLLMENT: 60,000** **SETTING: Urban** **CITY POPULATION: 4,000,000**

The University of Toronto (U of T) is the largest university in Canada and has a worldwide reputation for academic excellence. The university has three campuses: the St. George Campus, located in the heart of the city; the U of T at Missausauga, 20 miles west of downtown; and the U of T at Scarborough, 20 miles east of the city core. The university also has three affiliated colleges: St. Michael's College, Trinity College, and Victoria University. Students at each campus and college enjoy a distinctive learning environment and sense of community within the larger university setting.

The University of Toronto offers the widest range of programs of any Canadian university, with over 300 bachelor's programs. The university is recognized for innovation. It houses the fifth largest library in North America, and professors of international caliber bring leading research and scholarship to bear on their teaching and provide opportunities for study and discovery at the forefront of the sciences, social sciences, and humanities. Admission to the U of T is competitive.

Students will find that the U of T offers support services for nearly every imaginable aspect of academic and personal life. There is residence space for close to 6,000 students, but many students choose to live off campus. Toronto has a clean, efficient public transportation system that makes getting around the city easy.

Home to major theaters, movie complexes, international dining, and the Blue Jays, Raptors and Maple Leafs, Toronto is truly a cosmopolitan city. The Royal Ontario Museum and Ontario Art gallery are only blocks away from the downtown campus. The University of Toronto challenges students from around the world in a vibrant learning environment.

GENERAL INFORMATION

Year founded:	1827
Undergraduate enrollment, full-time:	50,000
Graduate enrollment, full-time:	10,000
Faculty, full-time:	2937
Number of international students:	2467
Male/female ratio (%):	44:56
Residence spaces available:	6000
Residence space guaranteed for 1st-year students:	Yes
Student media website:	www.varsity.utoronto.ca

UNDERGRADUATE ADMISSIONS

Office of Admissions
315 Bloor Street West
Toronto, ON   M5S 1A3
PH: 416.978.2190   FAX: 416.978.7022
WEBSITE: www.utoronto.ca

Minimum high school average:	80
Rolling admissions:	No
Fall application deadline:	Feb 1
Application fee:	$105
Electronic application accepted:	Yes
Admissions notification by:	Apr-Jun
Required with application:	HS transcripts, SAT I (1200 minimum), interview for some programs

UNDERGRADUATE FINANCES

Undergraduate tuition:		
International students:	$17,000	(US $15,300)
Canadian students:	$4400	(US $3960)
Estimated annual health insurance:	$500	(US $450)
Estimated annual books & supplies:	$1200	(US $1080)
Financial aid & Scholarships available for		
international students:	Yes	
Application deadline:	Mar 1	
Annual room/board cost for students in residence:	$7000-10,000	(US $6300-9000)
Average monthly rent for students living off campus:		
1 bedroom: $700-950, 2 bedroom: $1000-1200		
Federal School Code: G06688		

UNDERGRADUATE INSTRUCTIONAL PROGRAM

Most popular majors: Biology, Economics, History, Sociology
Percentages by program: N/A
Special study options: Co-op programs, internships, study abroad, language programs, special summer programs, distance learning programs

Liberal Arts and Sciences, General Studies, and Humanities

Aboriginal Studies, African Studies, Anthropology, Art, Art History, Asian Studies, Canadian Studies, Canadian Music, Caribbean Studies, Ceramic Arts & Ceramics, Classics & Classical Languages & Literature, Communications, Comparative Literature, Design & Applied Arts, Divinity/Ministry, Drama/Theater Arts, East Asian Studies, English Language & Literature, Fine/Studio Arts, Film/Cinema Studies, Finnish Studies, French Language & Literature, Gender/Sexuality Studies, German Language & Literature, History, Humanities/Humanistic Studies, International Relations & Affairs, Islamic Studies, Italian Language & Literature, Irish/Celtic Studies, Jewish/Judaic Studies, Middle Eastern Languages & Literature, Linguistics, Museum Studies, Music, Native Studies, Near Eastern Studies, Pacific Area Studies, Painting, Philosophy, Playwriting & Screenwriting, Political Science, Policy Analysis, Portuguese Language & Literature, Psychology, Religion/Religious Studies, Russian & Slavic Area Studies, Russian Languages & Literature, Sculpture, Slavic Languages & Literature, Social Work, Sociology, South Asian Studies, Spanish Language & Literature, Translation, Ukrainian Studies, Urban Affairs/Studies, Visual & Performing Arts, Women's Studies, Writing

Science and Mathematics

Agriculture Sciences, Animal Sciences, Archaeology, Astronomy/Astrophysics, Atmospheric Sciences & Meteorology, Biochemistry, Biological Sciences/Life Sciences, Biology, Biophysics, Biotechnology Research, Botany, Chemistry, Entomology, Environmental Sciences, Forestry Sciences, Genetics: Plant/ Animal, Geography, Geology, Horticulture Science, Marine/Aquatic Biology, Mathematics, Microbiology, Physics, Statistics, Zoology

Computer Science and Engineering

Aerospace Engineering, Bioengineering & Biomedical Engineering, Chemical Engineering, Civil Engineering, Computer & Information Sciences, Computer Engineering, Electrical/ Electronics & Communication Engineering, Engineering Science, Environmental Health Engineering, Industrial/Manufacturing Engineering, Mechanical Engineering, Metallurgical/ Mining & Mineral Engineering, Nuclear Engineering

Professional Studies

Architecture, Child Growth/ Care & Development Studies, City/Urban/ Community & Regional Planning, Criminal Justice Studies, Education, Journalism, Landscape Architecture, Law

Business and Economics

Accounting, Actuarial Science, Business Administration & Management/Commerce, Economics, Entrepreneurship, Human Resources Management, Information Sciences & Systems, International Business, Labor/Personnel Relations & Studies, Management Science, Management Information Sciences & Systems, Marketing Management & Research, Operations Management & Supervision, Organizational Behavior Studies, Public Administration, Public Relations & Organizational Communications, Sport & Fitness Administration/Management.

Health Professions and Related Sciences

Chiropractic, Counseling, Dental Hygiene, Diagnostic & Treatment Services, Environmental Health, Health Services Administration, Nursing, Occupational Therapy, Optometry, Pharmacology, Pharmacy, Physical Therapy, Pre-Dentistry, Pre-Medicine, Pre-Veterinary Medicine, Public Health, Speech-Language Pathology & Audiology

GRADUATE ADMISSIONS

School of Graduate Studies
University of Toronto
63 St. George Street
Toronto, ON   M5S 2Z9
PH: **416.978.6614**   FAX: **416.978.4367**
WEBSITE: **www.sgs.utoronto.ca**

International fall application deadline:	Apr 15
Application fee:	$105
Fall application deadline:	Jun 1
Application fee:	$105
Required with application:	College transcript, departmental requirements
Graduate student housing:	Various options available including Graduate Housing with 3 & 4 single bedroom apartments and family apartments on the St. George campus

GRADUATE FINANCES

Graduate tuition:

International students:	$12,000	(US $10,800)
Canadian students:	$6000	(US $5400)
Financial aid & Scholarships available for		
international students:	Yes	
Application deadline:	Varies	

GRADUATE INSTRUCTIONAL PROGRAM

Liberal Arts and Sciences, General Studies, and Humanities

Anthropology, Art History, Asian Studies, Canadian Studies, Classics & Classical Languages & Literature, Comparative Literature, Drama/Theater Arts, East Asian Studies, English Language & Literature, French Language & Literature, German Language & Literature, Gerontology, Greek Language & Literature, History, Humanities/Humanistic Studies, International Relations & Affairs, Italian Language & Literature, Linguistics, Medieval & Renaissance Studies, Museum Studies, Music, Near & Middle Eastern Civilizations, Philosophy, Political Science, Portuguese, Psychology, Religion/Religious Studies, Russian & Slavic Area Studies, Russian Languages & Literature, Slavic Languages & Literature, Social Work, Sociology, Spanish Language & Literature, Urban Affairs/Studies, Women's Studies

Science and Mathematics

Astronomy/Astrophysics, Biochemistry, Biological Sciences/ Life Sciences, Botany, Chemistry, Environmental Sciences, Forestry Sciences, Genetics: Plant/Animal, Geography, Geology, Metallurgy & Materials Science, Mathematics, Physics, Statistics, Toxicology, Wood Science, Zoology

Computer Science and Engineering

Aerospace Engineering, Bioengineering & Biomedical Engineering, Chemical Engineering, Civil Engineering, Computer & Information Sciences, Computer Engineering, Electrical/ Electronics & Communication Engineering, Engineering Physics, Engineering Science, Environmental/ Environmental Health Engineering, Mechanical Engineering, Metallurgical Engineering, Nuclear Engineering, Software Engineering, Welding Engineering, Wood Engineering

Professional Studies

Adult Education, Alcohol & Tobacco Substance Studies, Criminal Justice Studies, Education, Family & Community Studies, Law

Business and Economics

Business Administration & Management/Commerce, Economics, Entrepreneurship, Industrial Relations, Information Sciences & Systems, Human Resources Management, International Business, Labour/Personnel Relations & Studies, Management Science, Management Information Systems, Marketing Management & Research

Health Professions and Related Sciences

Anatomy & Cell Biology, Biomedical Studies, Cardiovascular Sciences, Dentistry, Health Administration, Immunology, Medical Biophysics, Medicine, Molecular & Medical Genetics, Neuroscience, Nursing, Nutritional Sciences, Pharmaceutical Sciences, Physiology, Rehabilitation Science, Speech-Language Pathology

UNIVERSITY OF TRINITY COLLEGE

Toronto, Ontario

SCHOOL CATEGORY: Bachelor's/Liberal Arts　**TOTAL ENROLLMENT: 1400**　**SETTING: Urban**　**CITY POPULATION: 4,000,000**

Trinity College is a small liberal arts college of Anglican heritage, federated with the University of Toronto since 1904 and sharing its campus and facilities.

Trinity admits 400 students annually who are enrolled in the faculty of Arts and Science of the University of Toronto. The College sponsors four interdisciplinary programs in Ethics, Society and Law, Immunology, International Relations and Social Policy.

Residence is guaranteed to all first-year students. Off-campus housing is also widely available nearby. Toronto has an excellent public transportation system that makes getting to and from campus easy.

Students enjoy the use of all services and facilities of the University of Toronto. Through the University of Toronto, students also have access to excellent cultural and athletic activities.

Home to major theaters, movie complexes, international dining, and the Blue Jays and Maple Leafs, Toronto is truly a cosmopolitan city. The Royal Ontario Museum and the Ontario Art gallery are only blocks away from the Trinity campus.

GENERAL INFORMATION

Year founded:	1852
Undergraduate enrollment, full-time:	1600
Graduate enrollment, full-time:	100
Faculty, full-time:	N/A
Number of international students:	N/A
Male/female ratio (%)	N/A
Residence spaces available:	500
Residence space guaranteed for 1st-year students:	Yes (if accepted before Jul 1)

UNDERGRADUATE ADMISSIONS

Registrar's Office
6 Hoskin Avenue
Toronto, ON   M5S 1H8
PH: **416.978.2533**   FAX: **416.978.2797**
WEBSITE: **www.trintiy.utoronto.ca**

Minimum high school average:	70
Rolling admissions:	N/A
Fall application deadline:	Feb 1
Application fee:	$105
Required with application:	HS transcript

UNDERGRADUATE FINANCES

Undergraduate tuition:		
International students:	$17,000	(US $15,300)
Canadian students:	$4400	(US $3960)
Estimated annual health insurance:	$500	(US $450)
Estimated annual books & supplies:	$1000	(US $900)
Financial aid & Scholarships available for		
international students:	N/A	
Application deadline:	N/A	
Annual room/board cost for students in residence:	$9000-10,000	(US 8100-9000)
Average monthly rent for students living off campus:		
1 bedroom: $700-950, 2 bedroom: $1000-1200		

UNDERGRADUATE INSTRUCTIONAL PROGRAM

Most popular majors: Arts & Science, Theology
Percentages by program: N/A
Special study options: University of Toronto Programs

Liberal Arts and Sciences, General Studies, and Humanities

University of Toronto offerings. University of Trinity sponsors: International Relations, Ethics, Criminal Justice Studies

Science and Mathematics

Immunology

Computer Science and Engineering

Computer Science

Business and Economics

Commerce

GRADUATE ADMISSIONS

Faculty of Divinity
University of Trinity College
6 Hoskin Avenue
Toronto, ON   M5S 1H8

Fall application deadline:	Mar 1
Application fee:	$100
Required with application:	College transcript, essay, recommendations portfolio required for some programs
Graduate student housing:	Available

GRADUATE FINANCES

Graduate tuition:		
International students:	$12,000+	(US $10,800)
Canadian students:	$6000+	(US $5400)
Financial aid & Scholarships available for		
international students:	Yes	
Application deadline:	May 1	

GRADUATE INSTRUCTIONAL PROGRAM

Liberal Arts and Sciences, General Studies, and Humanities

Divinity/Ministry, Religion/Religious Studies, Theology/Theological Studies

UNIVERSITY OF WATERLOO

Waterloo, Ontario

SCHOOL CATEGORY: Master's **TOTAL ENROLLMENT: 25,000** **SETTING: Suburban** **CITY POPULATION: 300,000**

The University of Waterloo is one of Canada's leading comprehensive universities. Since it was founded, Waterloo has been an innovative institution, and the tradition continues to this day. It was the first university in the world to establish a faculty of mathematics and the first university in North America to make computers available to undergraduates. Located in a suburban section of the city of Waterloo, the university's modern campus spans over 800 acres. Four affiliated colleges are located on the campus: Conrad Grebel College, Renison College, St. Jerome's University, and St. Paul's United College. The affiliated colleges offer smaller communities, and some have a religious orientation.

With over 100 areas of study leading to undergraduate degrees, the university also offers 49 master's degree programs and 31 programs at the doctoral level. Areas of strength include engineering, computer science, applied health sciences, arts, environmental studies, mathematics, and science. Waterloo was the first university in Canada to offer the co-op system of study, which balances classroom theory and real-world experience. Today, Waterloo has the largest cooperative education program in the world, with more than 10,000 students engaged in work-study programs. Admission requirements are very selective. The world's top technology companies, including Microsoft, Nortel, and others, heavily recruit Waterloo graduates. Waterloo attracts students, professors, and staff of very high quality, and receives substantial amounts of research funding. Waterloo offers a wide variety of residence options and excellent athletic facilities.

Waterloo students really do believe in the adage of working hard and playing hard. Waterloo is a clean, safe, student-friendly city that offers excellent entertainment, dining, and shopping opportunities. The city of Toronto is about an hour's drive away.

GENERAL INFORMATION

Year founded:	1957
Undergraduate enrollment, full-time:	21,000
Graduate enrollment, full-time:	2000
Faculty, full-time:	700
Number of international students:	669
Male/female ratio (%):	53:47
Residence spaces available:	5000
Residence space guaranteed for 1st-year students:	Yes
Student media website:	www.imprint.uwaterloo.ca

UNDERGRADUATE ADMISSIONS

Office of the Registrar
200 University Avenue W
Waterloo, ON   N2L 3G1
PH: 519.888.4567 ext.3614   FAX: 519.888.8009
WEBSITE: www.findoutmore.uwaterloo.ca

Minimum high school average:	70%
Rolling admissions:	N/A
International fall application deadline:	May 1
Application fee:	$140
Domestic fall application deadline:	May 1
Application fee:	$80
Electronic application accepted:	Yes
Admissions notification by:	June
Required with application:	HS transcripts, (SAT, ACT, essay, recommendations required for some programs)

UNDERGRADUATE FINANCES

Undergraduate tuition:		
International students:	$16,000	(US $14,400)
Canadian students:	$4200	(US $3800)
Estimated annual health insurance:	$600	(US $540)
Estimated annual books & supplies:	$1000	(US $900)
Financial aid available for international students:	No	
Application deadline:	N/A	
Scholarships available for international students:	Yes	
Application deadline:	N/A	
Annual room/board cost for students in residence:	$5450-6450	(US $4900-5800)
Average monthly rent for students living off campus:		
1 bedroom: $500+, 2 bedroom: $600+		
Federal School Code: G08526		

UNDERGRADUATE INSTRUCTIONAL PROGRAM

Most popular majors: Computer Science, Kinesiology, Mechanical Engineering
Percentages by program: 30% Liberal Arts, 28% Engineering/Computer Science, 12% Science, 8% Business, 8% Health Professions
Special study options: Co-op programs, internships, study abroad, language programs, special summer programs, distance learning programs

Liberal Arts and Sciences, General Studies, and Humanities

Anthropology, Canadian Studies, Classics & Classical Languages & Literature, Drama/Theater Arts, East Asian Studies, English Language & Literature, Fine/Studio Arts, French Language & Literature, German Language & Literature, Gerontology, History, Humanities/Humanistic Studies, International Relations & Affairs, Medieval & Renaissance Studies, Music, Philosophy, Political Science, Psychology, Religion/Religious Studies, Russian & Slavic Area Studies, Social Work, Sociology, Spanish Language & Literature, Women's Studies

Science and Mathematics

Biochemistry, Bioinformatics, Biological Sciences/Life Sciences, Biotechnology Research, Chemistry, Earth & Planetary Science, Ecology, Entomology, Environmental Sciences, Geography, Geology, Mathematics, Physics, Statistics

Computer Science and Engineering

Chemical Engineering, Civil Engineering, Computer & Information Sciences, Computer Engineering, Electrical/Electronics & Communication Engineering, Engineering Science, Environmental/Environmental Health Engineering, Geological Engineering, Mechanical Engineering, Software Engineering, Systems Design Engineering

Professional Studies

Architecture, Education, Leisure & Recreational Activities

Business and Economics

Accounting, Actuarial Science, Business Administration & Management/Commerce, Economics, Human Resources Management, International Business, Management Sciences, Marketing Management & Research, Operations Management & Supervision

Health Professions and Related Sciences

Health Sciences, Pre-Optometry, Speech-Language Pathology

GRADUATE ADMISSIONS

Graduate Studies Office
University of Waterloo
200 University Avenue West
Needles Hall, Room 3021
Waterloo, ON   N2L 3G1
PH: **519.888.4567 ext.5411**   FAX: **519.746.3051**
WEBSITE: **www.grad.uwaterloo.ca**

Fall application deadline:	Jan-Mar
Application fee:	$75
Required with application:	College transcript, (GRE, GMAT, essay, recommendations, portfolio may be required per department)
Graduate student housing:	Single student residence at Miota Hagey, apartments available for married students

GRADUATE FINANCES

Graduate tuition:

International students:	$9500	(US $8550)
Canadian students:	$4200	(US $3800)
Financial aid & Scholarships available for international students:	Yes	
Applications deadline:	N/A	

GRADUATE INSTRUCTIONAL PROGRAM

Liberal Arts and Sciences, General Studies, and Humanities

English Language & Literature, Fine/Studio Arts, French Language & Literature, Gerontology, German Language & Literature, History, Philosophy, Political Science, Psychology, Sociology

Science and Mathematics

Architecture, Biochemistry, Biology, Chemistry, Combinatorics & Optimization, Earth & Planetary Science, Environmental Sciences, Geography, Mathematics, Physics, Statistics

Computer Science and Engineering

Chemical Engineering, Civil Engineering, Computer & Information Sciences, Computer Engineering, Electrical/ Electronics & Communication Engineering, Engineering Sciences, Mechanical Engineering, Systems Design Engineering

Professional Studies

Architecture, City/Urban/ Community & Regional Planning, Kinesiology, Leisure & Recreational Activities

Business and Economics

Accounting, Actuarial Science, Economics, Management Science, Local Economic Development

Health Professions and Related Sciences

Health Sciences, Optometry

THE UNIVERSITY OF WESTERN ONTARIO

London, Ontario

SCHOOL CATEGORY: Doctoral/Research   **TOTAL ENROLLMENT: 30,000**   **SETTING: Suburban**   **CITY POPULATION: 330,000**

The University of Western Ontario is one of the oldest and largest universities in Canada. Located in picturesque southwestern Ontario, between Windsor and Toronto, its main campus is an inviting combination of older limestone buildings and modern construction.

The university has three smaller affiliated colleges: Brescia College is a Catholic liberal arts college for women. Huron College offers small classes and an intimate environment in the arts and social sciences. Finally, King's College is a Catholic coed liberal arts college.

The University of Western Ontario is known for its teaching and research excellence, as well as for its professional schools of business, dentistry, engineering, law, and medicine. More than 200 individual and combined three-year general and four-year honors degrees are offered. Students can choose from more than 60 programs in their first year of study. Admission to Western is competitive.

There are 4,200 residence spaces available. First-year students are guaranteed a spot if they are accepted by May 15. The school offers a wide range of athletic and extracurricular activities. School spirit is very strong at Western, and the school prides itself on its varsity teams.

London, with a population of over 300,000, is Canada's tenth largest city, situated midway between Toronto and Detroit, roughly two hours' drive from each. The city offers all the urban amenities—shopping, dining, theaters, clubs, art galleries, and parks—but also has a comfortable "college town" feeling. Throughout the year there are many festivals in the area, including the world famous Stratford Theatre Shakespeare festival. Students are drawn to the University of Western Ontario by the certainty that they will be studying with outstanding faculty members and will be exposed to leading research and teaching.

GENERAL INFORMATION

Year founded:	1878
Undergraduate enrollment, full-time:	25,000
Graduate enrollment, full-time:	3000
Faculty, full-time:	1181
Number of international students:	N/A
Male/female ratio (%):	45:55
Residence spaces available:	4200
Residence space guaranteed for 1st-year students:	Yes
Student media website:	www.usc.uwo.ca/gazette/

UNDERGRADUATE ADMISSIONS

Office of the Registrar
1151 Richmond Street
London, ON   N6G 5B8
PH: **519.661.2100**
WEBSITE: **WWW.UWO.ca**

Minimum high school average:	77
Applications, 2000-2001:	N/A
Rolling admissions:	No
International fall application deadline:	Feb 1
Application fee:	$105
Domestic fall application deadline:	Jun 1
Application fee:	$105
Electronic application accepted:	Yes
Admissions notification by:	N/A
Required with application:	HS transcripts, SAT

UNDERGRADUATE FINANCES

Undergraduate tuition:		
International students:	$12,600	(US $11,300)
Canadian students:	$4200	(US $3800)
Estimated annual health insurance:	$500	(US $450)
Estimated annual books & supplies:	$1000	(US $900)
Financial aid & Scholarships available for		
International students:	N/A	
Application deadline:		
Annual room/board cost for students in residence:	$5000-8500	(US $4500-7650)
Average monthly rent for students living off campus:		
1 bedroom: $300-400, 2 bedroom: $400-600		
Federal School Code: G08446		

UNDERGRADUATE INSTRUCTIONAL PROGRAM

Most popular majors: Business, Education, Engineering, Health Sciences
Percentages by program: N/A
Special study options: Co-op programs, internships, study abroad, language programs, special summer programs, distance learning programs

Liberal Arts and Sciences, General Studies, and Humanities

Anthropology, Art, Classics & Classical Languages & Literature, Communications, Comparative Literature, Dance, English Language & Literature, Film/Cinema, French Language & Literature, German Language & Literature, Greek Language & Literature, Hebrew, History, Humanities/Humanistic Studies, International Relations & Affairs, Italian Language & Literature, Japanese Language & Literature, Jewish/Judaic Studies, Latin Language & Literature, Linguistics, Middle Eastern Languages & Literature, Music, Philosophy, Polish, Political Science, Psychology, Religion/Religious Studies, Social Work, Sociology, Spanish Language & Literature, Visual & Performing Arts, Women's Studies, Writing

Science and Mathematics

Applied Mathematics, Astronomy, Biochemistry, Biology, Biophysics, Chemistry, Earth & Planetary Science, Epidemiology, Environmental Sciences, Genetics Plant /Animal, Geography, History of Science, Horticulture Science, Mathematics, Microbiology, Physics, Statistics, Zoology

Computer Science and Engineering

Chemical Engineering, Civil Engineering, Computer & Information Sciences, Computer Engineering, Electrical/ Electronics & Communication Engineering, Environmental/ Environmental Health Engineering, Engineering Science, Materials Engineering, Mechanical Engineering, Software Engineering

Professional Studies

Child Growth/Care/Development Studies, Human Ecology, Human Kinetics/Kinesiology, Family & Community Studies, Education, Law

Business and Economics

Actuarial Science, Business Administration & Management/ Commerce, Economics

Health Professions and Related Sciences

Anatomy, Health Sciences, Nursing, Nutritional Sciences, Pathology, Pharmacology, Physical Therapy, Speech-Language Pathology & Audiology

GRADUATE ADMISSIONS

Faculty of Graduate Studies
Room 149, Stevenson-Lawson Building
1151 Richmond Street
London, ON   N6A 5B8
PH: **519.661.2102**   FAX: **519.661.3730**
WEBSITE: **www.uwo.ca/grad**

Fall application deadline:	Feb - Apr
Application fee:	$105
Required with application:	College transcript, GMAT, essay, recommendations portfolio (dependant upon program)
Graduate student housing:	Various accommodations including family apartments

GRADUATE FINANCES

Graduate tuition:		
International students:	$16,000	(US $14,400)
Canadian students:	$6000	(US $5400)
Financial aid & Scholarships available for		
international students:	Yes	
Application deadline:	May 1	

GRADUATE INSTRUCTIONAL PROGRAM

Liberal Arts and Sciences, General Studies, and Humanities

Anthropology, Classics & Classical Languages & Literature, Communications, Comparative Literature, English Language & Literature, French Language & Literature, History, Music, Philosophy, Political Science, Psychology, Public Administration, Sociology, Spanish Language & Literature, Theory & Criticism, Visual & Performing Arts

Science and Mathematics

Applied Mathematics, Astronomy, Biochemistry, Chemistry, Geography, Geology, Geophysics & Seismology, Horticulture Science, Library Science, Mathematics, Microbiology, Physics, Statistics, Zoology

Computer Science and Engineering

Engineering Science

Professional Studies

Education, Journalism, Law

Business and Economics

Business Administration & Management/Commerce, Economics

Health Professions and Related Science

Anatomy & Cell Biology, Dentistry, Epidemiology, Family Medicine, Medical Biophysics, Medicine, Neuroscience, Nursing, Occupational Therapy, Orthodontics, Pathology, Pharmacology & Toxicology, Physical Therapy, Physiology, Rehabilitation Sciences

UNIVERSITY OF WINDSOR

Windsor, Ontario

SCHOOL CATEGORY: **Master's**	TOTAL ENROLLMENT: **13,000**	SETTING: **Urban**	CITY POPULATION: **280,000**

The University of Windsor (UW) is a medium-sized comprehensive university founded in 1857. The university is located near downtown Windsor across the Ambassador Bridge from Detroit.

The university offers over 100 undergraduate programs in the arts and sciences, business, engineering, and applied sciences. Professional degrees include nursing and law. The university maintains close partnerships with business and industry. With strong support from the automotive industry, UW is able to offer students many opportunities for coop placements and internships. UW has also formed many agreements with universities in the United States to provide students with cross-border learning opportunities. UW is home to the Great Lakes Environmental Research Center, one of the leading freshwater research centers in North America.

The university has six residences that can accommodate close to 1,500 students. First-year students are guaranteed a residence spot. Off-campus housing is readily available nearby.

Windsor offers comprehensive extracurricular and athletic programming. The nearby Great Lakes provide plenty of opportunities for outdoor activities like swimming and boating.

GENERAL INFORMATION

Year founded:	1857
Undergraduate enrollment, full-time:	12,000
Graduate enrollment, full-time:	1000
Faculty, full-time:	500
Number of international students:	900
Male/female ratio (%):	46:54
Residence spaces available:	1500
Residence space guaranteed for 1st-year students:	Yes (if accepted before 6/8)
Student media website:	www.flipside.org/

UNDERGRADUATE ADMISSIONS

Admissions Office
401 Sunset Avenue
Windsor, ON   N9B 3P4
PH: **519.253.3000 ext.3324**
WEBSITE: **www.uwindsor.ca**

Minimum high school average:	70
Applications, 2000-2001:	N/A
Rolling admissions:	Yes
International fall application deadline:	Feb 1
Application fee:	$105
Domestic fall application deadline:	Feb 1
Application fee:	$105
Electronic application accepted:	Yes
Admissions notification by:	N/A
Required with application:	HS transcripts, letter of recommendations

UNDERGRADUATE FINANCES

Undergraduate tuition:		
International students:	$11,000	(US $9900)
Canadian students:	$4400	(US $4000)
Estimated annual health insurance:	$500	(US $450)
Estimated annual books & supplies:	$1000	(US $900)
Financial aid available for international students:	Yes (work/study)	
Application deadline:	N/A	
Scholarships available for international students:	No	
Application deadline:	N/A	
Annual room/board cost for students in residence:	$5000-8000	(US $4500-7200)
Average monthly rent for students living off campus:		
1 bedroom: $500+, 2 bedroom: $650+		
Federal School Code: G06689		

UNDERGRADUATE INSTRUCTIONAL PROGRAM

Most popular majors: Business, Computer Science, Criminal Justice Studies, Education
Percentages by program: N/A
Special study options: Co-op programs, internships, study abroad, language programs, special summer programs, distance learning programs

Liberal Arts and Sciences, General Studies, and Humanities

Anthropology, Canadian Studies, Communications, Comparative Literature, Drama/Theater Arts, English Language & Literature, French Language & Literature, German Language & Literature, Greek Language & Literature, History, Humanities/Humanistic Studies, International Relations & Affairs, Italian Language & Literature, Languages, Latin Language & Literature, Multicultural Studies, Music, Philosophy, Political Science, Psychology, Social Work, Sociology, Spanish Language & Literature, Visual & Performing Arts, Women's Studies, Writing

Science and Mathematics

Biochemistry, Biological Sciences/Life Sciences, Chemistry, Earth & Planetary Science, Geology, Geography, Mathematics, Physics, Statistics

Computer Science and Engineering

Automotive Engineering, Civil Engineering, Computer & Information Sciences, Electrical/ Electronics & Communication Engineering, Engineering Science, Environmental/ Environmental Health Engineering, Industrial/ Manufacturing Engineering, Materials Engineering, Mechanical Engineering

Professional Studies

Criminal Justice Studies, Education, Law

Business and Economics

Accounting, Business Administration & Management/Commerce, Economics, Finance, Labour/Personnel Relations and Studies, Management Science, Marketing Management & Research, Operations Management & Supervision, Organizational Behavior Studies, Public Administration

Health Professions and Related Sciences

Nursing

GRADUATE ADMISSIONS

Faculty of Graduate Studies and Research
University of Windsor
360 Chrysler Hall Tower
401 Sunset Avenue
Windsor, ON N9B 3P4
PH: **519.253.3000 ext.2109** FAX: **519.971.3667**
WEBSITE: **www.uwindsor.ca/graduate**

Fall application deadline:	Jul 1
Application fee:	$105
Required with application:	College transcript, essay, recommendations GMAT, GRE
Graduate student housing:	Single student accommodations

GRADUATE FINANCES

Graduate tuition:		
International students:	$6000+	(US $5400+)
Canadian students:	$3500+	(US $3150+)
Financial aid & Scholarships available for		
international students:	Yes	
Application deadline:	N/A	

GRADUATE INSTRUCTIONAL PROGRAM

Liberal Arts and Sciences, General Studies, and Humanities

English Language & Literature, History, Philosophy, Political Science, Psychology, Sociology, Visual Arts, Writing

Science and Mathematics

Biochemistry, Biological Sciences/Life Sciences, Chemistry, Earth & Planetary Science, Mathematics, Physics, Statistics

Computer Science and Engineering

Civil Engineering, Computer & Information Sciences, Electrical/Electronics & Communication Engineering, Engineering Materials, Engineering Science, Environmental/Environmental Health Engineering Engineering, Industrial/Manufacturing Engineering, Mechanical Engineering

Professional Studies

Criminal Justice Studies, Education, Human Kinetics/Kinesiology

Business and Economics

Business Administration & Management/Commerce, Economics

Health Professions and Related Sciences

Nursing

VICTORIA UNIVERSITY

Toronto, Ontario

SCHOOL CATEGORY: Bachelor's/Liberal Arts **TOTAL ENROLLMENT: 4000** **SETTING: Urban** **CITY POPULATION: 4,000,000**

Victoria University is a small college federated with the University of Toronto and sharing its campus. Students have access to all courses offered at the University of Toronto and the Toronto School of Divinity. Victoria admits approximately 750 students annually.

Students enjoy the use of all services and facilities of the University of Toronto. Through the University of Toronto, students also have access to excellent cultural and athletic activities

Residence is guaranteed to all first-year students. Off-campus housing is also widely available nearby. Toronto has a clean, efficient public transportation system that makes getting around the city easy.

Home to major theaters, movie complexes, international dining, and the Blue Jays and Maple Leafs, Toronto is truly a cosmopolitan city. The Royal Ontario Museum and the Ontario Art gallery are only blocks away from the downtown campus.

GENERAL INFORMATION

Year founded:	1836
Undergraduate enrollment, full-time:	3000
Graduate enrollment, full-time:	129
Faculty, full-time:	N/A
Number of international students:	N/A
Male/female ratio (%)	43:57
Residence spaces available:	750
Residence space guaranteed for 1st-year students:	Yes
Student media website:	N/A

UNDERGRADUATE ADMISSIONS

73 Queen's Park Crescent East
Toronto, ON   M5S 1K7
PH: **416.585.4524**   FAX: **416.585.4584**
WEBSITE: **www.vicu.utoronto.ca**

Minimum high school average:	70
Applications, 2000-2001:	N/A
Rolling admissions:	N/A
Fall application deadline:	Feb 1
Application fee:	$105
Electronic application accepted:	N/A
Admissions notification by:	N/A
Required with application:	HS transcript
Recommended:	SAT/ACT

UNDERGRADUATE FINANCES

Undergraduate tuition:		
International students:	$17,000	(US $15,300)
Canadian students:	$4400	(US $4000)
Estimated annual health insurance:	$500	(US $450)
Estimated annual books & supplies:	$1000	(US $900)
Financial aid available for international students:	N/A	
Application deadline:	N/A	
Scholarships available for international students:	N/A	
Application deadline:	Mar 1	
Annual room/board cost for students in residence:	$8000-9000	(US $7200-8100)
Average monthly rent for students living off campus:		
1 bedroom: $700+, 2 bedroom: $800+		

UNDERGRADUATE INSTRUCTIONAL PROGRAM

Most popular majors: Communication, Literacy Studies
Percentages by program: N/A
Special study options: University of Toronto offerings

Liberal Arts and Sciences, General Studies, and Humanities

Classics, Communications, Comparative Literature, English Language & Literature, French Language & Literature, German Language & Literature, Medieval & Renaissance Studies, Near East Studies, Philosophy, Religion/Religious Studies

GRADUATE ADMISSIONS

Office of Graduate Admissions
73 Queen's Park Crescent East
Toronto, ON   M5s 1K7

International fall application deadline:	Jan 1	
Application fee:	$105	
Domestic fall application deadline:	Mar 1	
Application fee:	$105	
Required with application:	GRE, college transcript, essay, recommendations, portfolio required for some programs	

GRADUATE FINANCES

Graduate tuition:		
International students:	$12,000	(US $10,800)
Canadian students:	$6000	(US $5400)
Financial aid & Scholarships available for		
international students:	Yes	
Application deadline:	May 1	

GRADUATE INSTRUCTIONAL PROGRAM

Liberal Arts and Sciences, General Studies, and Humanities

Divinity/Ministry, Jewish Studies, Religion/Religious Studies, Theology/Theological Studies

WILFRID LAURIER UNIVERSITY

Waterloo, Ontario

SCHOOL CATEGORY: Bachelor's/General　　**TOTAL ENROLLMENT: 14,000**　　**SETTING: Suburban**　　**CITY POPULATION: 300,000**

Wilfrid Laurier is one of Canada's leading small universities, and is known for its strong sense of community. Located in a suburban section of Waterloo, the modern main campus is minutes away from the larger University of Waterloo. A second campus recently opened in Branford to offer BA degrees.

The university offers undergraduate programs in a wide range of areas including arts, science, music and business. The school of business is ranked very highly. Approximately half of business students participate in co-op programs across the country and around the globe. Admission is competitive.

The school has residence spaces for 1000 students on campus. Students can choose from dormitory- or apartment-style settings as well as all-male, all-female or co-ed. Off-campus housing is readily available nearby. The school has good athletic facilities and the many cultural and social clubs make the campus a vibrant place.

Waterloo and its twin city of Kitchener are located in southwestern Ontario and have a combined population of close to 300,000. The area is home to numerous colleges and universities and is very student-friendly. Waterloo is a clean, safe city that offers excellent entertainment, dining and shopping opportunities. The city of Toronto is an hour's drive away.

GENERAL INFORMATION

Year founded:	1911
Undergraduate enrollment, full-time:	11,000
Graduate enrollment, full-time:	500
Faculty, full-time:	314
Number of international students:	166
Male/female ratio (%)	43:57
Residence spaces available:	1800
Residence space guaranteed for 1st-year students:	Yes
Student media website:	www.wlusu.com

UNDERGRADUATE ADMISSIONS

Office of the Registrar
75 University Avenue West
Waterloo, ON N2L 3C5
PH: 519.884.0710 FAX: 519.886.9351
WEBSITE: www.wlu.ca

Minimum high school average:	75
Rolling admissions:	N/A
International fall application deadline:	May 1
Application fee:	$105
Domestic fall application deadline:	Jan 11
Application fee:	$105
Electronic application accepted:	Yes
Admissions notification by:	N/A
Required with application:	HS transcripts
Recommended:	SAT I/II, recommendations

UNDERGRADUATE FINANCES

Undergraduate tuition:		
International students:	$10,000	(US $9000)
Canadian students:	$4200	(US $3800)
Estimated annual health insurance:	$600	(US $540)
Estimated annual books & supplies:	$1000	(US $900)
Financial aid & Scholarships available for		
international students:	N/A	
Annual room/board cost for students in residence:	$5300-7025	(US $4800-6300)
Average monthly rent for students living off campus:		
1 bedroom: $650-750, 2 bedroom: $750-850		

UNDERGRADUATE INSTRUCTIONAL PROGRAM

Most popular majors: Business, Computer Science, Economics, Physical Education, Psychology
Percentages by program: 41% Liberal Arts, 27% Business, 20% Science
Special study options: Co-op programs, internships, study abroad, language programs, distance learning programs

Liberal Arts and Sciences, General Studies, and Humanities

Archaeology, Art, Art History, Asian Studies, Canadian Studies, Classics & Classical Languages & Literature, Communications, Contemporary Studies, English Language & Literature, Fine/Studio Arts, French Language & Literature, German Language & Literature, Greek Language & Literature, History, Humanities/Humanistic Studies, International Relations & Affairs, Latin Language & Literature, Linguistics, Languages & Literature, Music, Philosophy, Political Science, Psychology, Religion/Religious Studies, Social Work, Sociology, Spanish Language & Literature, Urban Affairs/Studies, Visual & Performing Arts, Women's Studies

Science and Mathematics

Biological Sciences/Life Sciences, Biology, Biochemistry/Biotechnology, Chemistry, Environmental Sciences, Geography, Mathematics, Physics

Computer Science and Engineering

Computer & Information Sciences

Professional Studies

Physical Education Teaching & Coaching, Journalism

Business and Economics

Accounting, Business Administration & Management/Commerce, Economics, Finance, Human Resources Management, Management Information Systems & Business Data Processing, Marketing Management & Research, Operations Management & Supervision, Organizational Behavior Studies

GRADUATE ADMISSIONS

Faculty of Graduate Studies
Alvin Woods Building
Wilfred Laurier University
Waterloo, ON   N2L 3C5
PH: **519.884.0710 ext.3324**   FAX: **519.884.1020**
WEBSITE: **www.wlu.ca/wwwgrads**

Fall application deadline:	Feb- Mar
Application fee:	$50 ($100 for MBA & MSW)
Electronic application accepted:	Yes
Required with application:	College transcript, recommendations & departmental requirements
Graduate student housing:	Bricker Residence for single students

GRADUATE FINANCES

Graduate tuition:		
International students:	$11,000	(US $9900)
Canadian students:	$6000	(US $5400)
Financial aid & Scholarships available for		
international students:	Yes	
Application deadline:	Varies	

GRADUATE INSTRUCTIONAL PROGRAM

Liberal Arts and Sciences, General Studies, and Humanities
Comparative Literature, Divinity/Ministry (Waterloo Lutheran Seminary), English Language & Literature, History, Philosophy, Political Science, Psychology, Religion/Religious Studies, Social Work, Theology/Theological Studies

Science and Mathematics
Geography

Business and Economics
Business Administration & Management/Commerce

YORK UNIVERSITY

Toronto, Canada

SCHOOL CATEGORY: Master's   **TOTAL ENROLLMENT: 40,000**   **SETTING: Suburban**   **CITY POPULATION: 4,000,000**

York, the third-largest university in Canada, is home to approximately 40,000 students and has earned international and national recognition for research and academics. It offers a wide selection of innovative graduate, professional, and undergraduate courses on two campuses within the metropolitan area of Toronto. York emphasizes interdisciplinary thinking, students are allowed to combine majors in completely different fields, and both students and faculty are encouraged to take a broader look at the world.

The main campus, located in Toronto's north end, offers a modern learning environment and extensive facilities. The Glendon campus in midtown Toronto is a small liberal arts college with less than 2,000 students. York offers more than 100 degree programs. Renowned programs include the Sculach School of Business and Osgoode Hall Law School. The Glendon campus offers liberal arts programs in both English and French and specialized programs such as translation. Admission to York is selective.

York's athletic facilities are among the best in Canada and include an indoor track and field center, six ice rinks, Olympic-size swimming pools, and numerous tennis courts.

The fifth-largest city in North America, Toronto is one of the world's most cosmopolitan cities and a very exciting place to live. The city is home to hundreds of restaurants, theaters, clubs, and other cultural opportunities. Sports fans can choose to watch college basketball games or some of the area's many professional sports teams, including baseball's Blue Jays and hockey's Maple Leafs. York is a place where the curious thrive, and where a climate of innovation celebrates daring thinking and uncommon approaches.

GENERAL INFORMATION

Year founded:	1959
Undergraduate enrollment, full-time:	38,000
Graduate enrollment, full-time:	3000
Faculty, full-time:	1125
Number of international students:	N/A
Male/female ratio (%):	40:60
Residence spaces available:	1850
Residence space guaranteed for 1st-year students:	Yes (for applicants with 85% avg)
Student media website:	www.excal.on.ca

UNDERGRADUATE ADMISSIONS

Department of Admissions
4700 Keele Street
Toronto, ON   M3J 1P3
PH: **416.736.2100**   FAX: **416.736.5700**
WEBSITE: **www.yorku.ca**

Minimum high school average	75%
Applications, 2000-2001:	N/A
Rolling admissions:	Yes
International fall application deadline:	Feb 1- Apr 1
Application fee:	$105
Domestic fall application deadline:	June 30
Application fee:	$105
Electronic application accepted:	Yes
Admissions notification by:	N/A
Required with application:	HS transcripts, SAT (1100 min), ACT (24min) audition for Fine Arts

UNDERGRADUATE FINANCES

Undergraduate tuition:		
International students:	$14,000	(US $12,600)
Canadian students:	$4200	(US $3800)
Estimated annual health insurance:	$820	(US $740)
Estimated annual books & supplies:	$1000	(US $900)
Financial aid & Scholarships available for		
international students:	N/A	
Application deadline:	N/A	
Annual room/board cost for students in residence:	$5000-7000	(US $4500-6300)
Average monthly rent for students living off campus:		
1 bedroom: $600+, 2 bedroom: $700+		
Federal School Code: G07679		

UNDERGRADUATE INSTRUCTIONAL PROGRAM

Most popular majors: Business, Computer Science, Fine Arts, Physical Education Teaching & Coaching
Percentages by program: N/A
Special Study Options: Co-op, internships, study abroad, language programs, distance learning

Liberal Arts and Sciences, General Studies, and Humanities

African Studies, Anthropology, Art, Asian Studies, Canadian Studies, Classics & Classical Languages & Literature, Communications, Comparative Literature, Cultural Studies, Dance, Design & Applied Arts, Drama/Theater Arts, East Asian Studies, English Language & Literature, Film/Cinema, Fine/ Studio Arts, French Language & Literature, German Language & Literature, Hispanic Studies, History, Humanities/Humanistic Studies, International Relations & Affairs, Italian Language & Literature, Japanese Language & Literature, Jewish/Judaic Studies, Latin American Studies, Linguistics, Music, Philosophy, Political Science, Portuguese Language & Literature, Psychology, Religion/Religious Studies, Russian & Slavic Area Studies, Russian Languages & Literature, Social Work, Sociology, Spanish Language & Literature, Translation, Urban Affairs/Studies, Visual & Performing Arts, Women's Studies

Science and Mathematics

Astronomy, Applied Mathematics, Atmospheric Sciences & Meteorology, Biological Sciences/Life Sciences, Biology, Biophysics, Chemistry, Earth & Planetary Science, Environmental Sciences, Geography, Mathematics, Natural Science, Science & Technology Studies, Space & Communications Science, Statistics

Computer Science and Engineering

Computer & Information Sciences, Computer Engineering, Electrical/Electronics & Communication Engineering, Environmental/Environmental Health Engineering, Geometrics Engineering, Information Science & Systems

Professional Studies

Criminal Justice Studies, Education, Human Kinetics/ Kinesiology, Physical Education Teaching & Coaching

Business and Economics

Business Administration & Management/Commerce, Economics, Entrepreneurship, Human Resources Management, Labour/ Personnel Relations & Studies

Health Professions and Related Sciences

Health Sciences, Nursing

GRADUATE ADMISSIONS

Faculty of Graduate Studies
York University
P.O. Box GA 2300/4700 Keele Street
Toronto, ON   M3J 1P3
PH: **416.736.5329**   FAX: **416.736.5592**
WEBSITE: **www.yorku.ca/grads/**

Fall application deadline:	Varies, early applications encouraged
Application fee:	N/A
Required with application:	College transcript, essay, recommendations portfolio (GRE & GMAT per department)
Graduate student housing:	Various accommodations for singles, couples and families

GRADUATE FINANCES

Graduate tuition:

International students:	$8000 +	(US $7200)
Canadian students:	$3200 +	(US $2900)

Financial aid & Scholarships available for

international students:	Yes
Application deadline:	Varies

GRADUATE INSTRUCTIONAL PROGRAM

Liberal Arts and Sciences, General Studies, and Humanities

Anthropology, Art History, Dance, English Language & Literature, Film/Cinema, History, Linguistics, Music, Philosophy, Political Science, Psychology, Social Work, Sociology, Translation, Visual & Performing Arts, Women's Studies

Science and Mathematics

Astronomy, Atmospheric Sciences & Meteorology, Biology, Chemistry, Earth & Planetary Science, Environmental Sciences, Geography, Mathematics, Physics, Statistics

Computer Science and Engineering

Computer & Information Sciences

Professional Studies

Education, Human Kinetics/Kinesiology, Law

Business and Economics

Business Administration & Management/Commerce, Economics

MANITOBA

BRANDON UNIVERSITY

Brandon, Manitoba

SCHOOL CATEGORY: Bachelor's/Liberal Arts   **TOTAL ENROLLMENT: 3550**   **SETTING: Suburban**   **CITY POPULATION: 40,000**

Brandon University is a small liberal arts college located in Manitoba's second-largest city. Small class sizes, a safe and compact campus, and a low student/faculty ratio combine to provide a unique educational experience.

Brandon offers programs in a wide range of subject areas. Brandon University's school of music and affiliated conservatory are very highly regarded.

Residence space is limited and is offered on a first-come, first-served basis. The school is located on the edge of a residential district, with good public transportation and easy access to downtown and shopping. Athletic facilities on campus include a gymnasium and playing fields.

Brandon is known as the "Wheat City" and is dotted with parks, many along the Assiniboine River that winds its way through the city. The city offers a wide range of indoor and outdoor recreational activities for all seasons. Brandon stages a Film Festival and a Jazz Festival as well as hosting the Royal Manitoba Winter Fair every year.

GENERAL INFORMATION

Year founded:	1899
Undergraduate enrollment, full-time:	2400
Graduate enrollment, full-time:	15
Faculty, full-time:	193
Number of international students:	N/A
Male/female ratio (%)	35:65
Residence spaces available:	420
Residence space guaranteed for 1st-year students:	N/A
Student media website:	www.brandonu.ca/busu

UNDERGRADUATE ADMISSIONS

Office of Admissions
270-18th Street
Brandon, MB   R7A 6A9
PH: 204.727.9784   FAX: 204.728.3221
WEBSITE: www.discover.brandonu.ca

Minimum high school average:	70
Rolling admissions:	Yes
International fall application deadline:	Aug 1
Application fee:	$60
Domestic fall application deadline:	Aug 1
Application fee:	$125
Electronic application accepted:	Yes
Admissions notification by:	N/A
Required with application:	HS transcript
Recommended:	Essays

UNDERGRADUATE FINANCES

Undergraduate tuition:		
International students:	$5700	(US $5130)
Canadian students:	$3000	(US $2700)
Estimated annual health insurance:	$500	(US $450)
Estimated annual books & supplies:	$900	(US $810)
Financial aid available for international students:	Yes (not to entering students)	
Application deadline:	N/A	
Scholarships available for international students:	Yes (available in senior year)	
Application deadline:	N/A	
Annual room/board cost for students in residence:	$5200	(US $4700)
Average monthly rent for students living off campus:		
1 bedroom: $400-500, 2 bedroom: $500-600		
Federal School Code: G09421		

UNDERGRADUATE INSTRUCTIONAL PROGRAM

Most popular majors: Business, Computer Science, Psychology, Sociology
Percentages by program: 44% Liberal Arts, 21% Science, 7% Health
Special study options: Co-op programs, study abroad, language programs, special summer programs, distance learning programs

Liberal Arts and Sciences, General Studies, and Humanities

Art, Anthropology, Canadian Studies, Classics & Classical Languages & Literature, Drama/Theater Arts, English Language & Literature, Fine/Studio Arts, History, Music, Native Studies, Philosophy, Political Science, Psychology, Religion/Religious Studies, Social Work, Sociology, Women's Studies

Science and Mathematics

Agriculture, Astronomy, Botany, Chemistry, Geography, Geology, Pre-Engineering, Environmental Sciences, Forestry Sciences, Horticulture Science, Mathematics, Physics, Water Quality Technology, Wildlife Management, Zoology

Professional Studies

Counseling (first nations & aboriginal), City/Urban/ Community Regional Planning, Education (music, native teacher), Human Ecology, Interior Design, Journalism

Business and Economics

Business Administration & Management/Commerce, Economics, Entrepreneurship

Health Professions and Related Sciences

Health Sciences, Nursing

GRADUATE ADMISSIONS

Department of Education/Music/Rural Development
Brandon University
270-18th Street
Brandon, MB   R7A 6A9
PH: **800-888-9770**   FAX: **204.728.3326**
WEBSITE: **www.discover.brandon.ca/graduate**

Fall application deadline:	Mar 1
Application fee:	$35
Electronic application accepted:	Yes
Required with application:	College transcript, departmental requirements

GRADUATE FINANCES

Graduate tuition:	$4200	(US $3800)
Financial aid & Scholarships available	Yes	
Application deadline:	May 1	
Graduate student housing:	N/A	

GRADUATE INSTRUCTIONAL PROGRAM

Liberal Arts and Sciences, General Studies, and Humanities

Music

Professional Studies

Education, City/Urban/Community & Regional Planning

THE UNIVERSITY OF MANITOBA

Winnipeg, Manitoba

SCHOOL CATEGORY: Doctoral/Research   **TOTAL ENROLLMENT: 27,000**   **SETTING: Suburban**   **CITY POPULATION: 700,000**

The University of Manitoba (U of M) is a large comprehensive university whose main campus is in the Winnipeg suburb of Fort Garry, about 7 miles from the city center. The Health Science campus is located next to Manitoba's largest medical complex in central Winnipeg. The university has recently opened a new research park that will attract advanced technology firms and research facilities.

The U of M offers a diverse and outstanding range of courses and studies in over 65 areas. Degrees are offered at the undergraduate, master's, doctoral, and postdoctoral level.

The U of M has five residence halls. Admission to residence is on a first-come, first-served basis. Excellent athletic facilities are a legacy of the school's hosting of the Thirteenth Pan American Games.

Winnipeg is a large, cosmopolitan city located at the geographic center of Canada. Winnipeg's position at the confluence of the Red and Assiniboine Rivers made it an important trading center for Native Americans going back 6,000 years. Today this attractive city, with its museums, historic buildings, and excellent restaurants, offers an enjoyable environment for study.

GENERAL INFORMATION

Year founded:	1977
Undergraduate enrollment, full-time:	18,000
Graduate enrollment, full-time:	2,300
Faculty, full-time:	1346
Number of international students:	754
Male/female ratio (%)	46:54
Residence spaces available:	950
Residence space guaranteed for 1st-year students:	No
Student media website:	www.umanitoba.ca/student/group

UNDERGRADUATE ADMISSIONS

Admissions Office
66 Chancellors Circle
Winnipeg, MB   R3T 2N2
PH: 204.474. 8810   FAX: 204.474.7536
WEBSITE: www.umanitoba.ca

Minimum high school average:	65%
Rolling admissions:	Yes
International fall application deadline:	May 1
Application fee:	$60
Domestic fall application deadline:	May 1
Application fee:	$35
Electronic application accepted:	Yes
Admissions notification by:	Jul 1
Required with application:	HS transcripts

UNDERGRADUATE FINANCES

Undergraduate tuition:		
International students:	$5700	(US $5130)
Canadian students:	$3000	(US $2700)
Estimated annual health insurance:	$500	(US $450)
Estimated annual books & supplies:	$1000	(US $900)
Financial Aid & Scholarships available for		
international students:	Yes	
Application deadline:	Varies	
Annual room/board cost for students in residence:	$4050	(US $3600)
Average monthly rent for students living off campus:		
1 bedroom: $400-500, 2 bedroom: $500-600		
Federal School Code: G06684		

UNDERGRADUATE INSTRUCTIONAL PROGRAM

Most popular majors: Business, Engineering, Education, Nursing
Percentages by program: 12% Liberal Arts, 10% Science, 6% Business, 7% Engineering/Computer Science, 7% Health Professions
Special study options: Co-op programs, study abroad, language programs, special summer programs, distance learning programs

Liberal Arts and Sciences, General Studies, and Humanities

Anthropology, Asian Studies, Canadian Studies, Catholic Studies, Classics & Classical Languages & Literature, Drama/Theater Arts, English Language & Literature, Film/Cinema, Fine/Studio Arts, French Language & Literature, German Language & Literature, Gerontology, History, Icelandic Language & Literature, Italian Language & Literature, Medieval & Renaissance Studies, Music, Native Studies, Philosophy, Political Science, Psychology, Religion/Religious Studies, Slavic Languages & Literature, Social Work, Ukrainian Canadian Heritage Studies, Sociology, Women's Studies

Science and Mathematics

Agriculture Sciences, Animal Science, Astronomy, Biology, Botany, Chemistry, Ecology, Entomology, Environmental Sciences, Food Sciences & Technology, Geography, Geology, Mathematics, Microbiology, Physics, Plant Science, Soil Science, Statistics, Zoology

Computer Science and Engineering

Biosystems Engineering, Computer & Information Sciences, Computer Engineering, Civil Engineering, Electrical/Electronics & Communications Engineering, Geological Engineering, Industrial/Manufacturing Engineering, Mechanical Engineering

Professional Studies

Architecture, Education, Family & Community Studies, Interior Design, Landscape Architecture, Leisure & Recreation Activities, Physical Education Teaching & Coaching, Textile Sciences

Business and Economics

Accounting, Business Administration & Management/Commerce, Economics, Entrepreneurship, Human Resources Management, Information Sciences & Systems, International Business, Labor/Personnel Relations & Studies, Management Science, Management Information Systems, Marketing Management & Research, Natural Resources Management & Protective Services, Operations Management & Supervision

Health Professions and Related Sciences

Nursing, Nutritional Sciences, Pharmacy, Physical Therapy, Pre-Dentistry, Pre-Medicine, Pre-Veterinary Medicine, Public Health, Speech-Language Pathology & Audiology, Veterinary Medicine

GRADUATE ADMISSIONS

Faculty of Graduate Studies
University of Manitoba
500 University Centre
Winnipeg, MB   R3T 2N2
PH: **204.474.9377**   FAX: **204.474.7553**
WEBSITE: **www.umanitoba.ca/graduate_studies/**

International fall application deadline:	Jan 15
Application fee:	$50
Domestic fall application deadline:	Jul 12
Application fee:	$50
Required with application:	College transcript, recommendations, (GRE & GMAT may be required)
Graduate student housing:	Accommodations for single students at Spechly/ Tache Hall

GRADUATE FINANCES

Graduate tuition:		
International students:	$8000	(US $7200)
Canadian students:	$3700	(US $3330)
Financial aid & Scholarships available for		
international students:	Yes	
Application deadline:	Jan 15	

GRADUATE INSTRUCTIONAL PROGRAM

Liberal Arts and Sciences, General Studies, and Humanities

Anthropology, Classics & Classical Languages & Literature, English Language & Literature, French Language & Literature, German Language & Literature, History, Icelandic Language & Literature, Italian Language & Literature, Linguistics, Native Studies, Philosophy, Political Science, Psychology, Religion/Religious Social Work, Slavic Languages & Literature, Sociology, Spanish Language & Literature

Science and Mathematics

Agriculture Sciences, Animal Science, Biochemistry, Botany, Chemistry, Entomology, Food Science & Technology, Geography, Geology, Mathematics, Microbiology, Physics, Plant Science, Soil Science, Zoology

Computer Science and Engineering

Bioengineering & Biomedical Engineering, Civil Engineering, Computer & Information Sciences, Electrical/Electronics & Communication Engineering, Geological Engineering

Professional Studies

Architecture, City/Urban/Community & Regional Planning, Education, Family & Community Studies, Interior Design, Law, Landscape Architecture, Physical Education Teaching & Coaching, Textile Sciences

Business and Economics

Agricultural Business /Economics & Farm Management, Economics, Information Sciences & Systems, Management Information Systems, Natural Resource Management & Protective Services, Public Administration

Health Professions and Related Sciences

Community Health Science, Dentistry, Genetics, Health Studies, Human Anatomy & Cell Biology, Immunology, Medicine, Medical Microbiology, Medical Rehabilitation, Nursing, Nutritional Science, Pathology, Pharmacy, Pharmacology & Therapy, Physiology, Psychiatry

THE UNIVERSITY OF WINNIPEG

Winnipeg, Manitoba

SCHOOL CATEGORY: Bachelor's/General   **TOTAL ENROLLMENT: 9000**   **SETTING: Suburban**   **CITY POPULATION: 700,000**

Founded in 1967, the University of Winnipeg is a medium-sized university located in downtown Winnipeg. The school attracts students from all across Manitoba, across Canada and from around the world.

The Faculty of Arts and Science offers undergraduate degree programs in the arts, sciences and education, with over 800 courses in 40 major areas. Students may obtain three- or four-year Bachelor of Arts and Science degrees, or a five-year Education degree. In addition, the University offers pre-professional programs (from one to three years) which prepare students for admission to everything from law to medicine.

Students have rated the university very highly in the areas of teaching quality, class sizes, faculty-student interaction, and the availability of faculty outside classroom hours.

The new Global Challenge, through its four centers—the Institute of Health, Security, and Human Potential; the Institute for Human Rights and Global Studies; the Climate Studies Institute; and the Global Information Commons Center—is a place where students, faculty and the community—local, national, and international—meet to research, discuss, and debate issues of global citizenship.

Residence space is limited, but off-campus housing is readily available nearby. The school offers a mix of recreational and cultural activities. Athletic facilities include a gymnasium, swimming pool, fitness center and playing fields.

Winnipeg is a large, cosmopolitan city located at the geographic center of Canada. This attractive city with its many museums, historic buildings and excellent restaurants, provides an enjoyable environment for learning.

GENERAL INFORMATION

Year founded:	1967
Undergraduate enrollment, full-time:	6251
Graduate enrollment, full-time:	28
Faculty, full-time:	300
Number of international students:	500
Male/female ratio (%):	38:64
Residence spaces available:	160
Residence space guaranteed for 1st-year students:	Yes
Student media website:	www.uwinnipeg.ca/uwsaweb/

UNDERGRADUATE ADMISSIONS

Admissions Office
515 Portgage Avenue
Winnipeg, MB   R3B 2E9
PH: **204.786.9159**   FAX: **204.786.8656**
WEBSITE: **www.uwinnipeg.ca**

Minimum high school average:	60
Applications, 2005:	N/A
Rolling admissions:	Yes
Fall application deadline:	May 31
Application fee:	$125
Electronic application accepted:	Yes
Admissions notification by:	N/A
Required with application:	HS transcripts

UNDERGRADUATE FINANCES

Undergraduate tuition:		
International students:	$6241	(US $5617)
Canadian students:	$2800	(US $2520)
Estimated annual health insurance:	$423	(US $380)
Estimated annual books & supplies:	$1000	(US $700)
Financial aid & Scholarships available for		
international students:	N/A	
Application deadline:	N/A	
Annual room cost for students in residence:	$2960	(US $2664)
Average monthly rent for students living off campus:		
1 bedroom: $400 +, 2 bedroom: $500 +		
Federal School Code: G08148		

UNDERGRADUATE INSTRUCTIONAL PROGRAM

Most popular majors: Business, Biology, English, Psychology
Percentages by program: N/A
Special study options: Co-op programs, internships

Liberal Arts and Sciences, General Studies, and Humanities

Anthropology, Art History, Classics & Classical Languages & Literature, Communications, Dance, Drama/Theater Arts, English Language & Literature, French Language & Literature, German Language & Literature, International Relations & Affairs, Music, Philosophy, Political Science, Psychology, Religion/Religious Studies, Sociology, Spanish Language & Literature, Theology/Theological Studies, Translation, Urban Affairs/Studies, Visual & Performing Arts, Women's Studies, Writing

Science and Mathematics

Biochemistry, Biology, Chemistry, Environmental Sciences, Geography, Mathematics, Physics, Statistics

Computer Science and Engineering

Computer & Information Sciences, Engineering Science

Professional Studies

Conflict Resolution Studies, Criminal Justice Studies, Education, Kinesiology, Sport & Fitness Administration/Management

Business and Economics

Business Administration & Management/Commerce, Economics

GRADUATE ADMISSIONS

Faculty of Graduate Studies
The University of Winnipeg
Winnipeg, MB   R3B 2E9

Faculty of Graduate Studies
University of Manitoba
Room 500, University Centre
Winnipeg, MB   R3T 2N2

Fall application deadline:	N/A
Application fee:	N/A
Required with application:	College transcript
Graduate student housing:	No

GRADUATE FINANCES

Graduate tuition:

International students:	$8000	(US $7200)
Canadian students:	$4000	(US $3600)
Financial aid & Scholarships available for		
international students:	N/A	
Application deadline:	N/A	

GRADUATE INSTRUCTIONAL PROGRAM

Liberal Arts and Sciences, General Studies, and Humanities
Divinity/Ministry, History,* Religion/Religious Studies,*
Theology/Theological, Sacred Theology

Professional Studies
Counseling

Business and Economics
Public Administration*

*Offered Jointly with the University of Manitoba

SASKATCHEWAN

CAMPION COLLEGE AT THE UNIVERSITY OF REGINA

Regina, Saskatchewan

SCHOOL CATEGORY: Bachelor's/Liberal Arts   **TOTAL ENROLLMENT: 1200**   **SETTING: Suburban**   **CITY POPULATION: 200,000**

Campion College is a Catholic co-educational institution. It provides a liberal arts education in the Jesuit tradition. Founded in 1917, Campion is federated with the University of Regina and named for the Jesuit priest and scholar St. Edmund Campion.

Campion offers innovative programs in partnership with the University of Regina. Campion students can register for courses offered by the University of Regina, as well as courses offered through the college.

Campion students have access to the University of Regina's residences and a variety of conveniently located houses and apartments are readily available for renting off campus. Students will find a wide variety of opportunities to participate in recreational, social, and cultural activities either through Campion or through the University of Regina.

Regina is a friendly, bustling city and the home of the internationally famous Royal Canadian Mounted Police. The RCMP museum is located here, and daily parades are a staple of city life. Saskatchewan is situated in the heart of North America, bordering the states of Montana and North Dakota to the south and the provinces of Alberta and Manitoba.

GENERAL INFORMATION

Year founded:	1917
Undergraduate enrollment, full-time:	1050
Graduate enrollment, full-time:	100
Faculty, full-time:	N/A
Number of international students:	N/A
Male/female ratio (%)	45:55
Residence spaces available:	573
Residence space guaranteed for 1st-year students:	No
Student media website:	N/A

UNDERGRADUATE ADMISSIONS

Office of the Registrar
3737 Wascana Parkway
Regina, SK S4S 0A2
PH: 306.586.4242   FAX: 306.359.1200
WEBSITE: www.campioncollege.sk.ca

Minimum high school average:	65
Applications, 2005:	N/A
Rolling admissions:	N/A
International fall application deadline:	Apr 1
Application fee:	$60
Domestic fall application deadline:	Jul 1
Application fee:	$60
Electronic application accepted:	No
Admissions notification by:	N/A
Required with application:	HS transcripts

UNDERGRADUATE FINANCES

Undergraduate tuition:		
International students:	$8152	(US $7336)
Canadian students:	$4076	(US $3670)
Estimated annual health insurance:	$250	(US $225)
Estimated annual books & supplies:	$1000	(US $900)
Financial aid & Scholarships available		
for international students:	Yes, after 1st year	
Application deadline:	N/A	
Annual room/board cost for students in residence:	$5031-6940	(US $4530-6250)
Average monthly rent for students living off campus:		
1 bedroom: $400-600, 2 bedroom: $500-700		

UNDERGRADUATE INSTRUCTIONAL PROGRAM

Most popular majors: Sciences, Fine/Studio Arts
Percentages by program: N/A
Special study options: Internships, study abroad, language programs, special summer programs, distance learning programs (available through the University of Regina)

Liberal Arts and Sciences, General Studies, and Humanities

Anthropology, Art, Art History, Chinese Language & Literature, English Language & Literature, French Language & Literature, German Language & Literature, History, Humanities/Humanistic Studies, Japanese Language & Literature, Jewish/Judaic Studies, Latin Language & Literature, Linguistics, Mandarin, Music, Native American Studies, Philosophy, Political Science, Psychology, Religion/Religious Studies, Russian Languages & Literature, Social Work, Sociology, Spanish Language & Literature, Theology/Theological Studies, Women's Studies

Science and Mathematics

Pre-Agriculture, Astronomy, Biology, Biochemistry, Chemistry, Geography, Mathematics, Physics, Statistics

Computer Science and Engineering

Computer & Information Sciences

Professional Studies

Pre-Criminal Justice Studies, Pre-Journalism, Pre-Law

Business and Economics

Pre-Business Administration & Management/Commerce

Health Professions & Related Sciences

Health Studies, Pre-Chiropractic, Pre-Dentistry, Pre-Medicine, Pre-Nutritional Sciences, Pre-Occupational Therapy, Pre-Optometry, Pre-Pharmacy, Pre-Physical Therapy, Pre-Veterinary Science

LUTHER COLLEGE

Regina, Saskatchewan

SCHOOL CATEGORY: Bachelor's/Liberal Arts   **TOTAL ENROLLMENT: 1000**   **SETTING: Urban**   **CITY POPULATION: 200,000**

Luther College is a small liberal arts college that is federated with and shares the campus of the University of Regina. Founded in 1913, Luther College provides a solid university education in a Christian context within a smaller, supportive community.

Academic programs at Luther include liberal arts, fine arts and science. The school also offers an extensive summer center for International Languages. These classes fulfill the language requirements for degree programs.

About a quarter of the students live in coed residences, and a variety of conveniently located houses and apartments are readily available for renting off campus. Students will find a wide variety of opportunities to participate in recreational, social, and cultural activities.

Regina is a friendly, bustling city and the home of the internationally famous Royal Canadian Mounted Police. The RCMP museum is located here, and daily parades are a staple of city life. Saskatchewan is situated in the heart of North America, bordering the states of Montana and North Dakota to the south and the provinces of Alberta and Manitoba on the east and west.

GENERAL INFORMATION

Year founded:	1913
Undergraduate enrollment, full-time:	830
Graduate enrollment, full-time:	100
Faculty, full-time:	12
Number of international students:	N/A
Male/female ratio (%)	62:38
Residence spaces available:	218
Residence space guaranteed for 1st-year students:	N/A
Student media website:	N/A

UNDERGRADUATE ADMISSIONS

Department of Admissions
3737 Wascana Parkway, Suite 100
Regina, SK   S4S 0A2
PH: 306.585.5083   FAX: 306.585.5267
WEBSITE: **www.luthercollege.edu**

Minimum high school average:	65
Applications, 2005:	N/A
Rolling admissions:	Yes
International fall application deadline:	Apr 1
Application fee:	$60
Domestic fall application deadline:	July 1
Application fee:	$60
Electronic application accepted:	Yes
Admissions notification by:	N/A
Required with application:	HS transcript

UNDERGRADUATE FINANCES

Undergraduate tuition:		
International students:	$8152	(US $7336)
Canadian students:	$4076	(US $3670)
Estimated annual health insurance:	$250	(US $225)
Estimated annual books & supplies:	$1000	(US $900)
Financial aid available for international students:	No	
Application deadline:	N/A	
Scholarships available for international students:	Yes	
Application deadline:	May 18	
Annual room/board cost for students in residence:	$4500-4800	(US $4050-4320)
Average monthly rent for students living off campus:		
1 bedroom: $400-600, 2 bedroom: $500-700		

UNDERGRADUATE INSTRUCTIONAL PROGRAM

Most popular majors: Psychology, Computer Science, Pre-Administration, English
Percentages by program: 68% Liberal Arts, 32% Science
Special study options: Co-op programs, study abroad, language programs, special summer programs

Liberal Arts and Sciences, General Studies, and Humanities

Anthropology, Art, Art History, Cree, English Language & Literature, Dakota, Film/Cinema, French Language & Literature, German Language & Literature, Greek Language & Literature, Hebrew, History, Humanities/Humanistic Studies, Indian Art/History, Japanese Language & Literature, Latin Language & Literature, Linguistics, Mandarin, Music, Nakota, Native Studies, Philosophy, Religion/Religious Studies, Russian Languages & Literature, Social Work, Sociology, (pre) Theology/Theological Studies, Visual & Performing Arts, Women's Studies

Science and Mathematics

Pre- Agricultural Science, Pre-Architecture, Astronomy, Biochemistry, Biology, Chemistry, Geography, Geology, Mathematics, Physics, Statistics

Computer Science and Engineering

Computer & Information Sciences

Professional Studies

Criminal Justice Studies, Journalism, Pre-Law

Business and Economics

Actuarial Science, Pre-Business Administration & Management/Commerce, Economics

Health Professions and Related Sciences

Health Sciences

ST. THOMAS MORE COLLEGE

Saskatoon, Saskachewan

SCHOOL CATEGORY: Bachelor's/Liberal Arts   **TOTAL ENROLLMENT: 1800**   **SETTING: Suburban**   **CITY POPULATION: 200,000**

St. Thomas More College (STM) is a small Catholic liberal arts institution affiliated with the University of Saskatchewan. It offers the benefits of a small institution alongside the academic excellence of a larger university. STM offers classes in the Humanities and Social Sciences that supplement course offerings of the University of Saskatchewan's College of Arts and Science.

The college offers students an active student life including recreational sports, socials, choir and drama. There are approximately 100 residence spaces available in a variety of co-ed settings. Off-campus housing is also widely available in Saskatoon. Students enjoy the use of all services and facilities of the University of Saskatchewan.

Saskatoon is a picturesque city located on the banks of the South Saskatchewan River in the center of the Canadian prairies. The city receives the most sunshine of any city in Canada. The province of Saskatchewan has a rich Western and Aboriginal heritage. From golden wheat fields in the south to lush forests and crystal-clear lakes in the north, Saskatchewan's diversity has much to charm new residents.

GENERAL INFORMATION

Year founded:	1936
Undergraduate enrollment, full-time:	1800
Graduate enrollment, full-time:	N/A
Faculty, full-time:	25
Number of international students:	N/A
Male/female ratio (%)	45:55
Residence spaces available:	100
Residence space guaranteed for 1st-year students:	No
Student media website:	N/A

UNDERGRADUATE ADMISSIONS

Office of Admissions
1437 College Drive
Saskatoon, SK   S7N 0W6
PH: **306.966.8900**   FAX: **306.966.8904**
WEBSITE: **www.usask.ca/stm**

Minimum high school average:	70
Applications, 2000-2001:	N/A
Rolling admissions:	No
International fall application deadline:	Apr 1
Application fee:	$50
Domestic fall application deadline:	May 15
Application fee:	$50
Electronic application accepted:	Yes
Admissions notification by:	N/A
Required with application:	HS transcripts
Recommended:	SAT

UNDERGRADUATE FINANCES

Undergraduate tuition:		
International students:	$11,400-17,800	(US $10,260-16,020)
Canadian students:	$4380-4950	(US $3950-4455)
Estimated annual health insurance:	$240	(US $216)
Estimated annual books & supplies:	$1000	(US $900)
Financial aid & Scholarships available for		
international students:	Yes	
Application deadline:	Apr 1	
Annual room/board cost for		
students in residence:	$5500-6300	(US $4950-5670)
Average monthly rent for students living off campus: 1 bedroom: $400-600, 2 bedroom: $500-800		

UNDERGRADUATE INSTRUCTIONAL PROGRAM

Most popular majors: Humanities, Social Science
Percentages by program: 95% Liberal Arts
Special study options: Study abroad

Liberal Arts and Sciences, General Studies, and Humanities

Anthropology, Classics & Classical Languages & Literature, English Language & Literature, History, Philosophy, Political Science, Psychology, Religion/Religious Studies, Sociology

Professional Studies
Archaeology

Business and Economics
Economics

THE UNIVERSITY OF REGINA

Regina, Saskatchewan

SCHOOL CATEGORY: Master's　　**TOTAL ENROLLMENT: 13,000**　　**SETTING: Suburban**　　**CITY POPULATION: 200,000**

The University of Regina is a large comprehensive university located in Regina, the capital of Saskatchewan, with a city population of 200,000. The university has two main campuses, both conveniently located just outside the city center. The new campus and the historic old campus offer an attractive work and study environment. There are three federated colleges: Campion College (Jesuit affiliation), Luther College (Lutheran affiliation), and the First Nations University of Canada.

The University of Regina offers its students programs leading to bachelor's, master's, and doctoral degrees in nine faculties and over 40 areas of specialization. The university offers many innovative and highly recognized programs. L' Institut Francais offers both credit and noncredit programs in French.

There are four separate residences on campus with many options for students. A variety of conveniently located houses and apartments are readily available for renting off campus. Students will find a wide variety of opportunities to participate in recreational, social, and cultural activities at both campuses.

Regina is a friendly, bustling city and the home of the internationally famous Royal Canadian Mounted Police. The RCMP museum is located here as well as many other landmarks and tourist destinations. Saskatchewan is situated in the heart of North America, bordering the states of Montana and North Dakota on the south and the provinces of Alberta and Manitoba.

GENERAL INFORMATION

Year founded:	1910
Undergraduate enrollment, full-time:	7245
Graduate enrollment, full-time:	588
Faculty, full-time:	449
Number of international students:	895
Male/female ratio (%)	40:60
Residence spaces available:	1233
Residence space guaranteed for 1st-year students:	N/A
Student media website:	N/A

UNDERGRADUATE ADMISSIONS

Admissions Office
3737 Wascana Parkway
Regina, SK   S4S 0A2
PH: **800-644-4756**   FAX: **306.585.5203**
WEBSITE: **www.uregina.ca**

Minimum high school average:	65
Applications, 2005:	1405 Received; 1220 Accepted
Rolling admissions:	N/A
Fall application deadline:	Apr 1
Application fee:	$60
Electronic application accepted:	Yes
Admissions notification by:	N/A
Required with application:	HS transcripts

UNDERGRADUATE FINANCES

Undergraduate tuition:		
International students:	$8152	(US $7336)
Canadian students:	$4076	(US $3670)
Estimated annual health insurance:	N/A	
Estimated annual books & supplies:	$1000	(US $900)
Financial aid available for international students:	No	
Application deadline:	N/A	
Scholarships available for international students:	No	
Application deadline:	N/A	
Annual room/board cost for students in residence:	$4000-6000	(US $3600-5400)
Average monthly rent for students living off campus:		
1 bedroom: $400-600, 2 bedroom: $500-700		
Federal School Code: G08448		

UNDERGRADUATE INSTRUCTIONAL PROGRAM

Most popular majors: Business, Computer Science, Education, Engineering, Liberal Arts
Percentages by program: N/A
Special study options: Co-op programs, internships, study abroad, language programs

Liberal Arts and Sciences, General Studies, and Humanities

Anthropology, Canadian Studies, Classics, English Language & Literature, Film/Cinema, Fine Arts, French Language & Literature, International Studies, History, Humanities/Humanistic Studies, Social Work, Linguistics, Music, Native Studies, Philosophy, Political Science, Psychology, Religion/Religious Studies, Social Work, Sociology, Theatre, Ukrainian, Visual Arts, Women's Studies

Science and Mathematics

Biochemistry, Biology, Chemistry, Geography, Geology, Mathematics, Physics, Statistics, Software Systems Development

Computer Science and Engineering

Computer & Information Sciences, Electrical/ Electronics & Communication Engineering, Environmental Engineering, Industrial/Manufacturing Engineering, Petroleum Engineering, Software Systems Engineering

Professional Studies

Criminal Justice Studies, Education, Health Studies, Human Kinetics/Kinesiology, Journalism, Law, Leisure & Recreational Activities, Police Studies, Radio & Television Broadcasting

Business and Economics

Accounting, Actuarial Science, Business Administration & Management/Commerce, Economics, Finance, Human Resources Management, Labour/Personnel Relations & Studies, Marketing Management & Research, Operations Management & Supervision, Public Policy/Relations & Organizational Communications

GRADUATE ADMISSIONS

Faculty of Graduate Studies & Research
University of Regina
Regina, Saskatchewan S4S 0A2
PH: **306.585.4161** FAX: **306.337.2444**
WEBSITE: **www.uregina.ca/gradstudies/**

International fall application deadline:	Feb 15 most programs
Application fee:	$100
Required with application:	College transcript, references, CV, test scores
Graduate student housing:	Single student accommodations

GRADUATE FINANCES

Graduate tuition:

International students:	$8172	(US $7336)
Canadian students:	$4076	(US $3670)
Financial aid & Scholarships available for		
international students:	N/A	
Application deadline:	N/A	

GRADUATE INSTRUCTIONAL PROGRAM

Liberal Arts and Sciences, General Studies, and Humanities
Anthropology, Canadian Studies, English Language & Literature, French Language & Literature, History, Linguistics, Music, Native Studies, Philosophy, Political Science, Psychology, Religion/Religious Studies, Social Work, Sociology, Visual & Performing Arts, Women's Studies

Science and Mathematics
Biology, Biochemistry, Chemistry, Geography, Geology, Mathematics, Physics, Statistics

Computer Science and Engineering
Computer & Information Sciences, Engineering Science

Professional Studies
Education, Human Kinetics/Kinesiolgy, Justice, Police Studies

Business and Economics
Business Administration & Management/Commerce, Economics

UNIVERSITY OF SASKATCHEWAN

Saskatoon, Saskatchewan

SCHOOL CATEGORY: Doctoral/Research **TOTAL ENROLLMENT: 20,000** **SETTING: Suburban** **CITY POPULATION: 200,000**

The University of Saskatchewan (U of S) is a medium-sized comprehensive University located in the heart of the Canadian prairies. The U of S enjoys a reputation for excellence in both teaching and research and prides itself on delivering innovative programs in a comfortable environment. The University is situated on 300 acres, which are occupied by the campus; the Canadian Light Source, the only national facility for synchrotron light research and the fourth most powerful in the world; Innovation Place, Canada's largest operating research park; as well as the University's farm and experimental plots. The U of S is located in the heart of Saskatoon, on the scenic South Saskatchewan River. St. Thomas More College is affiliated with the University.

The University offers more than 100 areas of specialization for undergraduate and graduate education. Synergy between the university, government, and the private sector has created a vibrant R&D environment. Superb facilities and broad expertise have made Saskatoon one of the world's leading centers in agricultural biotechnology. Research at the University of Saskatchewan has produced the first genetically engineered vaccine for animals, the first Canadian experiment undertaken aboard a space shuttle, and the introduction of more than 100 new crop varieties.

Saskatoon is a picturesque city located on the banks of the South Saskatchewan River in the centre of the Canadian prairies. The city enjoys more hours of sunshine than any other major city in Canada. The province of Saskatchewan has a rich Western and Aboriginal heritage. From golden wheat fields in the south to lush forests and crystal-clear lakes in the north, Saskatchewan's diversity has much to charm new residents.

GENERAL INFORMATION

Year founded:	1907
Undergraduate enrollment, full-time:	13,798
Graduate enrollment, full-time:	1,589
Faculty, full-time:	900
Number of international students:	1,675
Male/female ratio (%)	43:57
Residence spaces available:	1850
Residence space guaranteed for 1st-year students:	No
Student media website:	www.thesheaf.com

UNDERGRADUATE ADMISSIONS

Recruitment & Admissions
105 Administration Place
Saskatoon, SK S7N 5A2
PH: 306.966.5788 FAX: 306.966-2115
WEBSITE: **www.usask.ca, www.explore.usask.ca**

Minimum high school average:	65-80%
Applications, 2005:	9250
Rolling admissions:	N/A
International fall application deadline:	Apr 1
Application fee:	$75
Domestic fall application deadline:	May 1
Application fee:	$75
Electronic application accepted:	Yes
Admissions notification by:	N/A
Required with application:	HS transcripts (essay & interview for some)

UNDERGRADUATE FINANCES

Undergraduate tuition:		
International students:	$11,400-17,800	(US $10,260-16,020)
Canadian students:	$4380-4950	(US $3950-4455)
Estimated annual health insurance:	$240	(US $216)
Estimated annual books & supplies:	$1000-1500	(US $900-1350)
Financial aid available for international students:	N/A	
Application deadline:	N/A	
Scholarships available for international students:	Yes	
Application deadline:	Feb 15	
Annual room/board cost for students in residence:	$4894-5434	(US $4400-4892)
Average monthly rent for students living off campus:		
1 bedroom: $400-600, 2 bedroom: $500-800		
Federal School Code: G22192		

UNDERGRADUATE INSTRUCTIONAL PROGRAM

Most popular majors: Biology, English, Native Sites, Psychology, Sociology
Percentages by program: N/A
Special study options: Co-op programs, internships, study abroad, language programs, distance learning programs

Liberal Arts and Sciences, General Studies, and Humanities

Anthropology, Art, Art History, Classics & Classical Languages & Literature, Drama/Theater Arts, English Language & Literature, History, Linguistics, Music, Native Studies, Philosophy, Political Science, Psychology, Religion/Religious Studies, Sociology, Women's Studies

Science and Mathematics

Agriculture Sciences, Animal Science, Applied Microbiology, Food Sciences & Technology, Biology, Chemistry, Genetics/Plant & Animal, Geography, Horticulture Science, Mathematics, Microbiology, Physics, Physiology/Human & Animal, Statistics, Soil Science, Toxicology

Computer Science and Engineering

Agricultural Engineering, Chemical Engineering, Civil Engineering, Computer Engineering, Computer & Information Sciences, Electrical/ Electronics & Communications Engineering, Mechanical Engineering

Professional Studies

Archaeology, Education (curriculum studies, educational administration, educational foundations, educational psychology and special education), Human Kinetics/Kinesiology, Pre-Law

Business and Economics

Accounting, Agribusiness, Business Administration & Management/Commerce, Information Sciences & Systems, Labour/Personnel Relations & Studies, Management Science, Management Information Systems & Business Data Processing, Marketing Management & Research, Operations Management & Supervision, Organizational Behavior Studies

Health Professions and Related Sciences

Nursing, Nutrition, Pharmacy, Physical Therapy, Toxicology

GRADUATE ADMISSIONS

College of Graduate Studies and Research
University of Saskatchewan
Room 50 Murray Building, 3 Campus Drive
Saskatoon, SK   S7N 5A2
PH: **306.966.5751**   FAX: **306.966.5756**
WEBSITE: **WWW.USASK.CA/CGSR**

Fall application deadline:	Feb 1 (for financial support)
Application fee:	$75
Required with application:	College transcript, essay, recommendations portfolio required for some programs
Graduate student housing:	Apartment accommodations for singles, couples & families in apartments

GRADUATE FINANCES

Graduate tuition:	$2000	(US $1800)
Financial aid & Scholarships available for international students:	Yes	
Application deadline:	Varies	

GRADUATE INSTRUCTIONAL PROGRAM

Liberal Arts and Sciences, General Studies, and Humanities

Anthropology, Art, Art History, Classics & Classical Languages & Literature, Drama/Theater Arts, English Language & Literature, French Language & Literature, History, Modern Languages, Native Studies, Philosophy, Political Science, Psychiatry, Psychology, Religion/Religious Studies, Sociology, Women's Studies

Science and Mathematics

Agriculture Sciences, Applied Microbiology, Biochemistry, Biology, Chemistry, Food Science & Technology, Geography, Geology, Horticulture Science, Mathematics, Microbiology, Physics, Soil Science, Statistics

Computer Science and Engineering

Agricultural Engineering, Bioengineering & Biomedical Engineering, Biotechnology Research, Chemical Engineering, Civil Engineering, Computer & Information Sciences, Electrical/Electronics & Communication Engineering, Environmental/Environmental Health Engineering, Engineering Physics, Mechanical Engineering

Professional Studies

Archaeology, Education (administration, exceptional children, foundations), Law

Business and Economics

Agricultural Economics, Business Administration & Management/Commerce, Economics, Finance, Management Science

Health Professions and Related Sciences

Anatomy, Community Health & Epidemiology, Dentistry, Health Science, Herb Medicine & Theriogenology, Medicine, Nursing, Nutritional Sciences, Pathology, Pharmacology, Pharmacy, Physiology, Surgery, Toxicology, Veterinary Medicine

ALBERTA

ALBERTA COLLEGE OF ART & DESIGN

Calgary, Alberta

SCHOOL CATEGORY: Arts   **TOTAL ENROLLMENT: 1000**   **SETTING: Urban**   **CITY POPULATION: 861,000**

Alberta College of Art and Design (ACAD) is a specialized four-year university devoted exclusively to the education of professional artists and designers. The college is located in Calgary, close to the downtown. ACAD offers extremely spacious studios and small class sizes.

ACAD offers four-year programs leading to a Bachelor of Design or Bachelor of Fine Arts degree or to a Diploma in Visual Arts. Studio majors include Ceramics, Drawing, Fiber, Glass, Jewelry and Metals, Media Arts and Digital Technologies, Painting, Photographic Arts, Printmaking, Sculpture, and Visual Communications. Complementary Liberal Studies are also required in every year. The Foundation Year is a required first-year program designed to give students a solid grounding in fundamental techniques and an understanding of artistic traditions.

All students interested in attending ACAD must participate in a portfolio review and interview held each spring. Interviews are scheduled after applications have been received. A student's portfolio should contain 15 pieces of original artwork in a variety of media, and should represent a student's best work.

ACAD's location near downtown Calgary offers students easy access via public transportation to the city's galleries, museums, and cultural events. The city of Calgary is a vibrant, modern center of high technology and natural resources development. It has a fast-paced, can-do attitude. Each summer, the city celebrates the famous Calgary Stampede. Calgary is close to the Rocky Mountains and Banff National Park. The mountains provide abundant opportunities for four-season recreational activities.

GENERAL INFORMATION

Year founded:	1926
Undergraduate enrollment, full-time:	1000
Graduate enrollment, full-time:	N/A
Faculty, full-time:	47
Number of international students:	16
Male/female ratio (%)	39:61
Residence spaces available:	N/A
Residence space guaranteed for 1st-year students:	No
Student media website:	N/A

UNDERGRADUATE ADMISSIONS

Office of the Registrar
1407-14 Ave NW
Calgary, AB   T2N 4R3
PH: 800.251.8290   FAX: 902.289.6682
WEBSITE: www.acad.ab.ca

Minimum high school average:	60
Rolling admissions:	No
International fall application deadline:	Apr
Application fee:	$50
Domestic fall application deadline:	Apr 1- May 1
Application fee:	$50
Electronic application accepted:	No
Admissions notification by:	Jun 1- Jun 15
Required with application:	HS transcript, essay, portfolio

UNDERGRADUATE FINANCES

Undergraduate tuition:		
International students:	$11,270	(US $10,143)
Canadian students:	$5635	(US $5072)
Estimated annual health insurance:	$183	(US $165)
Estimated annual books & supplies:	$2500	(US $2250)
Financial aid available for international students:	No	
Application deadline:	N/A	
Scholarships available for international students:	Yes	
Application deadline:	Apr 11	
Annual room/board cost for students in residence:	N/A	
Average monthly rent for students living off campus:		
1 bedroom: $350-650, 2 bedroom: $500-750		
Federal School Code: G32983		

UNDERGRADUATE INSTRUCTIONAL PROGRAM

Most popular majors: Communications, Media Arts, Digital Technologies
Percentages by program: 100% Arts
Special study options: Study abroad, special summer programs

Liberal Arts and Sciences, General Studies, and Humanities

Art, Art History, Ceramic Arts & Ceramics, Design & Applied Arts, Fine/Studio Arts, Jewelry & Metals, Glass, Fibre & Interdisciplinary Studies, Humanities/Humanistic Studies, Media Arts & Digital Technologies, Painting, Photography, Printmaking, Sculpture, Visual & Performing Arts

ATHABASCA UNIVERSITY

Athabasca, Alberta

SCHOOL CATEGORY: Non-Traditional **TOTAL ENROLLMENT: 30,000** **SETTING: Suburban** **CITY POPULATION: 8000**

Athabasca University is Canada's leading distance-education university. Located 87 miles (145 kilometers) north of Edmonton, Athabasca is dedicated to removing barriers that traditionally restrict access to and success in university-level studies, and to increasing educational opportunity regardless of a student's geographic location or academic credentials. Athabasca is an open university, without formal admission or individual requirements for most programs, Any person 18 years of age or older who resides in Canada, the United States, or Mexico is eligible for admission. About 6 percent of students come from outside Canada.

Athabasca offers full bachelor's degree programs in Arts, General Studies, Science, Business, and Nursing. Master's degree programs are offered in Business Administration (MBA), Distance Education (MDE), and Health Studies.

Instructional methods include print-based material as well as video, audio, and Internet communications. Students study in their home communities using specially designed course materials, supplemented by toll-free access to tutor support. Students set their own study schedules within the time allowed for course completion. With most courses starting at the beginning of every month, the university provides maximum flexibility for students.

GENERAL INFORMATION

Year founded:	1970
Undergraduate enrollment, part-time:	19,055
Graduate enrollment, part-time:	1945
Faculty, full-time:	93
Number of international students:	N/A
Male/female ratio (%)	37:63
Residence spaces available:	No
Residence space guaranteed for 1st-year students:	N/A

UNDERGRADUATE ADMISSIONS

Office of the Registrar
1 University Drive
Athabasca, AB   T93 3A3
PH: **800-788-9041**   FAX: **780.427.0423**
WEBSITE: **www.athabascau.ca**

Minimum high school average:	N/A
Applications, 2000-2001:	N/A
Rolling admissions:	Yes
Fall application deadline:	N/A
Application fee:	$60
Electronic application accepted:	Yes
Admissions notification by:	N/A
Required:	HS transcript

UNDERGRADUATE FINANCES

Undergraduate tuition:		
International students:	$856 per course	(US $770)
Canadian students:	$578 per course	(US $520)
Estimated annual health insurance:	N/A	
Estimated annual books & supplies:	Included in tuition fee	
Financial aid available for international students:	No	
Application deadline:	N/A	
Scholarships available for international students:	Yes	
Application deadline:	N/A	
Annual room/board cost for students in residence:	N/A	
Average monthly rent for students living off campus:	N/A	

UNDERGRADUATE INSTRUCTIONAL PROGRAM

Most popular majors: Arts, Administration, Business Administration & Management/Commerce
Percentages by program: N/A
Special study options: Language programs, distance learning programs

Liberal Arts and Sciences, General Studies, and Humanities

Anthropology, Art, Art History, Canadian Studies, Communications, English Language & Literature, French Language & Literature, German Language & Literature, History, Humanities/Humanistic Studies, Music, Native Studies, Philosophy, Political Science, Psychology, Religion/Religious Studies, Scandinavian Languages & Literature, Sociology, Spanish Language & Literature, Women's Studies

Science and Mathematics

Astronomy, Biological Sciences/Life Sciences, Biology, Chemistry, Environmental Sciences, Geography, Geology, Mathematics, Physics

Computer Science and Engineering

Computer & Information Sciences

Professional Studies

Criminal Justice Studies, Education

Business and Economics

Accounting, Business Administration & Management/Commerce, Economics, Entrepreneurship, Finance, Human Resources Management, Labour/Personnel Relations & Studies, Management Science, Management Information Systems, Marketing, Management & Research, Organizational Behavior Studies, Public Administration

Health Professions and Related Sciences

Health Sciences, Nursing, Nutritional Sciences

GRADUATE ADMISSIONS

Graduate Studies
Athabasca University
1 University Drive
Athabasca, AB   T9S 3A3
PH: 780.675.6185   FAX: 780.675.6431
WEBSITE: www.athabascau.ca/main/grads

Fall application deadline:	Mar 1
Application fee:	$60
Electronic application accepted:	Yes
Required with application:	College transcript, essay (additional requirement per academic departments)
Graduate student housing:	N/A

GRADUATE FINANCES

Graduate tuition:

International students:	$1040 per course	(US $936)
Canadian students:	$1240 per course	(US $1116)
Financial Aid & Scholarships Available for international Students:	N/A	

GRADUATE INSTRUCTIONAL PROGRAM

Liberal Arts and Sciences, General Studies, and Humanities
Counseling (Proposed)

Computer Science and Engineering
Computer & Information Sciences

Professional Studies
Distance Education

Business and Economics
Agriculture Business Administration, Business Administration & Management/Commerce, Information Sciences & Systems, Management Information Systems

Health Professions and Related Sciences
Health Services Administration, Nursing

CONCORDIA UNIVERSITY COLLEGE OF ALBERTA

Edmonton, Alberta

SCHOOL CATEGORY: **Liberal Arts**	TOTAL ENROLLMENT: **1700**	SETTING: **Suburban**	CITY POPULATION: **650,000**

Concordia University College (CUC) is a small, Christian liberal arts university. It is located in a scenic setting that overlooks the beautiful valley of the North Saskatchewan River, minutes from downtown Edmonton.

CUC offers degrees in arts, science, and education. Classes are small, and faculty are able to provide students with individual attention.

Residence space is limited and is offered on a first-come, first-served basis. The school is located on the edge of a residential district, with good public transportation and easy access to downtown and shopping. Athletic facilities on campus include a gymnasium and playing fields.

Edmonton, originally established as a Hudson's Bay Company trading post in 1795, is now the center of Canada's oil industry. It occupies the valley of the North Saskatchewan River and is a city of great natural beauty, with dozens of parks and woodland trails. For outdoor enthusiasts, the Canadian Rockies and Jasper National Park are within easy driving distance.

GENERAL INFORMATION

Year founded:	1921
Undergraduate enrollment, full-time:	1400
Graduate enrollment, full-time:	N/A
Faculty, full-time:	N/A
Number of international students:	21
Male/female ratio (%)	42:58
Residence spaces available:	Limited
Residence space guaranteed for 1st-year students:	No
Student media website:	www.csa.concordia.ab.ca/

UNDERGRADUATE ADMISSIONS

Admissions and Financial Aid Office
7218 Ada Boulevard
Edmonton, AB T5B 4E4
PH: **780.479.9220**   FAX: **780.474.1933**
WEBSITE: **www.concordia.ab.ca**

Minimum high school average:	60
Applications, 2005:	N/A
Rolling admissions:	No
International fall application deadline:	Mar 1
Application fee:	N/A
Domestic fall application deadline:	Jun 1
Application fee:	N/A
Electronic application accepted:	Yes
Admissions notification by:	N/A
Required with application:	HS transcript

UNDERGRADUATE FINANCES

Undergraduate tuition:		
International students:	$8434	(US $7590)
Canadian students:	$5810	(US $5229)
Estimated annual health insurance:	N/A	
Estimated annual books & supplies:	$1000	(US $900)
Financial aid & Scholarships available for		
international students:	Yes (limited)	
Application deadline:	N/A	
Annual room/board cost for students in residence:	$4800	(US $4320)
Average monthly rent for students living off campus:		
1 bedroom: $400 +, 2 bedroom: $500 +		

UNDERGRADUATE INSTRUCTIONAL PROGRAM

Most popular majors: Education, Psychology, Environmental Health, Sociology
Percentages by program: 65% Liberal Arts, 23% Science, 12% Education
Special study options: Internships, study abroad, language programs, special summer programs

Liberal Arts and Sciences, General Studies, and Humanities

Canadian Studies, English Language & Literature, French Language & Literature, History, Music, Philosophy, Political Science, Psychology, Religion/Religious Studies, Sociology, Spanish Language & Literature, Theology/Theological Studies, Translation, Urban Affairs/Studies, Visual & Performing Arts, Women's Studies, Writing

Science and Mathematics

Biology, Chemistry, Environmental/Environmental Health Engineering, Environmental Sciences, Mathematics, Physics

Computer Science and Engineering

Computer & Information Sciences

Professional Studies

Education

Business and Economics

Business Administration & Management/Commerce, Economics, Information Sciences & Systems

THE KING'S UNIVERSITY COLLEGE

Edmonton, Alberta

SCHOOL CATEGORY: Liberal Arts   **TOTAL ENROLLMENT: 600**   **SETTING: Suburban**   **CITY POPULATION: 650,000**

The King's University College is a nondenominational Christian college located in Edmonton, the capital of Alberta. It is a relatively young school, founded in 1979, and has a new, fully equipped campus. King's offers programs in the arts, sciences, business, education, and music. The university's small size allows for close interaction between faculty and students.

Residence space is limited and is offered on a first-come, first-served basis. The school is located on the edge of a residential district, with good public transportation and easy access to downtown and shopping. Athletic facilities on campus include a gymnasium and playing fields.

Edmonton, originally established as a Hudson's Bay Company trading post in 1795, is now the center of Canada's oil industry. It occupies the valley of the North Saskatchewan River and is a city of great natural beauty, with dozens of parks and woodland trails. For outdoor enthusiasts, the Canadian Rockies and Jasper National Park are within easy driving distance.

GENERAL INFORMATION

Year founded:	1979
Undergraduate enrollment, full-time:	580
Graduate enrollment, full-time:	60
Faculty, full-time:	38
Number of international students:	50
Male/female ratio (%)	40:60
Residence spaces available:	164
Residence space guaranteed for 1st-year students:	No
Student media website:	N/A

UNDERGRADUATE ADMISSIONS

Enrollment Services
9125-50 Street NW
Edmonton, AB   T6B 2H3
PH: **780.465.3500**   FAX: **780.465.3534**
WEBSITE: **www.kingsu.ab.ca**

Minimum high school average:	60
Rolling admissions:	No
Fall application deadline:	Aug 15
Application fee:	$100
Electronic application accepted:	Yes
Admissions notification by:	1 week after documentation received
Required with application:	HS transcripts, recommendations
Recommended:	SAT I/II, ACT (if available)

UNDERGRADUATE FINANCES

Undergraduate tuition:	$7130	(US $6417)
Estimated annual health insurance:	$200	(US $180)
Estimated annual books & supplies:	$1000	(US $900)
Financial aid & Scholarships available for		
international students:	Yes	
Application deadline:	Mar 31	
Annual room/board cost for students in residence:	$5200	(US $4680)
Average monthly rent for students living off campus:		
1 bedroom: $400+, 2 bedroom: $600+		
Federal School Code: G26119		

UNDERGRADUATE INSTRUCTIONAL PROGRAM

Most popular majors: Business, Environmental Studies, Psychology
Percentages by program: 65% Liberal Arts, 20% Science, 10% Business, 3% Engineering/Computer Science
Special study options: Internships, study abroad

Liberal Arts and Sciences, General Studies, and Humanities

Art, Art History, Drama/Theater Arts, English Language & Literature, History, Music, Philosophy, Political Science, Psychology, Sociology, Theology/Theological Studies

Science and Mathematics

Astronomy, Biology, Chemistry, Environmental Sciences, Geography, Mathematics

Computer Science and Engineering

Computer & Information Sciences

Professional Studies
Education

Business and Economics

Business Administration & Management/Commerce, Economics

MOUNT ROYAL COLLEGE

Calgary, Alberta

SCHOOL CATEGORY: Comprehensive   **TOTAL ENROLLMENT: 22,000**   **SETTING: Suburban**   **CITY POPULATION: 861,000**

Mount Royal College is a medium sized postsecondary institution that celebrated its ninetieth anniversary in 2001. The school has three Calgary campuses, with the main campus, Lincoln Park, located in the southwestern section of the city.

Among the degree programs offered are arts, public relations, journalism, technical writing, electronic publishing, business, accounting, child studies, ecotourism and outdoor leadership, justice studies, and nursing. MRC also has a wide range of diploma and certificate programs. The Mount Royal Conservatory offers well-respected diploma programs in theater and music.

The Lincoln Park campus offers residence space for over 400 students. Off-campus housing is readily available nearby. The school offers a good mix of recreational and cultural activities. Athletic facilities include a gymnasium, swimming pool, fitness center, and playing fields.

Calgary is a vibrant modern city with a fast-paced, can-do attitude. It is a center of high technology and natural resources development. Each summer, the city celebrates the famous Calgary Stampede. Calgary is close to the Rocky Mountains and Banff National Park. The mountains provide abundant four-season recreational activities.

GENERAL INFORMATION

Year founded:	1910
Undergraduate enrollment, full-time:	7000
Graduate enrollment, full-time:	N/A
Faculty, full-time:	N/A
Number of international students:	400
Male/female ratio (%):	37:63
Residence spaces available:	1000
Residence space guaranteed for 1st-year students:	N/A
Student media website:	www.mtroyal.ab.ca/news/

UNDERGRADUATE ADMISSIONS

Office of the Registrar
4825 Richard Road S.W.
Calgary, AB   T3E 6K6
PH: 403.240.5419   FAX: 403.240.6740
WEBSITE: www.mtroyal.ab.ca

Minimum high school average:	70
Applications, 2005:	N/A
Rolling admissions:	N/A
Fall application deadline:	Aug 1
Application fee:	$50
Electronic application accepted:	Yes
Admissions notification by:	N/A
Required with application:	HS transcript
Recommended:	SAT

UNDERGRADUATE FINANCES

Undergraduate tuition:		
International students:	$5900	(US $5310)
Canadian students:	$4000	(US $3600)
Estimated annual health insurance:	N/A	
Estimated annual books & supplies:	$1200	(US $1080)
Financial aid & Scholarships available for		
international students:	No	
Application deadline:	N/A	
Annual room cost for students in residence:	$3800-5700	(US $3420-5130)
Average monthly rent for students living off campus:		
1 bedroom: $300-350, 2 bedroom: $300-500		

UNDERGRADUATE INSTRUCTIONAL PROGRAM

Most popular majors: Arts, Business, Communications, Computer Science
Percentages by program: N/A
Special study options: Co-op programs, internships, study abroad, language programs, distance learning programs

Liberal Arts and Sciences, General Studies, and Humanities

Anthropology, Art, Canadian Studies, Chinese Language & literature, Classics & Classical Languages & Literature, Communications, Comparative Literature, Design & Applied Arts, Drama/Theater Arts, English Language & Literature,* French Language & Literature, Gerontology, History,* Music, Pacific Area Studies, Philosophy, Political Science, Psychology,* Religion/Religious Studies, Romance Studies, Social Work, Sociology, Spanish Language & Literature, Women's Studies, Writing

Science and Mathematics

Astronomy, Archeology, Aviation & Airway Science, Biochemistry, Biology, Biophysics, Chemistry, Geography, Geology, Mathematics, Microbiology, Natural Sciences, Physics, Zoology

Computer Science and Engineering

Computer & Information Sciences, Engineering Science

Professional Studies

Child Growth/Care & Development Studies, Criminal Justice Studies, Ecotourism, Education, Family & Community Studies, Hospitality/Administration Management, Interior Design, Leisure & Recreational Activities, Physical Education Teaching & Coaching, Tourism

Business and Economics

Business Administration & Management/Commerce, Economics, Entrepreneurship, International Business

Health Professions and Related Sciences

Community Rehabilitation, Health Science, Nursing,* Public Health, Speech-Language Pathology and Audiology

*Through Athabasca University

UNIVERSITY OF ALBERTA

Edmonton, Alberta

SCHOOL CATEGORY: Doctoral/Research   **TOTAL ENROLLMENT: 30,924**   **SETTING: Suburban**   **CITY POPULATION: 650,000**

Founded in 1908, the University has been a renowned centre of learning and research for nearly a century. With its history of excellence in teaching, research, services and athletics, it has garnered a reputation as one of the best universities in Canada.

The U of A's original site—and the largest of its four campuses—covers a 50-city-block park-like area on the southern banks of the North Saskatchewan River across from downtown Edmonton. Its architecture features stately old brick and stone, as well as outstanding examples of contemporary architecture. Other campuses include Campus Saint-Jean, Augustana Campus, and the South Campus.

The U of A offers more than 200 undergraduate areas of study through 17 faculties and schools, and elite learning experiences through 110 master's and 75 doctoral programs in 300 research areas, to over 36,000 full- and part-time students from Alberta, Canada, and the world.

There are eight different residences at the U of A, each offering a unique style and community. Students enjoy a wide variety of recreational, athletic, and social events, and there are over 300 student clubs.

Edmonton is a vibrant, cosmopolitan city and the U of A is right in the heart of it. The capital of the province of Alberta, Edmonton has a greater metropolitan population over one million. The city is a few hours' drive from Banff and Jasper in Alberta's majestic Rocky Mountains. With Canada's leading economy, Alberta offers one of the country's highest standards of living and no provincial sales tax. The economy in Alberta is diverse and competitive, with an abundance of natural resources, and one of the lowest unemployment rates.

GENERAL INFORMATION

Year founded:	1908
Undergraduate enrollment, full-time:	27,145
Graduate enrollment, full-time:	4356
Faculty, full-time:	1526
Number of international students:	2600
Male/female ratio (%)	43:57
Residence spaces available:	4000
Residence space guaranteed for 1st-year students:	N/A
Student media website:	www.su.albert.ca/

UNDERGRADUATE ADMISSIONS

Office of the Registrar & Student Awards
201 Administration Building
Edmonton, AB   T6G 2M7
PH: 780.492.3113   FAX: 780.492.7172
WEBSITE: **www.registrar.ualberta.ca**

Minimum high school average:	70
Applications, 2005:	25,713
Rolling admissions:	No
Fall application deadline:	Varies
Application fee:	$100
Electronic application accepted:	Yes
Admissions notification by:	Jul
Required with application:	HS transcripts, SAT I, (essay, recommendations, interview dependent upon program)

UNDERGRADUATE FINANCES

Undergraduate tuition:		
International students:	$16,300	(US $14,670)
Canadian students:	$5100	(US $4590)
Estimated annual health insurance:	$500	(US $450)
Estimated annual books & supplies:	$1000	(US $900)
Financial aid available for international students:	No	
Scholarships available for international students:	Yes	
Application deadline:	Varies	
Annual room/board cost for students in residence:	$4700	(US $4230)
Average monthly rent for students living off campus:		
1 bedroom: $600, 2 bedroom: $800		
Federal School Code: G08362		

UNDERGRADUATE INSTRUCTIONAL PROGRAM

Most popular majors: Biology, Engineering, English, Political Science, Psychology
Percentages by program: 22% Science, 21% Liberal Arts, 13% Engineering/Computer Science, 13% Health Professions, 8% Business
Special study options: Co-op programs, internships, study abroad, language programs, special summer programs

Liberal Arts and Sciences, General Studies, and Humanities

Anthropology, Art, Art History, Chinese Studies, Classics & Classical Languages & Literature, Comparative Literature, Design & Applied Arts, Drama/Theater Arts, East Asian Studies, English Language & Literature, Film Studies, French Language & Literature, History, Humanities/Humanistic Studies, Linguistics, Medieval & Renaissance Studies, History, Middle Eastern Languages/Literature Studies, Modern Languages, Music, Native Studies, Philosophy, Political Science, Psychology, Religion/Religious Studies, Women's Studies

Science and Mathematics

Agriculture, Atmospheric Sciences, Biochemistry, Bioinformatics, Biological Sciences/Life Sciences, Cell Biology, Biology, Chemistry, Earth & Atmospheric Science, Ecology, Environmental Sciences, Forestry, Geography, Geology, Geophysics & Seismology, Marine/Aquatic Science, Mathematics, Paleontology, Physics, Statistics, Zoology

Computer Science and Engineering

Chemical Engineering, Civil Engineering, Computer & Information Sciences, Computer Engineering, Electrical/Electronics & Communications Engineering, Engineering Physics, Engineering Science, Materials Engineering, Mechanical Engineering, Mining & Mineral Engineering, Petroleum Engineering, Software Engineering

Professional Studies

Coaching, Education, Family & Community Studies Studies, Human Ecology, Human Kinetics/Kinesiology, Leisure & Recreational Activities, Retailing & Services, Tourism

Business and Economics

Accounting, Business Economics & Law, Business Administration
& Management/Commerce, Distribution Management,
Economics, Entrepreneurship, Human Resources Management,
Information Sciences & Systems, International Business,
Labor/Personnel Relations & Studies, Management Science,
Management Information Systems, Marketing, Operations
Management, Organizational Behavior Studies

Health Professions and Related Sciences

Dental Hygiene, Medical Laboratory Science, Neuroscience,
Nursing, Pharmacy, Pharmacology, Physiology, Pre-Veterinary
Medicine

GRADUATE ADMISSIONS

Faculty of Graduate Studies and Research
105 Administration Building
Edmonton, AB   T6G 2M7
PH: **780.492.3499**   FAX: **780.492.0692**
WEBSITE: **www.ualberta.ca/gradstudies**

International fall application deadline:	Jul 1
Application fee:	$100
Domestic fall application deadline:	Varies
Application fee:	$100
Required with application:	College transcript, essay, recommendations, GRE & GMAT per department
Graduate student housing:	Various accommodations for mature students including dormitory style (singles), apartments and townhouses (for couples and families)

GRADUATE FINANCES

Graduate tuition:		
International students:	$7325 +	(US $6590)
Canadian students:	$3950 +	(US $3555)
Financial aid & Scholarships available for		
international students:	Yes	
Application deadline:	Varies	

GRADUATE INSTRUCTIONAL PROGRAM

Liberal Arts and Sciences, General Studies, and Humanities

Anthropology, Art & Design, Classics & Classical Languages
& Literature, Communications and Technology, Comparative
Literature, Drama/Theater Arts, East Asian Studies, English
Language & Literature, History, Human Ecology, Linguistics,
Modern Languages, Music, Philosophy, Political Science,
Psychology, Religious Studies, Sociology

Science and Mathematics

Agriculture Sciences, Biochemistry, Biological Sciences/Life
Sciences, Chemistry, Earth & Atmospheric Science, Mathematics,
Physics, Renewable Resources, Rural Economy

Computer Science and Engineering

Chemical Engineering, Civil Engineering, Computer &
Information Sciences, Computer Engineering, Electrical/
Electronics & Communication Engineering, Environmental/
Environmental Health Engineering, Internetworking, Materials
Engineering, Mechanical Engineering

Professional Studies

Education, Law, Library Sciences

Business and Economics

Business Administration & Management/Commerce (agriculture,
engineering, forestry, international business, leisure & sport
management, natural resources, technology), Economics

Health Professions and Related Sciences

Biomedical Engineering, Cell Biology, Dentistry, Health
Sciences, Laboratory Medicine & Pathology, Medical Genetics,
Medical Microbiology, Medicine, Neuroscience, Nursing,
Occupational Therapy, Oncology, Opthalmology, Oral Health
Sciences, Orthodontics, Pediatrics, Pharmacology, Pharmacy &
Pharmaceutical Sciences, Physical Therapy, Psychiatry, Physiology,
Public Health Sciences, Radiology & Diagnostic Imagining,
Rehabilitation Medicine, Speech Pathology & Audiology, Surgery

THE UNIVERSITY OF CALGARY

Calgary, Alberta

SCHOOL CATEGORY: Comprehensive   **TOTAL ENROLLMENT: 30,000**   **SETTING: Urban**   **CITY POPULATION: 861,000**

The University of Calgary is a comprehensive research and teaching university that ranks among the finest institutions in Canada. The university offers quality undergraduate education that is characterized by the synthesis of research, teaching and learning. The 400-plus-acre campus is a beautiful and dynamic setting for scholars in 15 faculties, 53 departments and more than 30 research institutes and centers. All major fields of study are represented as a number of specialty areas.

Campus facilities are extensive and include one of Canada's largest libraries, a world-class concert hall, an art gallery, a museum, performance theaters and on-campus residences. The school offers a variety of residence settings ranging from traditional dormitories to larger apartments. Off-campus housing is readily available in Calgary.

Calgary, a vibrant, modern city with a fast-paced, can-do attitude, is a center of high technology and natural resources development. Each summer, the city celebrates the famous Calgary Stampede. Calgary is close to the Rocky Mountains and Banff National Park. The mountains provide abundant four-season recreational activities.

GENERAL INFORMATION

Year founded:	1945
Undergraduate enrollment, full-time:	20,000
Graduate enrollment, full-time:	4000
Faculty, full-time:	1750
Number of international students:	900
Male/female ratio (%)	46:54
Residence spaces available:	1860
Residence space guaranteed for 1st-year students:	N/A
Student media website:	www.gauntlet.ucalgary.ca

UNDERGRADUATE ADMISSIONS

2500 University Drive N.W.
Calgary, AB   T2N 1N4
PH: **430.220.4380**   FAX: **430.282.7298**
WEBSITE: **www.ucalgary.ca**

Minimum high school average:	70% (varies)
Applications, 2000-2001:	N/A
Rolling admissions:	No
International fall application deadline:	Feb 1
Application fee:	$65
Domestic fall application deadline:	Feb 1
Application fee:	$65
Electronic application accepted:	Yes
Admissions notification by:	6-8 weeks after application received
Required with application:	HS Transcripts, SAT I/II
Recommended:	Interview (for music)

UNDERGRADUATE FINANCES

Undergraduate tuition:		
International students:	$15,630	(US $14,000)
Canadian students:	$5000	(US $4500)
Estimated annual health insurance:	$400	(US $360)
Estimated annual books & supplies:	$1000	(US $900)
Financial aid available for international students:	No	
Application deadline:	N/A	
Scholarships available for international students:	Yes, after 1st year	
Application deadline:	N/A	
Annual room/board cost for students in residence:	$4000-7000	(US $3600-6300)
Average monthly rent for students living off campus:		
1 bedroom: $300-500, 2 bedroom: $500-750		
Federal School Code: G07874		

UNDERGRADUATE INSTRUCTIONAL PROGRAM

Most popular majors: Communications, Computer Science, Engineering, Management
Percentages by program: 50% Liberal Arts, 14 % Science, 13% Business, 8% Engineering, 6% Health Professions
Special study options: Co-op programs, internships, study abroad, language programs, special summer programs, distance learning programs

Liberal Arts and Sciences, General Studies, and Humanities

African Studies, Anthropology, Art, Art History, Canadian Studies, Chinese Language & Literature, Classics & Classical Languages & Literature, Communications, Comparative Literature, Dance, Drama/Theater Arts, Dutch Language & Literature, East Asian Studies, English Language & Literature, European Studies, Film/Cinema, Fine/Studio Arts, French Language & Literature, German Language & Literature, Greek Language & Literature, Hindi Language & Literature, History, Humanities/Humanistic Studies, International Relations & Affairs, Italian Language & Literature, Japanese Language & Literature, Latin American Studies, Latin Language & Literature, Linguistics, Museum & Heritage Studies, Music, Native Studies, Pacific Area Studies, Philosophy, Political Science, Psychology, Religion/Religious Studies, Romance Studies, Russian & Slavic Area Studies, Russian Languages & Literature, Slavic Languages & Literature, Social Work, Sociology, South Asian Studies, Spanish Language & Literature, Urban Affairs/Studies, Visual & Performing Arts, Women's Studies

Science and Mathematics

Applied Mathematics, Applied Physics, Astronomy, Astrophysics, Biochemistry, Biological Sciences/Life Sciences, Biology, Biophysics, Biotechnology Research, Botany, Chemistry, Ecology, Entomology, Environmental Sciences, General Sciences, Geography, Geology, Geophysics & Seismology, Marine/Aquatic Science, Mathematics, Physics, Space Physics, Statistics, Transportation Science, Zoology

Computer Science and Engineering

Chemical Engineering, Civil Engineering, Computer & Information Sciences, Electrical/Electronics & Communication Engineering, Engineering Science, Environmental/Environmental Health Engineering, Geometrics Engineering, Industrial/Manufacturing Engineering, Mechanical Engineering, Petroleum Engineering, Software Engineering

Professional Studies

Archaeology, City/Urban/Community Regional Planning, Criminal Justice Studies, Education (preparation, policy, psychology, research), Exercise Sciences/Physiology & Movement Studies, Family & Community Studies, Hospitality/Administration Management, Human Kinetics/Kinesiology, Law, Leisure & Recreational Activities, Physical Education Teaching & Coaching, Tourism

Business and Economics

Accounting, Actuarial Science, Business Administration & Management/Commerce, Economics, Entrepreneurship, Finance, Human Resources Management, International Business, Management & Protective Services, Management Science, Management Information Systems & Business Data Processing, Marketing Management & Research, Northern Planning & Development Studies, Operations Management & Supervision, Organizational Behavior Studies, Risk Management & Insurance, Strategic Studies, Strategy & General Management

Health Professions and Related Sciences

Nursing

GRADUATE ADMISSIONS

Faculty of Graduate Studies
University of Calgary
Earth Science Building Room 720
2500 University Drive N.W.
Calgary, AB T2N 1N4
PH: **403.220.5417** FAX: **403.289.7635**
WEBSITE: **www.ucalgary.ca/Uof C/faculties/GS/**

Fall application deadline:	Jan - Mar
Application fee:	N/A
Required with application:	College transcript, essay, recommendations, portfolio required for some programs
Graduate student housing:	Various accommodations including couples & family housing

GRADUATE FINANCES

Graduate tuition:

International students:	$10,000 +	(US $9000)
Canadian students:	$5000 +	(US $4500)

Financial aid & scholarships available for
international students: Yes
Application deadline: Varies

GRADUATE INSTRUCTIONAL PROGRAM

Liberal Arts and Sciences, General Studies, and Humanities

Anthropology, Applied Psychology, Art, Clinical Psychology, Communications, English Language & Literature, East Asian Studies, French Language & Literature, German Language & Literature, History, Linguistics, Music, Philosophy, Political Science, Psychology, Religion/Religious Studies, Slavic Languages & Literature, Social Work, Sociology

Science and Mathematics

Applied Mathematics, Astronomy, Biological Sciences/Life Sciences, Chemistry, Environmental Sciences, Geography, Geology, Geophysics & Seismology, Mathematics, Physics, Statistics

Computer Science and Engineering

Bioengineering & Biomedical Engineering, Computer & Information Science, Chemical Engineering, Civil Engineering, Computer Engineering, Electrical/Electronics & Communications Engineering, Environmental/Environmental Health Engineering, Geological Engineering, Mechanical Engineering

Professional Studies

Archaeology, Educational Research, Human Kinetics/Kinesiology, Law

Business and Economics

Actuarial Science, Business Administration & Management/Commerce, Economics, Military and Strategic Studies

Health Professions and Related Sciences

Biochemistry, Cardiovascular & Respiratory Sciences, Community Health Sciences, Gastrointestinal Studies, Medicine, Microbiology & Infectious Diseases, Neuroscience

THE UNIVERSITY OF LETHBRIDGE

Lethbridge, Alberta

SCHOOL CATEGORY: Bachelor's/General   **TOTAL ENROLLMENT: 8400**   **SETTING: Suburban**   **CITY POPULATION: 70,000**

The University of Lethbridge is a small liberal arts institution located in southern Alberta. The university has an attractive campus in suburban Lethbridge, a thriving center two hours' drive south of Calgary, in the foothills of the Rocky Mountains.

The school offers undergraduate degree programs in 17 academic disciplines. With more than 8,000 students, the U of L is big enough to ensure that you meet a lot of people, yet small enough to remain dedicated to small class sizes. 70% of first-year classes have fewer than 50 students and 80% of fourth-year classes have fewer than 50 students.

The university has a variety of accommodations ranging from traditional-style dormitory to larger apartments. Students can participate in a full range of recreational and competitive athletics. With over 12 miles of trails only minutes from campus, students can easily enjoy biking, in-line skating, and running.

Lethbridge's campus is only minutes away from the center of the city and has easy access to shopping, restaurants, and other services. The Canadian Rockies are within easy driving distance and offer exceptional year-round recreational activities: hiking, skiing, mountain biking, and rock climbing.

GENERAL INFORMATION

Year founded:	1967
Undergraduate enrollment, full-time:	7987
Graduate enrollment, full-time:	367
Faculty, full-time:	445
Number of international students:	486
Male/female ratio (%)	45:57
Residence spaces available:	550
Residence space guaranteed for 1st-year students:	Yes (for 200 students)
Student media website:	www.home.uleth.ca/stu

UNDERGRADUATE ADMISSIONS

Registrar's Office
4401 University Drive
Lethbridge, AB   T1K 3M4
PH: **403.329.2758**   FAX: **403.329.5159**
WEBSITE: **www.uleth.ca**

Minimum high school average:	65%
Applications, 2005:	6159
Rolling admissions:	Yes
Fall application deadline:	Jun 1
Application fee:	$60
Electronic application accepted:	Yes
Admissions notification by:	N/A
Required with application:	HS transcripts, SAT I/II, ACT

UNDERGRADUATE FINANCES

Undergraduate tuition:		
International students:	$10,475	(US $9425)
Canadian students:	$5635	(US $5075)
Estimated annual health insurance:	$245	(US $220)
Estimated annual books & supplies:	$1000	(US $900)
Financial aid available for international students:	No	
Application deadline:	N/A	
Scholarships available for international students:	Yes	
Application deadline:	Jul 15	
Annual room/board cost for students in residence:	$3664	(US $3300)
Average monthly rent for students living off campus:		
1 bedroom: $400+, 2 bedroom: $600+		

UNDERGRADUATE INSTRUCTIONAL PROGRAM

Most popular majors: Accounting, Biological Sciences, General Management, Kinesiology, Marketing
Percentages by program: 60% Arts & Science, 22% Business, 3% Computer Science, 2% Health Professions
Special study options: Co-op programs, internships, study abroad, language programs, special summer programs

Liberal Arts and Sciences, General Studies, and Humanities

Anthropology, Art, Art History, Canadian Studies, Ceramic Arts & Ceramics, Classics & Classical Languages & Literature, Communications, Comparative Literature, Design & Applied Arts, Drama/Theater Arts, English Language & Literature, Fine/Studio Arts, French Language & Literature, German Language & Literature, Greek, Hebrew, History, Humanities/Humanistic Studies, Jewish/Judaic Studies, Latin Language & Literature, Linguistics, Multimedia, Museum Studies, Music, Native Studies, Philosophy, Political Science, Psychology, Religion/Religious Studies, Sociology, Spanish Language & Literature, Visual & Performing Arts, Women's Studies

Science and Mathematics

Agriculture Sciences, Biochemistry, Biological Sciences/Life Sciences, Biology, Botany, Chemistry, Ecology, Environmental Science, Geography, Geology, Mathematics, Physics, Statistics, Zoology

Computer Science and Engineering

Agricultural Engineering, Computer & Information Sciences

Professional Studies

Archaeology, Education, Human Kinetics/Kinesiology, Leisure & Recreational Activities, Library Science, Physical Education Teaching & Coaching

Business and Economics

Aboriginal Management, Accounting, Agricultural Business, Business Administration & Management/Commerce, Economics, Finance, Human Resources Management, International Business, Labor/Personnel Relations & Studies, Management Science, Management Information Systems & Business Data Processing, Marketing Management & Research, Operations Management & Supervision

Health Professions and Related Sciences

Health Studies (Addictions Counseling), Nursing

GRADUATE ADMISSIONS

School of Graduate Studies
4401 University Drive
Lethbridge, AB   T1K 3M4
PH: **403.320.5700**   FAX: **403.329.5159**
WEBSITE: **www.uleth.ca/sgs/**

Fall application deadline:	Mar 1
Application fee:	$50
Required with application:	College transcript, GMAT, recommendations, CV
Graduate student housing:	Apartments, family housing

GRADUATE FINANCES

Graduate tuition:

International students:	$11,757	(US $10,600)
Canadian students:	$6147	(US $5530)
Financial aid & Scholarships available for		
international students:	Yes	
Application deadline:	Varies	

GRADUATE INSTRUCTIONAL PROGRAM

Liberal Arts and Sciences, General Studies, and Humanities

Anthropology, Drama/Theater Arts, English Language & Literature, Fine/Studio Arts, French Language & Literature, German Language & Literature, History, Modern languages, Music, Native Studies, Philosophy, Political Science, Psychology, Sociology, Spanish Language & Literature, Visual & Performing Arts

Science and Mathematics

Biochemistry, Biological Sciences/Life Sciences, Chemistry, Environmental Sciences, Geography, Mathematics, Physics

Computer Science and Engineering

Computer & Information Sciences

Professional Studies

Education, Human Kinetics/Kinesiology

Business and Economics

Business Administration & Management/Commerce, Economics, Management Science

Health Professions and Related Sciences

Health Science

BRITISH COLUMBIA

EMILY CARR INSTITUTE OF ART & DESIGN

Vancouver, British Columbia

SCHOOL CATEGORY: **Specialized**	TOTAL ENROLLMENT: **1500**	SETTING: **Suburban**	CITY POPULATION: **2,000,000**

Named in honor of one of British Columbia's most famous artists, the Emily Carr Institute of Art and Design is a professional school devoted to the development of emerging artists. The Emily Carr campus is situated in the popular Granville Island area of Vancouver, which offers an inspiring view of the Northshore Mountains.

Emily Carr offers a variety of degree and diploma programs. All first-year students must follow a Foundation Year program of study designed to give students a solid grounding in fundamental techniques and an understanding of artistic traditions. This general training is followed by three years of specialized study in either the School of Design, the School of Media Arts, or the School of Visual Arts.

Interviews are scheduled after applications have been received. A student's portfolio should contain 15 pieces of original artwork in a variety of media, and should represent a student's best work.

Emily Carr offers no student housing, but apartments are readily available in Vancouver. Emily Carr students have a chance to study in one of the world's most beautiful cities, where they can also enjoy a mild climate and an extraordinary natural setting.

GENERAL INFORMATION

Year founded:	1926
Undergraduate enrollment, full-time:	1300
Graduate enrollment, full-time:	N/A
Faculty, full-time:	N/A
Number of international students:	N/A
Male/female ratio (%)	N/A
Residence spaces available:	No
Residence space guaranteed for 1st-year students:	No
Student media website:	N/A

UNDERGRADUATE ADMISSIONS

Office of Student Services
1399 Johnston Street
Granville Island, Vancouver, BC   V6H 3R9
PH: **604.844.3800**   FAX: **604.844.3801**
WEBSITE: **www.eciad.bc.ca**

Minimum high school average:	70
Applications, 2000-2001:	N/A
Rolling admissions:	No
International fall application deadline:	Mar 3
Application fee:	$30
Domestic fall application deadline:	Mar 3
Application fee:	$30
Electronic application accepted:	Yes
Admissions notification by:	Jun 5
Required with application:	HS transcript, portfolio

UNDERGRADUATE FINANCES

Undergraduate tuition:		
International students:	$11,500	(US $10,350)
Canadian students:	$4000	(US $3600)
Estimated annual health insurance:	$500	(US $450)
Estimated annual books & supplies:	$2000	(US $1800)
Financial aid available for international students:	Yes	
Application deadline:	May 1	
Scholarships available for international students:	Yes, after 1st semester	
Application deadline:	May 1	
Annual room/board cost for students in residence:	N/A	
Average monthly rent for students living off campus:		
1 bedroom: $675+, 2 bedroom: $800+		
Federal School Code: G23388		

UNDERGRADUATE INSTRUCTIONAL PROGRAM

Most popular majors: Media Arts, Design & Applied Arts
Percentages by program: N/A
Special study options: Co-op programs, internships

Liberal Arts and Sciences, General Studies, and Humanities

Animation, Communications Design, Fine/Studio Arts, Industrial Design, Integrated Media, Photography, Visual & Performing Arts

KWANTLEN UNIVERSITY COLLEGE

Surrey, British Columbia

SCHOOL CATEGORY: Bachelor's/General   **TOTAL ENROLLMENT:** 24,000   **SETTING:** Suburban   **CITY POPULATION:** 2,000,000

Kwantlen University College is a medium-sized undergraduate school that offers all the services of an undergraduate university and a comprehensive community college. Both bachelor's and associate degrees are granted. It has four campuses in the Greater Vancouver area, in Langley, Newton, Richmond, and Surrey. The largest campus is located in Surrey.

Courses leading to a bachelor's degree are offered in business, accounting, nursing, information technology, fashion, and interior design. Students enjoy small class sizes as well as a personal and friendly atmosphere. Students may take their first two years of university studies at Kwantlen and then transfer to other universities. Kwantlen transfers the largest number of students to other universities in British Columbia.

The school does not offer any residence facilities, but off-campus housing is readily available. Kwantlen offers a good mix of recreational and cultural activities. Athletic facilities are limited.

Nestled between soaring mountains and the glimmering ocean, Vancouver is the largest city on Canada's west coast and is one of the world's most beautiful cities. Vancouver offers historic districts, lush gardens, and wilderness parks close by. Students can take advantage of the many cultural and recreational opportunities the city has to offer. The region enjoys the mildest climate in the country.

GENERAL INFORMATION

Year founded:	1981
Undergraduate enrollment, full-time:	7000
Graduate enrollment, full-time:	N/A
Faculty, full-time:	753
Number of international students:	296
Male/female ratio (%):	40:60
Residence spaces available:	No
Residence space guaranteed for 1st-year students:	No
Student media website:	www.kwantlen.bc.ca/ksa

UNDERGRADUATE ADMISSIONS

Office of the Registrar
12886 - 72nd Avenue
Surrey, BC   V3W 2M8
PH: **604.599.2000**   FAX: **604.599.2068**
WEBSITE: **www.kwantlen.bc.ca**

Minimum high school average:	High school completion or equivalent
Applications, 2000-2001:	N/A
Rolling admissions:	No
International fall application deadline:	Mar 31
Application fee:	$120
Domestic fall application deadline:	Jun 30
Application fee:	$20
Electronic application accepted:	Yes
Admissions notification by:	N/A
Required with application:	HS transcript (essay, recommendations & interview required for some programs)

UNDERGRADUATE FINANCES

Undergraduate tuition:		
International students:	$10,500	(US $9450)
Canadian students:	$3700	(US $3350)
Estimated annual health insurance:	$600	(US $540)
Estimated annual books & supplies:	$1200	(US $1080)
Financial aid available for international students:	No	
Application deadline:	Mar 31	
Scholarships available for international students:	Yes	
Application deadline:	Mar 31	
Annual room/board cost for students in residence:	N/A	

Average monthly rent for students living off campus:
  1 bedroom: $500+, 2 bedroom: $700+
Federal School Code: G33325

UNDERGRADUATE INSTRUCTIONAL PROGRAM

Most popular majors: Business, Information Technology, Arts & Sciences
Percentages by program: N/A
Special study options: Co-op programs, internships, study abroad, language programs

Liberal Arts and Sciences, General Studies, and Humanities

Anthropology, Art, Communication, Chinese Language & Literature, English Language & Literature, Fine/Studio Arts, French Language & Literature, German Language & Literature, History, Humanities/Humanistic Studies, Japanese Language & Literature, Linguistics, Music, Philosophy, Political Science, Psychology, Public Relations, Religion/Religious Studies, Russian Languages & Literature, Slavic Languages & Literature, Sociology, Spanish Language & Literature, Writing

Science and Mathematics

Animal Science, Astronomy, Biology, Chemistry, Equine Studies, Geography, Geology, Geophysics & Seismology, Horticulture Science, Mathematics, Physics, Science, Physiology/Human & Animal, Psychology, Statistics, Textile Sciences, Toxicology, Wood Science, Zoology

Computer Science and Engineering

Computer & Information Sciences, Computer Engineering, Electrical/ Electronics & Communication Engineering

Professional Studies

Criminal Justice Studies, Early Childhood Education

Business and Economics

Accounting, Business Administration & Management/Commerce, Economics, Entrepreneurship, Fashion Marketing, Human Resources Management, Marketing Management & Research, Public Administration, Public Relations & Organizational Communications

Health Professions and Related Sciences

Health Sciences, Nursing (refresher & EAL), Public Health

MALASPINA UNIVERSITY COLLEGE

Nanaimo, British Columbia

SCHOOL CATEGORY: Bachelor's/General   **TOTAL ENROLLMENT: 8200**   **SETTING: Suburban**   **CITY POPULATION: 80,000**

Malaspina University College is a medium-sized undergraduate school that offers all the services of an undergraduate university and a comprehensive community college. Both bachelor's and associate degrees are granted. The main campus is in the city of Nanaimo on the eastern shore of Vancouver Island. The campus is located on a hill and enjoys a spectacular view of the city; the Georgia Strait, which separates the island from the mainland; and the far-off Coastal Mountain range. The campus features two Japanese gardens, an arboretum, a museum, and an art gallery.

Courses leading to a bachelor's degree are offered in a wide range of areas, including business, education, fisheries and aquaculture, liberal arts, and nursing. Students enjoy small class sizes as well as a personal and friendly atmosphere. Students may take their first two years of university studies at Malaspina and then transfer to other universities.

The school has limited residence facilities, but international students are directed to home-stay programs offered through the University. Off-campus housing is readily available. MUC offers a good mix of athletic, recreational, and cultural activities.

Vancouver Island's ancient rain forest and impressive coastal scenery provide outdoor enthusiasts with a perfect playground to enjoy kayaking, hiking, skiing, and a variety of other sports.

GENERAL INFORMATION

Year founded:	1969
Undergraduate enrollment, full-time:	5400
Graduate enrollment, full-time:	N/A
Faculty, full-time:	N/A
Number of international students:	575
Male/female ratio (%)	40:60
Residence spaces available:	189
Residence space guaranteed for 1st-year students:	No
Student media website:	N/A

UNDERGRADUATE ADMISSIONS

Office of the Registrar
900 Fifth Street
Nanaimo, BC   V9R 5S5
PH: **250.755.8755**   FAX: **705.755.8725**
WEBSITE: **www.mala.bc.ca**

Minimum high school average:	60
Applications, 2000-2001:	N/A
Rolling admissions:	International only
International fall application deadline:	Jul 15
Application fee:	$100
Domestic fall application deadline:	Mar 1
Application fee:	$30
Electronic application accepted:	Yes
Admissions notification by:	N/A
Required with application:	Essay, recommendations, interview dependent upon program

UNDERGRADUATE FINANCES

Undergraduate tuition:		
International students:	$9700	(US $8730)
Canadian students:	$3400	(US $3060)
Estimated annual health insurance:	$425	(US $398)
Estimated annual books & supplies:	$1000	(US $900)
Financial aid available for international students:	No	
Application deadline:	N/A	
Scholarships available for international students:	Yes	
Application deadline:	Varies	
Annual room cost for students in residence:	$2800	(US $2500)
Average monthly rent for students living off campus:		
1 bedroom: $425-525, 2 bedroom: $550-650		
Federal School Code: G21365		

UNDERGRADUATE INSTRUCTIONAL PROGRAM

Most popular majors: Anthropology, Business, Education, Nursing
Percentages by program: N/A
Special study options: Co-op programs, study abroad, language programs, special summer programs

Liberal Arts and Sciences, General Studies, and Humanities

Anthropology, Art, Chinese Language & Literature, Classics & Classical Languages & Literature, English Language & Literature, Film Studies, French Language & Literature, History, Japanese Language & Literature, Liberal Studies, Linguistics, Media Studies, Modern Languages, Music, Philosophy, Political Science, Psychology, Religion/Religious Studies, Social Work, Sociology, Spanish Language & Literature, Visual & Performing Arts, Women's Studies, Writing

Science and Mathematics

Aquaculture Operations, Astronomy, Biology, Chemistry, Fishing & Fisheries Sciences & Management, Forestry Sciences, Genetics, Geography, Geology, Mathematics, Microbiology, Physics

Computer Science and Engineering

Computer & Information Sciences, Engineering Science

Professional Studies

Child Growth/Care & Development Studies, Criminal Justice Studies, Education, Hospitality/Administration Management, Interior Design, Journalism, Pre-Law, Leisure & Recreational Activities, Physical Education Teaching & Coaching

Business and Economics

Accounting, Business Administration & Management/Commerce, Economics, Finance, Information Sciences & Systems, Marketing Management & Research

Health Professions and Related Sciences

Health Sciences, Nursing

SIMON FRASER UNIVERSITY

Burnaby, British Columbia

SCHOOL CATEGORY: Master's   **TOTAL ENROLLMENT: 22,000**   **SETTING: Suburban**   **CITY POPULATION: 2,000,000**

Simon Fraser University (SFU) is a comprehensive medium-sized university. Its main campus is in Burnaby, just seven miles from the center of Vancouver. The Burnaby campus was designed by Arthur Erickson and is known for its distinctive, award-winning architecture. Buildings are terraced and enjoy spectacular views of Vancouver, the Coastal Mountains, and Georgia Strait. A second campus, the Harbor Center campus, is located downtown.

SFU is a comprehensive university with over 100 programs in the liberal and fine arts, sciences, applied sciences, business, and education. Students are given the opportunity to study across disciplines and to discover which subjects interest them. A trimester system offers students flexibility in scheduling their studies. Admission is competitive.

SFU has residence space for over 1,200 students, with the majority of spaces reserved for first-year students. A variety of off-campus housing is readily available. SFU offers a comprehensive extracurricular and athletic system. The school is a member of the National Association of Intercollegiate Athletics and competes against many U.S. varsity teams. The school has over 100 clubs, including an active Snowboard club.

Nestled between soaring mountains and the glimmering ocean, Vancouver is the largest city on Canada's west coast and one of the world's most beautiful cities. Vancouver offers historic districts, lush gardens, and wilderness parks close by. Students can take advantage of the many cultural and recreational opportunities the city has to offer. Vancouver enjoys the mildest climate of any city in Canada.

GENERAL INFORMATION

Year founded:	1965
Undergraduate enrollment, full-time:	11,000
Graduate enrollment, full-time:	2500
Faculty, full-time:	700
Number of international students:	N/A
Male/female ratio (%):	44:56
Residence spaces available:	1250
Residence space guaranteed for 1st-year students:	No
Student media website:	www.peak.sfu.ca

UNDERGRADUATE ADMISSIONS

Office of the Registrar
8888 University Drive
Burnaby, BC   V5A 1S6
PH: **604.291.3224**   FAX: **604.291.4969**
WEBSITE: **www.sfu.ca**

Minimum high school average:	80 (GPA 3.2)
Applications, 2000-2001:	15,000 Received; 7000 Accepted
Rolling admissions:	No
International fall application deadline:	Jul 15
Application fee:	$100
Domestic fall application deadline:	Mar 1
Application fee:	$30
Electronic application accepted:	Yes
Admissions notification by:	N/A
Required with application:	HS transcripts, essay, recommendations

UNDERGRADUATE FINANCES

Undergraduate tuition:		
International students:	$14,500	(US $13,050)
Canadian students:	$4900	(US $4400)
Estimated annual health insurance:	$500	(US $450)
Estimated annual books & supplies:	$1000	(US $900)
Financial aid available for international students:	Limited	
Application deadline:	Varies	
Scholarships available for international students:	Yes	
Application deadline:	May 1	
Annual room/board cost for students in residence:	$5000-6000	(US $4500-5400)

Average monthly rent for students living off campus:
    1 bedroom: $400+, 2 bedroom: $700+
Federal School Code: G08444

UNDERGRADUATE INSTRUCTIONAL PROGRAM

Most popular majors: Business, Biology, English, Engineering
Percentages by program: N/A
Special study options: Co-op programs, study abroad, language programs, special summer programs, distance learning programs

Liberal Arts and Sciences, General Studies, and Humanities

Art, Asian Studies, Canadian Studies, Communications, English Language & Literature, French Language & Literature, Gerontology, History, Humanities/Humanistic Studies, Latin American Studies, Linguistics, Philosophy, Political Science, Psychology, Publishing, Sociology, Women's Studies

Science and Mathematics

Actuarial Science, Actuarial Mathematics, Applied Mathematics, Biological Sciences/Life Sciences, Biochemistry, Chemistry, Cognitive Science, Earth & Planetary Science, Environmental Chemistry, Environmental Science, Environmental Toxicology, Geography, Marine/Aquatic Science, Nuclear Science, Physics, Statistics

Computer Science and Engineering

Computer & Information Sciences, Computer Engineering, Electrical/Electronics & Communication Engineering, Engineering Physics, Systems Engineering

Professional Studies

Archaeology, Criminal Justice Studies, Education, Human Kinetics/Kinesiology

Business and Economics

Accounting, Business Administration & Management/Commerce, Economics, Finance, Natural Resource Management & Protective Services, Management Science, Marketing Management & Research

Health Professions and Related Sciences

Pre-Medicine

GRADUATE ADMISSIONS

Office of Graduate Studies
Simon Fraser University
Maggie Benston Student Services Centre 1100
888 University Drive
Burnaby, BC   V5A 1S6
PH: **604.268.6568**   FAX: **604.291.3080**
WEBSITE: **www.sfu.ca/dean-gradstudies/**

Fall application deadline:	Varies
Application fee:	N/A
Required with application:	N/A
Graduate student housing:	Graduate residence in Louis Reil House (families) & Hamilton Hall (singles)

GRADUATE FINANCES

International Graduate tuition:	$5000-23,000	(US $4500-20,700)
Financial aid & Scholarships available for international students:	N/A	

GRADUATE INSTRUCTIONAL PROGRAM

Liberal Arts and Sciences, General Studies, and Humanities

Anthropology, Art, Communications, Gerontology, English Language & Literature, French Language & Literature, History, Humanities/Humanistic Studies, Latin American Studies, Liberal Studies, Linguistics, Philosophy, Political Science, Publishing, Sociology, Women's Studies

Science and Mathematics

Geography, Environmental Sciences

Computer Science and Engineering

Computer & Information Sciences, Engineering Science

Professional Studies

Archaeology, Education, Human Kinetics/Kinesiology

Business and Economics

Business Administration & Management/Commerce

THOMPSON RIVERS UNIVERSITY

Kamloops, British Columbia

SCHOOL CATEGORY: Bachelor's/General   **TOTAL ENROLLMENT: 15,000**   **SETTING: Suburban**   **CITY POPULATION: 80,000**

Thompson Rivers University is a medium-sized school located in Kamloops, a city of 80,000 people in the central southern interior of British Columbia. The school was founded in 1970 as a community college and achieved independent university status in 1995.

Thompson Rivers offers over 30 programs in a wide cross-section of areas, including business, education, the sciences, and the liberal arts. The school enjoys a close collaboration with business and industry.

Approximately 600 units of housing are located on or very close to the campus. The McGill facility offers 300 single rooms right on campus, while the Upper College Heights facility features 300 one-, two-, and three-bedroom apartment units. Conveniently located and reasonably priced off-campus housing is relatively easy to find in Kamloops. Thompson Rivers has good athletic facilities, including a gymnasium, stadium, numerous playing fields, an Olympic-sized indoor pool, and a fully equipped weight and exercise room.

Kamloops has long been a crossroads for trade. The name "Kamloops" means "where the rivers meet," and the north and south Thompson Rivers join here. The area, with its mild winters and warm summers, is a popular destination for outdoor enthusiasts, with excellent skiing and hiking nearby.

GENERAL INFORMATION

Year founded:	1970
Undergraduate enrollment, full-time:	5000
Graduate enrollment, full-time:	N/A
Faculty, full-time:	N/A
Number of international students:	750
Male/female ratio (%):	40:60
Residence spaces available:	600
Residence space guaranteed for 1st-year students:	No
Student media website:	N/A

UNDERGRADUATE ADMISSIONS

P.O. Box 3010, 900 McGill Road
Kamloops, BC V2C 5N3
PH: 250.828.5000   FAX: 250.828.5086
WEBSITE: **www.tru.ca**

Minimum high school average:	65
Applications, 2000-2001:	N/A
Rolling admissions:	Yes
International fall application deadline:	May 31
Application fee:	$100
Domestic fall application deadline:	Apr 15
Application fee:	$15
Electronic application accepted:	Yes
Admissions notification by:	N/A
Required with application:	HS transcripts, (essay, recommendations per department)

UNDERGRADUATE FINANCES

Undergraduate tuition:		
International students:	$12,000	(US $10,800)
Canadian students:	$3800	(US $3400)
Estimated annual health insurance:	$450	(US $405)
Estimated annual books & supplies:	$900	(US $810)
Financial aid available for international students:	Limited	
Application deadline:	N/A	
Scholarships available for international students:	Yes	
Application deadline:	Apr/Sep	
Annual room cost for students in residence:	$2400-2600	(US $2160-2340)
Average monthly rent for students living off campus:		
1 bedroom: $250-350, 2 bedroom: $400+		

UNDERGRADUATE INSTRUCTIONAL PROGRAM

Most popular majors: Business, Science, Natural Resource Science, Health Sciences
Percentages by program: 40% Liberal Arts, 25% Science, 9% Business, 8% Health Professions, 5% Engineering/Computer Science
Special study options: Co-op programs, internships, study abroad, language programs, special summer programs, distance learning programs

Liberal Arts and Sciences, General Studies, and Humanities

Anthropology, Art, Art History, Asian Studies, Canadian Studies, Ceramic Arts & Ceramics, Design & Applied Arts, Drama, English Language & Literature, Fine/Studio Arts, History, Native Studies, Modern Languages, Painting & Drawing, Printmaking & Photography, Psychology, Political Science, Psychology, Sculpture, Social Work, Sociology, Visual & Performing Arts

Science and Mathematics

Animal Sciences, Biology, Biochemistry, Cell Biology, Chemistry, Ecology, Environmental Sciences, Forestry Sciences, Genetics Plant/Animal, Geography, Geology, Marine/Aquatic Science, Mathematics, Microbiology, Natural Resource Science, Plant Science, Physics, Statistics

Computer Science and Engineering

Computer & Information Sciences, Engineering Science

Professional Studies

Education, Journalism, Leisure & Recreational Activities, Tourism

Business and Economics

Accounting, Business Administration & Management/Commerce, Economics, Finance, Human Resources Management, Marketing Management & Research, Natural Resource Management

Health Professions and Related Sciences

Nursing, Respiratory Therapy

TRINITY WESTERN UNIVERSITY

Langley, British Columbia

SCHOOL CATEGORY: Bachelor's/Liberal Arts   **TOTAL ENROLLMENT: 2700**   **SETTING: Suburban**   **CITY POPULATION: 80,000**

Trinity Western University (TWU) is a small, Christian, liberal arts institution located near Vancouver. At the undergraduate level, TWU offers bachelor's degrees in arts, business administration, education, science, nursing, and physical education. The School of Graduate Studies grants master's degrees in administrative leadership, biblical studies, counseling psychology, religion, culture, and ethics. A commitment to developing the whole student—academically, socially, physically, and spiritually—distinguishes TWU as an institute for leadership development.

The schools offers a variety of residence options ranging from traditional dorm-style to apartment-style accommodations. The school maintains an off-campus housing office which can help students find accommodations in the area.

Langley is located within an hour's drive of Vancouver. Nestled between soaring mountains and the glimmering ocean, Vancouver is the largest city on Canada's west coast and one of the world's most beautiful cities. Vancouver offers historic districts, lush gardens, and wilderness parks close by. Students can take advantage of the many cultural and recreational opportunities the city has to offer. The region enjoys the mildest climate in the country.

GENERAL INFORMATION

Year founded:	1962
Undergraduate enrollment, full-time:	2000
Graduate enrollment, full-time:	300
Faculty, full-time:	200
Number of international students:	270
Male/female ratio (%)	60:40
Residence spaces available:	900
Residence space guaranteed for 1st-year students:	No
Student media website:	www.student.twu.ca/twusa

UNDERGRADUATE ADMISSIONS

Department of Admissions
7600 Glover Road
Langley, BC V2Y 1Y1
PH: 640.513.2019   FAX: 640.513.2064
WEBSITE: **www.twu.ca**

Minimum high school average:	75
Applications, 2000-2001:	N/A
Rolling admissions:	Yes
International fall application deadline:	Feb 28
Application fee:	$35
Domestic fall application deadline:	N/A
Application fee:	$35
Electronic application accepted:	Yes
Admissions notification by:	N/A
Required with application:	HS transcripts, essay, SAT

UNDERGRADUATE FINANCES

Undergraduate tuition:		
All students:	$14,700	(US $13,200)
Estimated annual health insurance:	$600	(US $540)
Estimated annual books & supplies:	$900	(US $810)
Financial aid available for international students:	Yes	
Application deadline:	Feb 28	
Scholarships available for international students:	Yes	
Application deadline:	Feb 28	
Annual room/board cost for students in residence:	$8000-10,000	(US $7200-9000)
Average monthly rent for students living off campus:		
1 bedroom: $600+, 2 bedroom: $900+		
Federal School Code: G09486		

UNDERGRADUATE INSTRUCTIONAL PROGRAM

Most popular majors: Business, Psychology, Education
Percentages by program: N/A
Special study options: N/A

Liberal Arts and Sciences, General Studies, and Humanities

Art, Biblical Studies, Canadian Studies, Celtic/Irish Studies, Christianity & Culture, Communications, Drama/Theater Arts, English Language & Literature, Fine/Studio Arts, French Language & Literature, History, Humanities/Humanistic Studies, International Relations & Affairs, Missions, Music, Philosophy, Political Science, Psychology, Religion/Religious Studies, Social Work, Sociology, Theology/Theological Studies

Science and Mathematics

Applied Mathematics, Aviation & Airway Science, Biology, Chemistry, Environmental Sciences, Geography, Mathematics, Natural & Applied Science

Computer Science and Engineering

Computer & Information Sciences, Pre-Engineering

Professional Studies

Education, Human Kinetics/Kinesiology

Business and Economics

Accounting, Business Administration & Management/Commerce, Economics, Information Sciences & Systems

Health Professions and Related Sciences

Nursing, Pre-Dentistry, Pre-Medicine, Pre-Veterinary Medicine

GRADUATE ADMISSIONS

School of Graduate Studies
Langley, BC   V2Y 1Y1
PH: **604.888.7511**   FAX: **604.513.2010**
WEBSITE: **www.twu.ca/admissions/GradStudies**

Fall application deadline:	N/A
Application fee:	N/A
Required with application:	College transcript
Graduate student housing:	Apartment-style for senior students

GRADUATE FINANCES

Graduate tuition:
International & Canadian students:	$11,000-15,000	(US $9900-13,500)

Financial aid & Scholarships available for
international students:	N/A
Application deadline:	N/A

GRADUATE INSTRUCTIONAL PROGRAM

Liberal Arts and Sciences, General Studies, and Humanities
Administrative Leadership, Biblical Studies, Counseling Psychology, Culture & Ethics, Divinity/Ministry, Religion/Religious Studies, Theology/Theological Studies

UNIVERSITY COLLEGE OF THE FRASER VALLEY

Abbotsford, British Columbia

SCHOOL CATEGORY: Bachelor's/General   **TOTAL ENROLLMENT: 6500**   **SETTING: Suburban**   **CITY POPULATION: 140,000**

University College of the Fraser Valley (UCFV) is a medium-sized undergraduate school that offers all the services of an undergraduate university and a comprehensive community college. Both bachelor's and associate degrees are granted. It has four campuses in the Greater Vancouver area: in Abbotsford, Chilliwack, Mission, and Hope. The largest campus is located in Abbotsford.

Courses leading to a bachelor's degree are offered in Arts, Aviation, Adult Education, Business Administration, Child and Youth Care, Criminal Justice, Computer Information Systems, Nursing, Science, and Social Work. Students enjoy small class sizes as well as a personal and friendly atmosphere. Students may take their first two years of university studies at UCFV and then transfer to other universities.

The school does not offer any residence facilities, but off-campus housing is readily available. The school offers a good mix of recreational and cultural activities. Athletic facilities are limited.

Vancouver is the largest city on Canada's west coast and one of the world's most beautiful cities, with historic districts, lush gardens, and wilderness parks close by. Students can take advantage of the many cultural and recreational opportunities the city has to offer. The region enjoys the mildest climate in Canada.

GENERAL INFORMATION

Year founded:	1974
Undergraduate enrollment, full-time:	4500
Graduate enrollment, full-time:	N/A
Faculty, full-time:	325
Number of international students:	350
Male/female ratio (%)	35:65
Residence spaces available:	N/A
Residence space guaranteed for 1st-year students:	N/A
Student media website:	www.ucfv.bc.ca/sus/

UNDERGRADUATE ADMISSIONS

Office of the Registrar
33844 King Road
Abbotsford, BC   V2S 7M8
PH: **604.854.4544**   FAX: **604.855.7153**
WEBSITE: **www.ucfv.bc.ca**

Minimum high school average:	None
Applications, 2000-2001:	N/A
Rolling admissions:	Yes
International fall application deadline:	Mar 15
Application fee:	$100
Domestic fall application deadline:	Mar 31
Application fee:	$15
Electronic application accepted:	No
Admissions notification by:	N/A
Required with application:	HS transcripts, essay

UNDERGRADUATE FINANCES

Undergraduate tuition:		
International students:	$10,500	(US $9500)
Canadian students:	$3700	(US $3300)
Estimated annual health insurance:	$600	(US $540)
Estimated annual books & supplies:	$1000	(US $900)
Financial aid available for international students:	N/A	
Application deadline:	N/A	
Scholarships available for international students:	Yes	
Application deadline:	Varies	
Annual room/board cost for students in residence:	N/A	
Average monthly rent for students living off campus:		
1 bedroom: $500+, 2 bedroom: $700+		

UNDERGRADUATE INSTRUCTIONAL PROGRAM

Most popular majors: Arts, Business, Criminal Justice Studies, Computer & Information Science
Percentages by program: N/A
Special study options: Co-op programs, study abroad, language programs, special summer programs, distance learning programs

Liberal Arts and Sciences, General Studies, and Humanities

Anthropology, English Language & Literature, History, Latin American Studies, Psychology, Speech & Language, Social Work, Sociology, Visual & Performing Arts

Science and Mathematics

Agricultural Sciences, Aviation & Airway Science, Biological Sciences/Life Sciences, Biology, Chemistry, Geography, Mathematics, Physics, Statistics

Computer Science and Engineering

Computer & Information Sciences

Professional Studies

Criminal Justice Studies, Education, Human Kinetics/Kinesiology, Library Science

Business and Economics

Business Administration & Management/Commerce, Economics, Information Sciences & Systems

Health Professions and Related Sciences

Nursing

THE UNIVERSITY OF BRITISH COLUMBIA

Vancouver, British Columbia

SCHOOL CATEGORY: Doctoral/Research   **TOTAL ENROLLMENT: 40,000**   **SETTING: Urban**   **CITY POPULATION: 2,000,000**

The University of British Columbia (1908) is one of Canada's premier universities with a global reputation for excellence in teaching and research. Recognized journals consistently rank UBC in the top 10 universities in North America, and the top 40 worldwide. International students (including many from the US) choose UBC for its wide study programs, expert faculty, world-class facilities, international perspective, and vibrant student life.

Programs at undergraduate, professional, and postgraduate levels are available through 17 Faculties and 13 Schools, leading to globally recognized degrees and diplomas. Areas of study include: humanities, visual and performing arts, social sciences, business studies, life and physical sciences, health sciences, engineering sciences, computer science, earth and ocean sciences, food and nutritional sciences, education, architecture and landscape, law, human kinetics, and more, with literally hundreds of major, minor, double major, honors, and specialization options.

Over 98% of full-time faculty have PhDs, and the majority of undergraduate classes have 30 students or less, although there are some large first-year classes. The school has the second-largest research library in Canada.

UBC has two principal campuses – Vancouver on Canada's spectacular Pacific coast and Okanagan in British Columbia's beautiful interior. The main campus, UBC Vancouver, is 1,000 acres in size, and an award-winning model for environmental sustainability. Surrounded by forest, mountains and ocean, it is also located in one of the world's most livable cities. Vancouver is to host the 2010 Winter Olympic Games, and UBC will be one of the venues.

UBC Okanagan's college-size campus is located in the friendly lakeside city of Kelowna BC. The city is close to mountain, lake, and ski resorts, with a gentler pace of life than Vancouver's bustling metropolis.

About 20% of students live in high-quality campus housing, and first-year international students have guaranteed priority if they apply before May 1 and accept admission by May 31. Off-campus housing can be found in nearby neighborhoods.

At UBC Vancouver, there are over 300 student clubs and societies, and students can participate in athletics from varsity-level competition to spirited intramural events and solo pursuits. From both campuses there is ready access to numerous outdoor activities year-round, including beaches, forested parks, and world-class ski trails.

First-class academics and tremendous extracurricular opportunities make UBC a very popular choice.

GENERAL INFORMATION

Year founded:	1908
Undergraduate enrollment, full-time:	19,961
Graduate enrollment, full-time:	8976
Faculty, full-time:	2048
Number of international students:	5280
Male/female ratio (%)	46:54
Residence spaces available:	5000
Residence space guaranteed for 1st-year students:	Yes
Student media website:	www.ubc.ca/ubyssey

UNDERGRADUATE ADMISSIONS

Student Information
1874 East Mall, Brock Hall
Vancouver, BC   V6T 1Z1
PH: 604.822.9836   FAX: 604.822.9888
WEBSITE: www.welcome.ubc.ca

Minimum high school average:	Varies
Applications, 2005:	17001
Rolling admissions:	After Sep
International fall application deadline:	Mar 31
Application fee:	$100
Domestic fall application deadline:	Mar 31
Application fee:	$54
Electronic application accepted:	Yes
Admissions notification by:	Feb 15-Jul 15
Required with application:	HS transcripts
Recommended:	SAT, ACT, essay, recommendations

UNDERGRADUATE FINANCES

Undergraduate tuition:		
International students:	$17,577	(US $15,800)
Canadian students:	$4174	(US $3760)
Estimated annual health insurance:	$587	(US $530)
Estimated annual books & supplies:	$1100	(US $990)
Financial aid available for international students:	No	
Application deadline:	N/A	
Scholarships available for international students:	Yes	
Application deadline:	Apr 15	
Annual room/board cost for students in residence:	$6650	(US $5985)
Average monthly rent for students living off campus:		
1 bedroom: $675+, 2 bedroom: $800+		
Federal School Code: G08369		

UNDERGRADUATE INSTRUCTIONAL PROGRAM

Most popular majors: Biology, Computer Science, Economics, English, Psychology
Percentages by program: N/A
Special study options: Co-op programs, internships, study abroad, language programs, special summer programs, distance learning programs

Liberal Arts and Sciences, General Studies, and Humanities

Anthropology, Art, Asian Studies, Canadian Studies, Chinese Language & Literature, Classics & Classical Languages & Literature, Drama/Theater Arts, English Language & Literature, Film/Cinema, Fine/Studio Arts, French Language & Literature, German Language & Literature, History, Humanities/Humanistic Studies, International Relations & Affairs, Italian Language & Literature, Linguistics, Modern European Studies, Medieval & Renaissance Studies, Museum Studies, Music, Native Studies, Near Eastern Studies, Philosophy, Political Science, Psychology,

Religion/Religious Studies, Social Work, Sociology, Spanish Language & Literature, Visual & Performing Arts, Women's Studies, Writing

Science and Mathematics

Aviation & Airway Science, Agricultural Engineering, Agroecology, Atmospheric Sciences & Meteorology, Biochemistry, Biological Sciences/Life Sciences, Biology, Biophysics, Biotechnology Research, Chemistry, Environmental Sciences, Food Sciences & Technology, Forestry Sciences, General Science, Genetics, Geography, Geology, Geophysics & Seismology, Horticulture Science, Mathematics, Microbiology, Oceanography, Physics, Soil Sciences, Statistics, Wood Science

Computer Science and Engineering

Bioengineering & Biomedical Engineering, Chemical Engineering, Cognitive Systems, Computer Engineering, Computer & Information Sciences, Electrical Engineering/ Electronics & Communication Engineering, Engineering Physics, Geological Engineering, Integrated Engineering, Mechanical Engineering, Metals & Materials Engineering, Mining & Mineral Engineering, Software Engineering

Professional Studies

Archaeology, Architecture, City/Urban/Community & Regional Planning, Education, Family & Community Studies, Fashion, Home Economics, Human Kinetics/Kinesiology, Pre-Law, Leisure & Recreational Activities, Naval Architecture, Radio & Television Broadcasting, Physical Education Teaching & Coaching, Teacher Education

Business and Economics

Accounting, Agricultural Business, Business Administration & Management/Commerce, Economics, Food Market Analysis, General Business Management, Human Resources Management, International Business, Labor/Personnel Relations & Studies, Management Science, Management Information Systems & Business Data Processing, Marketing Management & Research, Natural Resources Management & Protective Services, Operations Management & Supervision, Public Relations & Organizational Communications, Sports & Fitness Administration/Management, Transportation & Logistics, Urban Land Economics

Health Professions and Related Sciences

Dental Hygiene, Dietetics, Diagnostic & Treatment Services, Environmental Health, Health & Fitness, Health Services Administration, Nursing, Nutritional Science, Occupational Therapy, Pharmacy, Pharmacology, Physical Therapy, Pre-Dentistry, Pre-Medicine, Pre-Veterinary Medicine, Public Health, Speech-Language Pathology & Audiology

GRADUATE ADMISSIONS

Faculty of Graduate Studies
The University of British Columbia
Vancouver, BC   V6T 1Z1
PH: **604.822.2848**   FAX: **604.822.5802**
WEBSITE: **www.grad.ubc.ca/**

Fall application deadline:	N/A
Application fee:	N/A
Required with application:	College transcript, essay, recommendations GRE & GMAT required for some programs
Graduate student housing:	Single residences at Green & St. John's College, family housing available

GRADUATE FINANCES

Graduate tuition:

International students:	$7200	(US $6480)
Canadian students:	$3786	(US $3407)

Financial aid & Scholarships available for

international students:	Yes
Application deadline:	Feb 1-Jun15

GRADUATE INSTRUCTIONAL PROGRAM

Liberal Arts and Sciences, General Studies, and Humanities

Anthropology, Asian Studies, Classical Archaeology, Classics & Classical Languages, Comparative Literature, English Language & Literature, European Studies, Film/Cinema, Fine Arts, French Language & Literature, German Language & Literature, Hispanic Studies, History, Latin American Studies, Linguistics, Music, Philosophy, Political Science, Psychology, Religion/Religious Studies, Social Work, Sociology, Visual & Performing Arts, Women's Studies

Science and Mathematics

Animal Science, Applied Mathematics, Astronomy, Atmospheric Sciences & Meteorology, Biochemistry, Botany, Chemistry, Environmental Sciences, Food Science, Forestry Sciences, Genetics, Geography, Geology, Geophysics & Seismology, Mathematics, Oceanography, Physics, Plant Science, Soil Science, Statistics, Wood Science

Computer Science and Engineering

Bioengineering & Biomedical Engineering, Chemical Engineering, Civil Engineering, Computer & Information Sciences, Electrical/Electronics & Communication Engineering, Computer Engineering, Engineering Physics, Engineering Science, Geological Engineering, Mechanical Engineering, Metals & Materials Engineering, Mining & Mineral Engineering, Pulp & Paper Engineering, Wood Science

Professional Studies

Architecture, Community & Regional Planning, Counseling, Curriculum Studies, Education, Family & Community Studies, Human Kinetics/Kinesiology, Journalism, Landscape Architecture, Law, Library Science

Business and Economics

Agricultural Business/Economics, Business Administration & Management/Commerce, Economics, Information Sciences & Systems

Health Professions and Related Sciences

Anatomy, Counseling Psychology, Dentistry, Experimental Medicine, Health Care, Epidemiology, Medical Genetics, Medicine, Microbiology & Immunology, Neuroscience, Nursing, Nutritional Sciences, Occupational Hygiene, Pathology & Laboratory Medicine, Pharmaceutical Sciences, Pharmacology & Therapeutics, Physiology, Rehabilitation Sciences, Reproductive & Developmental Sciences, Speech-Language Pathology & Audiology, Surgery

UNIVERSITY OF NORTHERN BRITISH COLUMBIA

Prince George, British Columbia

SCHOOL CATEGORY: Bachelor's/General **TOTAL ENROLLMENT: 3000** **SETTING: Suburban** **CITY POPULATION: 75,000**

The University of Northern British Columbia is a young, small university located in north central British Columbia. The main campus is located in a beautiful wooded setting overlooking Prince George, a growing community of 75,000 in the foothills of the Rocky Mountains. The campus blends into its environment through the use of stunningly modern wood and glass architecture.

The university offers a wide range of undergraduate and graduate degrees. Reflecting its rugged setting, the school's program in Natural Resource Management is one of it's most popular offerings. Other programs include arts and science, business, computer science, environmental studies, and resource-based tourism.

The university offers residence facilities for over 500 students, and off-campus housing is readily available. The school offers a good mix of athletic, recreational, and cultural activities. The area is rich in outdoor opportunities: five ski hills are within a two-hour radius, and there are many rivers in the area for canoeing and kayaking and many trails for hiking or mountain biking. Prince George is a service town for a wide geographic area and, as such, has many amenities, including fine dining and shopping, theaters, and clubs.

GENERAL INFORMATION

Year founded:	1994
Undergraduate enrollment, full-time:	2300
Graduate enrollment, full-time:	225
Faculty, full-time:	N/A
Number of international students:	575
Male/female ratio (%):	40:60
Residence spaces available:	548
Residence space guaranteed for 1st-year students:	No
Student media website:	www.web.unbc.ca/edge/

UNDERGRADUATE ADMISSIONS

Registrar's Office
3333 University Way
Prince George, BC   V2N 4Z9
PH: **250.960.5555**   FAX: **250.960.6330**
WEBSITE: **www.unbc.ca**

Minimum high school average:	70
Applications, 2000-2001:	N/A
Rolling admissions:	N/A
International fall application deadline:	N/A
Application fee:	$35
Domestic fall application deadline:	N/A
Application fee:	$10
Electronic application accepted:	Yes
Admissions notification by:	N/A
Required with application:	HS transcripts

UNDERGRADUATE FINANCES

Undergraduate tuition:		
International students:	$15,000	(US $13,500)
Canadian students:	$4900	(US $4400)
Estimated annual health insurance:	$500	(US $450)
Estimated annual books & supplies:	$800	(US $720)
Financial aid available for international students:	N/A	
Application deadline:	N/A	
Scholarships available for international students:	N/A	
Application deadline:	N/A	
Annual room/board cost for students in residence:	$4000-4500	(US $3600-4050)

Average monthly rent for students living off campus:
1 bedroom: $300-350, 2 bedroom: $300-500
Federal School Code: G36133

UNDERGRADUATE INSTRUCTIONAL PROGRAM

Most popular majors: Business, Biology, Environmental Studies, Natural Resource Management
Percentages by program: N/A
Special study options: Co-op programs, study abroad

Liberal Arts and Sciences, General Studies, and Humanities

Anthropology, English Language & Literature, Gender Studies, History, International Relations & Affairs, Native Studies, Nisga'a Studies, Northern Studies, Political Science, Psychology, Social Work, Women's Studies

Science and Mathematics

Biology, Chemistry, Environmental Sciences, Fishing & Fisheries Sciences, Forestry, Geography, Mathematics, Microbiology, Natural Resources, Physics, Wildlife Management

Computer Science and Engineering

Computer & Information Sciences

Professional Studies

Aboriginal Community Resource Planning, Leisure & Recreation Studies

Business and Economics

Business Administration & Management/Commerce, Economics

Health Professions and Related Sciences

Community Health Science, Nursing

GRADUATE ADMISSIONS

Office of Graduate Studies
University of Northern British Columbia
3333 University Way
Prince George, BC   V2N 4Z9
PH: 250.960.5795   FAX: 250.960.7300
WEBSITE: www.unbc.ca/calendar/Graduate/

International fall application deadline:	Feb 15
Application fee:	$35
Domestic fall application deadline:	Feb 15
Application fee:	$10
Required with application:	College transcript, GRE, essay, recommendations
Graduate student housing:	Single student accommodations

GRADUATE FINANCES

Graduate tuition:	$3000-10,000	(US $2700-9000)
Financial aid & Scholarships available for		
international students:	Yes	
Application deadline:	Varies	

GRADUATE INSTRUCTIONAL PROGRAM

Liberal Arts and Sciences, General Studies, and Humanities

Gender Studies, History, International Studies, Native Studies, Political Science, Psychology, Social Work

Science and Mathematics

Biology, Chemistry, Environmental Studies, Forestry Sciences, Geography, Geology, Mathematics, Physics, Physiology/Human & Animal, Plant Sciences, Psychology, Statistics, Textile Sciences & Engineering, Toxicology, Wood Science, Zoology

Computer Science and Engineering

Computer & Information Sciences

Professional Studies

Community Health Science, Education, Leisure & Recreational Activities, Tourism

UNIVERSITY OF VICTORIA

Victoria, British Columbia

SCHOOL CATEGORY: Master's   **TOTAL ENROLLMENT: 19,000**   **SETTING: Suburban**   **CITY POPULATION: 310,000**

The University of Victoria is a medium-sized comprehensive institution located on the west coast of Vancouver Island, 15 minutes from the provincial capital's downtown. The school, founded in 1963, has a stunning setting featuring botanical gardens and is bounded on one side by a forested ecological preserve.

Areas of academic and research strength include the study of aging, the Asia-Pacific region, biochemistry and microbiology, environmental studies, earth and ocean systems, physics, astronomy, law, and engineering. The school is a Canadian leader in co-operative education, integrating academic studies with relevant paid work experience in more than 40 academic areas.

On-campus housing is available for approximately 2,100 students, with a guaranteed dormitory space for 1st-year students, coming directly from high school. The university has an excellent athletic program and is home to the National Coaching Institute, which provides expert consultation to elite athletes from across North America.

Victoria is a quiet, attractive city of long tradition, with beautiful gardens and historic buildings at every turn for scholars to discover. Vancouver Island has the mildest climate in Canada, and its rugged terrain offers plenty of challenges for hikers, skiers, kayakers, and other outdoor enthusiasts.

GENERAL INFORMATION

Year founded:	1963
Undergraduate enrollment, full-time:	10,757
Graduate enrollment, full-time:	2003
Faculty, full-time:	790
Number of international students:	1536
Male/female ratio (%):	40:60
Residence spaces available:	2160
Residence space guaranteed for 1st-year students:	No
Student media website:	www.uvic.ca/ring

UNDERGRADUATE ADMISSIONS

P.O. Box 1700 STN CSC
Victoria, BC   V8W 2Y2
PH: 250.721.7211   FAX: 705.721.6225
WEBSITE: www.uvic.ca

Minimum high school average:	76%
Applications, 2005:	12,133
Rolling admissions:	N/A
International fall application deadline:	Apr 30
Application fee:	$100
Domestic fall application deadline:	May 15
Application fee:	$100
Electronic application accepted:	Yes
Admissions notification by:	6 weeks from application
Required with application:	HS transcripts (essay, recommendations, interview depende nt upon department)
Recommended:	SAT

UNDERGRADUATE FINANCES

Undergraduate tuition:		
International students:	$14,274	(US $12,850)
Canadian students:	$4412	(US $3970)
Estimated annual health insurance:	$120	(US $96)
Estimated annual books & supplies:	$1000	(US $900)
Financial aid & Scholarships available for		
international students:	No	
Application deadline:	N/A	
Annual room/board cost for students in residence:	$6500	(US $5,850)
Average monthly rent for students living off campus:		
1 bedroom: $550+, 2 bedroom: $700+		
Federal School Code: G08370		

UNDERGRADUATE INSTRUCTIONAL PROGRAM

Most popular majors: Biology, English, History, Psychology
Percentages by program: 23% Liberal Arts, 14% Science, 10% Human & Social Development, 9% Engineering/Computer Science, 4% Business
Special study options: Co-op programs, internships, study abroad, language programs, special summer programs, distance learning programs

Liberal Arts and Sciences, General Studies, and Humanities

Anthropology, Art, Art History, Asian Studies, Canadian Studies, Chinese Language & Literature, Classics & Classical Languages & Literature, Communications, Comparative Literature, English Language & Literature, Fine/Studio Arts, French Language & Literature, German Language & Literature, Greek Language & Literature, Hispanic Studies, History, Humanities, Italian Language & Literature, Linguistics, Medieval & Renaissance Studies, Latin American Studies, Music, Political Science, Psychology, Slavic Languages & Literature, Social Work, Sociology, Visual & Performing Arts, Women's Studies, Writing

Science and Mathematics

Astronomy, Biochemistry, Biology, Chemistry, Earth & Ocean Science, Environmental Studies, Geography, Mathematics, Oceanography, Physics, Statistics

Computer Science and Engineering

Computer & Information Sciences, Computer Engineering, Electrical/ Electronics & Communication Engineering, Mechanical Engineering, Software Engineering

Professional Studies

Child Growth/Care & Development Studies, Human Kinetics/ Kinesiology, Leisure & Recreational Activities, Pre-Education

Business and Economics

Accounting, Actuarial Science, Agricultural Business & Engineering, Aquaculture Operations & Production Management, Business Administration & Management/ Commerce, Economics, Entrepreneurship, Human Resources Management, Information Science & Systems, International Business, Labor/Personnel Relations & Studies, Management Science, Management Information Systems & Business Data Processing, Marketing Management & Research, Operations Management & Supervision, Organizational Behavior Studies, Public Relations & Organizational Communications, Sport & Fitness Administration/Management.

Health Professions and Related Sciences

Health Services Administration, Nursing

GRADUATE ADMISSIONS

Faculty of Graduate Studies
University of Victoria
P.O. Box 3025, STN CSC
Victoria, BC   V8W 3P2
PH: **250.721.7970**   FAX: **250.721.6225**
WEBSITE: **web.uvic.ca/grad/**

Fall application deadline:	Dec 15 - Feb 15
Application fee:	$50
Electronic application accepted:	N/A
Required with application:	College transcript, (GRE, GMAT, essay depending upon program)
Graduate student housing:	Various options available including family housing in 1-3 bedroom apartments

GRADUATE FINANCES

International Graduate tuition:	$3635	(US $3270)
Financial aid & Scholarships available for international students:	Yes	
Application deadline:	Feb	

GRADUATE INSTRUCTIONAL PROGRAM

Liberal Arts and Sciences, General Studies, and Humanities

Anthropology, Art History, English Language & Literature, French Language & Literature, German Language & Literature, Greek Language & Literature, History, Human & Social Development, Linguistics, Music, Political Science, Psychology, Sociology, Visual & Performing Arts

Science and Mathematics

Astronomy, Biochemistry, Biology, Chemistry, Criminal Justice Studies, Earth & Planetary Science, Geography, Geology, Mathematics, Microbiology, Oceanography, Physics, Statistics

Computer Science and Engineering

Electrical/ Electronics & Communication Engineering, Mechanical Engineering

Professional Studies

Education

Business and Economics

Business Administration & Management/Commerce, Economics, Public Administration

MAJORS INDEX

U = undergraduate degree, G = graduate degree

ACCOUNTING

Acadia University	U
Athabasca University	U
Bishop's University	U
Brock University	U, G
Cape Breton University	U
Carleton University	U
Concordia University	U, G
Dalhousie University	U
King's College	U
Kwantlen University	U
McGill University	U, G
McMaster University	U
Memorial University	U
Mount Allison University	U
Queen's University	U
Saint Francis Xavier University	U
Saint Mary's University	U
Simon Fraser University	U
Thompson Rivers University	U
Trinity Western University	U
Université de Moncton	U
Université de Montreal	U
Université de Sherbrooke	U, G
Université du Quebec	U, G
Université Laval	U
University of Alberta	U
University of British Columbia	U, G
University of Calgary	U
University of Guelph	U
University of Lethbridge	U
University of Manitoba	U
University of New Brunswick	U
University of Ontario	U
University of Ottawa	U
University of Prince Edward Island	U
University of Regina	U
University of Saskatchewan	U, G
University of Toronto	U, G
University of Victoria	U
University of Waterloo	U, G
University of Windsor	U
Wilfrid Laurier University	U
York University	U

ACTUARIAL SCIENCE

Cape Breton University	U
Concordia University	U
Luther College	U
McGill University	U
Simon Fraser University	U
University of Alberta	U
University of Calgary	U, G
University of Regina	U
University of Toronto	U
University of Victoria	U
University of Waterloo	U, G
University of Western Ontario	U

AEROSPACE, AERONAUTICAL ENGINEERING

Carleton University	U, G
Concordia University	G
McGill University	U
Ryerson University	U
Université de Montreal	G
Université de Sherbrooke	G
University of Toronto	U, G

AFRICAN STUDIES

Cape Breton University	U
Dalhousie University	U
McGill University	U
University of Calgary	U
University of Toronto	U
York University	U

AGRICULTURAL SCIENCES

Brandon University	U
Campion College	U
Cape Breton University	U
Dalhousie University	U, G
McGill University	U
Nova Scotia Agricultural College	U, G
Université de Moncton	U
Université Laval	U
University College of the Fraser Valley	U
University of Alberta	U, G
University of British Columbia	U
University of Guleph	U, G
University of Lethbridge	U
University of Manitoba	U, G
University of Moncton	U
University of Saskatchewan	U, G
University of Toronto	U

AGRICULTURAL BUSINESS & MANAGEMENT

Athabasca University	U, G
McGill University	U
Nova Scotia Agricultural College	U
University of Alberta	U, G
University of British Columbia	U, G
University of Guelph	U, G
University of Lethbridge	U
University of Manitoba	U, G
University of Saskatchewan	U, G
University of Victoria	U

AGRICULTURAL ENGINEERING

Dalhousie University	U
McGill University	U, G
Nova Scotia Agricultural College	U, G
University of British Columbia	U
University of Guleph	U, G
University of Saskatchewan	U, G

AMERICAN STUDIES

McGill University	U
Mount Allison University	U
University of New Brunswick	U, G

ANIMAL SCIENCE

Bishop's University	U
Kwantlen University College	U
McGill University	U, G
Nova Scotia Agricultural College	U
Université Sainte-Anne	U
University of British Columbia	U, G
University of Guelph	U, G
University of Manitoba	U, G
University of Prince Edward Island	U, G
University of Saskatchewan	U, G

ANTHROPOLOGY

Athabasca University	U
Bishop's University	U
Brandon University	U
Brescia College	U
Campion College	U
Carleton University	U, G
Concordia University	U, G
Concordia University College	U
Dalhousie University	U
Huron College	U
Kwantlen University	U
Lakehead University	U
Laurentian University	U
Luther College	U

Malaspina University	U
McGill University	U, G
McMaster University	U, G
Memorial University	U, G
Mount Allison University	U
Mount Royal College	U
Mount Saint Vincent University	U
Nipissing University	U
Queen's University	U
Saint Francis Xavier College	U
Saint Mary's University	U
Saint Thomas More University	U
St. Thomas University	U
Simon Fraser University	U, G
The King's University College	U
Thompson Rivers University	U
Trent University	U, G
Trinity Western University	U
Université de Montreal	U, G
Université de Moncton	U
Université Laval	U, G
University College of the Fraser Valley	U
University of Alberta	U, G
University of British Columbia	U, G
University of Calgary	U, G
University of Guelph	U
University of Lethbridge	U, G
University of Manitoba	U, G
University of New Brunswick	U, G
University of N. British Columbia	U
University of Regina	U, G
University of Saskatchewan	U, G
University of Toronto	U, G
University of Victoria	U, G
University of Waterloo	U
University of Western Ontario	U, G
University of Windsor	U
University of Winnipeg	U
Wilfrid Laurier University	U
York University	U, G

APPLIED MATHEMATICS

Carleton University	U, G
Dalhousie University	U, G
McGill University	U, G
McMaster University	U
Simon Fraser University	U
Trinity Western University	U
University of British Columbia	U, G
University of Alberta	U, G
University of British Columbia	U, G
University of Calgary	U, G

University of Guelph	U
University of Toronto	U, G
University of Waterloo	U, G
University of Western Ontario	U
York University	U

AQUACULTURE OPERATIONS

Malaspina University	U
Memorial University	U, G
University of British Columbia	U
University of Guelph	U, G

ARCHAEOLOGY

McGill University	U
McMaster University	U
Memorial University	U, G
Mount Royal College	U
Saint Thomas More University	U
St. Thomas University	U
Simon Fraser University	U, G
Université Laval	U, G
University of British Columbia	U, G
University of Calgary	U, G
University of Lethbridge	U
University of Saskatchewan	U, G
University of Toronto	U
Wilfrid Laurier University	U

ARCHITECTURE

McGill University	U, G
Ryerson University	U
Université de Montreal	U
Université Laval	U, G
University of British Columbia	U, G
University of Manitoba	U, G
University of Toronto	U, G
University of Waterloo	U, G

ART

ACAD	U
Athabasca University	U
Brandon University	U
Campion College	U
Carleton University	U, G
Concordia University	U
Dalhousie University	U
ECIAD	U
Kwantlen University	U
Luther College	U
Malaspina University	U
McGill University	U
McMaster University	U

Mount Royal College	U
Mount Saint Vincent University	U
NSCAD	U, G
OCAD	U
Queen's University	U, G
Redeemer College	U
Thompson Rivers University	U
Saint Mary's University	U
Simon Fraser University	U, G
The King's University College	U
Trinity Western University	U
Université de Montreal	U, G
Université du Quebec	U, G
University of the Fraser Valley	U
University of Alberta	U, G
University of British Columbia	U
University of Calgary	U, G
University of Guelph	U
University of King's College	U
University of Lethbridge	U
University of Manitoba	U
University of New Brunswick	U
University of N. British Columbia	U
University of Ottawa	U
University of Prince Edward Island	U
University of Regina	U
University of Saskatchewan	U, G
University of Toronto	U
University of Trinity	U
University of Victoria	U
University of Waterloo	U
University of Western Ontario	U
University of Windsor	U
University of Winnipeg	U
Wilfrid Laurier University	U
York University	U

ART HISTORY

Athabasca University	U
Campion College	U
Carleton University	U, G
Concordia University	U, G
ECIAD	U
Luther College	U
McGill University	U
McMaster University	U
Mount Allison University	U
Mount Saint Vincent University	U
Nova Scotia Agricultural College	U
OCAD	U
Queen's University	U, G
The King's University College	U

Thompson Rivers University	U
Université de Montreal	U, G
Université du Quebec	U, G
Université Laval	U, G
Université Sainte-Anne	U
University of Alberta	U
University of Calgary	U
University of Guelph	U, G
University of Lethbridge	U
University of Saskatchewan	U, G
University of Toronto	U, G
University of Victoria	U, G
University of Winnipeg	U
Wilfrid Laurier University	U
York University	U, G

ASIAN STUDIES

Concordia University	U
McGill University	U, G
Thompson Rivers University	U
Simon Fraser University	U
Université de Montreal	U
Université du Quebec	U
University of British Columbia	U, G
University of Calgary	U
University of Manitoba	U
University of Prince Edward Island	U
University of Toronto	U, G
University of Victoria	U
Wilfrid Laurier University	U
York University	U

ASTRONOMY/ASTROPHYSICS

Athabasca University	U
Brandon University	U
Campion College	U
Kwantlen University College	U
Luther College	U
Malaspina University	U
McGill University	U
McMaster University	U, G
Mount Royal College	U
Queen's University	U, G
Saint Mary's University	U
The King's University College	U
University of Alberta	U
University of British Columbia	U, G
University of Calgary	U, G
University of Manitoba	U
University of Toronto	U, G
University of Victoria	U, G

University of Western Ontario	U
York University	U

ATMOSPHERIC SCIENCES & METEOROLOGY

Dalhousie University	U
McGill University	U
Université du Quebec	U, G
University of Alberta	U
University of British Columbia	U, G
University of Toronto	U
York University	U, G

AUTOMOTIVE ENGINEERING

Kwantlen University College	U
University of Windsor	U

AVIATION & AIRWAYS SCIENCES

Concordia University	G
Mount Royal College	U
Trinity Western University	U
University College of the Fraser Valley	U
University of British Columbia	U
York University	U

BIOCHEMISTRY

Bishop's University	U
Brock University	U
Campion College	U
Carleton University	U
Concordia University	U, G
Dalhousie University	U
Laurentian University	U
Luther College	U
McGill University	U, G
McMaster University	U, G
Memorial University	U, G
Mount Allison University	U
Mount Royal College	U
Queen's University	U, G
Simon Fraser University	U
Trent University	U, G
Université de Moncton	U, G
Université de Montreal	U, G
Université de Sherbrooke	U, G
Université du Quebec	U
Université Laval	U
Université Sainte-Anne	U
University of Alberta	U, G
University of British Columbia	U, G
University of Calgary	U, G
University of Guelph	U, G
University of King's College	U

University of Lethbridge	U, G
University of Manitoba	U, G
University of New Brunswick	U
University of Ottawa	U, G
University of Regina	U
University of Saskatchewan	U, G
University of Toronto	U, G
University of Victoria	U, G
University of Western Ontario	U, G
University of Windsor	U, G
University of Winnipeg	U
University of Waterloo	U
Wilfrid Laurier University	U

BIOENGINEERING & BIOMEDICAL ENGINEERING

Dalhousie University	U, G
McGill University	U, G
Nova Scotia Agricultural College	U
Université de Montreal	U, G
University of Alberta	U, G
University of British Columbia	U, G
University of Calgary	U, G
University of Guelph	U, G
University of Manitoba	U, G
University of Toronto	U, G
University of Saskatchewan	U, G
University of Western Ontario	U, G

BIOLOGICAL/LIFE SCIENCES

Athabasca University	U
Brock University	U, G
Carleton University	U
Concordia University	U, G
Dalhousie University	U, G
McGill University	U
Memorial University	U, G
Nova Scotia Agricultural College	U
NSCAD	U
Simon Fraser University	U
Trinity Western University	U
Université de Montreal	U, G
Université du Quebec	U, G
University of the Fraser Valley	U
University of Alberta	U, G
University of British Columbia	U, G
University of Calgary	U, G
University of Guelph	U, G
University of Lethbridge	U, G
University of Toronto	U, G
University of Saskatchewan	U, G
University of Waterloo	U

University of Windsor	U, G
University of Western Ontario	U, G
Wilfrid Laurier University	U
York University	U

BIOLOGY

Acadia University	U, G
Athabasca University	U
Bishop's University	U
Brock University	U
Campion College	U
Cape Breton University	U
Carleton University	U, G
Concordia University	U, G
Concordia University College	U
Dalhousie University	U
Kwantlen University	U
Lakehead University	U, G
Laurentian University	U, G
Luther College	U
Malaspina University	U
McGill University	U, G
McMaster University	U, G
Memorial University	U, G
Mount Allison University	U, G
Mount Royal College	U
Mount Saint Vincent University	U
Nipissing University	U
Nova Scotia Agricultural College	U
OCAD	U
Queen's University	U, G
Redeemer College	U
Ryerson University	U
Saint Francis Xavier College	U, G
Saint Mary's University	U
The King's University	U
Thompson Rivers University	U
Trent University	U, G
Trinity Western University	U
Université de Moncton	U, G
Université de Montreal	U
Université de Sherbrooke	U, G
Université du Quebec	U
Université Laval	U
University College of the Fraser Valley	U
University of Alberta	U, G
University of British Columbia	U, G
University of Calgary	U, G
University of Guelph	U
University of King's College	U

University of Lethbridge	U
University of Manitoba	U
University of New Brunswick	U, G
University of N. British Columbia	U, G
University of Ontario	U
University of Ottawa	U, G
University of Prince Edward Island	U
University of Regina	U, G
University of Saskatchewan	U, G
University of Toronto	U, G
University of Trinity	U
University of Victoria	U, G
University of Waterloo	U, G
University of Western Ontario	U
University of Windsor	U
University of Winnipeg	U
Wilfrid Laurier University	U
York University	U, G

BIOPHYSICS

Bishop's University	U
Carleton University	U
Dalhousie University	U, G
McGill University	U
Mount Royal College	U
University of British Columbia	U
University of Calgary	U
University of Guelph	U, G
University of Toronto	U
University of Western Ontario	U
York University	U

BIOTECHNOLOGY

Brock University	U, G
Carleton University	U
Dalhousie University	U, G
McGill University	U
St. Thomas University	U
Université de Sherbrooke	U
Université du Quebec	U, G
Université Laval	U
University of Alberta	U
University of British Columbia	U
University of Calgary	U
University of Guelph	U
University of Ontario	U
University of Toronto	U
University of Saskatchewan	U, G
University of Waterloo	U
York University	U
Wilfrid Laurier University	U

BOTANY

Brandon University	U
Laurentian University	G
McGill University	U
Nova Scotia Agricultural College	U
Université Laval	G
University of British Columbia	U, G
University of Calgary	U
University of Guelph	U, G
University of Lethbridge	U
University of Manitoba	U, G
University of Toronto	U, G
University of Saskatchewan	U, G
University of Western Ontario	U

BUSINESS ADMINISTRATION & MANAGEMENT

Acadia University	U
Athabasca University	U, G
Bishop's University	U
Brandon University	U
Brescia College	U
Brock University	U
Campion College	U
Cape Breton University	U, G
Carleton University	U, G
Concordia University	U
Concordia University College	U
Dalhousie University	U, G
Huron College	U
King's College	U
Kwantlen University College	U
Lakehead University	U
Laurentian University	U, G
Malaspina University	U
McGill University	U
McMaster University	U
Memorial University	U, G
Mount Allison University	U
Mount Royal College	U
Mount Saint Vincent College	U
Nipissing University	U
Nova Scotia Agricultural College	U
Queen's University	U, G
Redeemer College	U
Ryerson University	U
Saint Francis Xavier University	U
Saint Mary's University	U, G
Simon Fraser University	U, G
St. Thomas University	U
The King's University College	U
Thompson Rivers University	U

Trent University	U
Trinity Western University	U
Université de Moncton	U, G
Université de Montreal	U
Université de Sherbrooke	U, G
Université du Quebec	U, G
Université Laval	U, G
Université Sainte-Anne	U
University of the Fraser Valley	U
University of Alberta	U, G
University of British Columbia	U
University of Calgary	U, G
University of Guelph	U, G
University of King's College	U
University of Lethbridge	U
University of Manitoba	U, G
University of New Brunswick	U, G
University of N. British Columbia	U
University of Ontario	U
University of Ottawa	U, G
University of Prince Edward Island	U
University of Regina	U
University of Saskatchewan	U, G
University of Toronto	U, G
University of Victoria	U, G
University of Waterloo	U
University of Western Ontario	U, G
University of Windsor	U, G
University of Winnipeg	U
Wilfrid Laurier University	U, G
York University	U, G

CANADIAN STUDIES

Acadia University	U
Brandon University	U
Brock University	U
Carleton University	U, G
Concordia University	U
Dalhousie University	U
Lakehead University	U, G
McGill University	U
Memorial University	U
Mount Allison University	U
Mount Royal College	U
Mount Saint Vincent College	U
Queen's University	U
Saint Mary's University	U, G
Simon Fraser University	U
Thompson Rivers University	U
Trent University	U, G
Trinity Western University	U

Université de Sherbrooke	U, G
Université Sainte-Anne	U
University of British Columbia	U
University of Calgary	U
University of Guelph	U
University of Lethbridge	U
University of Manitoba	U
University of Ottawa	U, G
University of Prince Edward Island	U
University of Regina	U, G
University of Toronto	U, G
University of Victoria	U
University of Waterloo	U
University of Windsor	U
University of Winnipeg	U
Wilfrid Laurier University	U
York University	U

CELTIC/IRISH STUDIES

St. Francis Xavier University	U, G
Saint Mary's University	U
Trinity Western University	U
University College of Cape Breton	U
University of St. Michael's College	U
University of Toronto	U

CERAMIC ARTS & CERAMICS

ACAD	U
NSCAD	U, G
OCAD	U
Thompson Rivers University	U
Université de Moncton	U
University of Lethbridge	U
University of Toronto	U

CHEMICAL ENGINEERING

Dalhousie University	U, G
Lakehead University	U
McGill University	U, G
McMaster University	U
Nova Scotia Agricultural College	U
Queen's University	U, G
Ryerson University	U, G
Université de Montreal	U, G
Université de Sherbrooke	G
Université Laval	U, G
University of Alberta	U, G
University of British Columbia	U, G
University of Calgary	U, G
University of New Brunswick	U, G
University of Ottawa	U, G
University of Saskatchewan	U, G

University of Toronto	U, G
University of Waterloo	U, G
University of Western Ontario	U

CHEMISTRY

Acadia University	U, G
Athabasca University	U
Bishop's University	U
Brandon University	U
Brescia College	U
Brock University	U, G
Campion College	U
Cape Breton University	U
Carleton University	U, G
Concordia University	U
Concordia University College	U
Dalhousie University	U, G
Kwantlen University	U
Lakehead University	U, G
Laurentian University	U, G
Luther College	U
Malaspina University	U
McGill University	U, G
McMaster University	U, G
Memorial University	U, G
Mount Allison University	U, G
Mount Royal College	U
Mount Saint Vincent College	U
Nipissing University	U
Queen's University	U, G
Redeemer College	U
Ryerson University	U
Saint Francis Xavier College	U, G
Simon Fraser University	U
The King's University College	U
Thompson Rivers University	U
Trent University	U, G
Trinity Western University	U
Université de Moncton	U, G
Université de Montreal	U, G
Université de Sherbrooke	U, G
Université du Quebec	U, G
Université Laval	U, G
University College of the Fraser Valley	U
University of Alberta	U, G
University of British Columbia	U, G
University of Calgary	U, G
University of Guelph	U, G
University of King's College	U
University of Lethbridge	U, G
University of Manitoba	U, G
University of New Brunswick	U

University of N. British Columbia	U, G
University of Ontario	U
University of Ottawa	U, G
University of Prince Edward Island	U
University of Regina	U, G
University of Saskatchewan	U, G
University of Toronto	U, G
University of Victoria	U, G
University of Waterloo	U, G
University of Western Ontario	U, G
University of Windsor	U, G
University of Winnipeg	U
Wilfrid Laurier University	U
York University	U, G

CHILD GROWTH, CARE & DEVELOPMENT STUDIES

Brock University	U, G
Carleton University	U
King's College	U
Malaspina University College	U
Mount Royal College	U
Mount Saint Vincent University	U, G
Ryerson University	U
Université de Montreal	U
Université de Sherbrooke	U
Université du Quebec	U
Université Laval	U, G
University of Guelph	U
University of Toronto	U
University of Victoria	U
University of Western Ontario	U

CHINESE LANGUAGE & LITERATURE

Campion College	U
Kwantlen University College	U
Malaspina University College	U
Mount Royal College	U
University of Alberta	U
University of British Columbia	U, G
University of Calgary	U
University of Toronto	U
University of Victoria	U, G

CITY/URBAN, COMMUNITY/REGIONAL PLANNING

Brandon University	U, G
Dalhousie University	G
McGill University	U
Ryerson University	U
Queen's University	U
Trent University	U
Université Laval	U
University of British Columbia	U

University of Calgary	U
University of Guelph	U
University of Manitoba	U
University of Toronto	U
University of Waterloo	U

CIVIL ENGINEERING

Cape Breton University	U
Carleton University	U, G
Concordia University	U
Dalhousie University	U, G
Lakehead University	U
McGill University	U, G
McMaster University	U
Memorial University	U, G
Nova Scotia Agricultural College	U
Queen's University	U, G
Ryerson Institute	U, G
Université de Moncton	U, G
Université de Montreal	U, G
Université de Sherbrooke	G
Université du Quebec	U, G
Université Laval	U, G
University of Alberta	U, G
University of British Columbia	U, G
University of Calgary	U, G
University of Manitoba	U, G
University of New Brunswick	U, G
University of Ottawa	U, G
University of Prince Edward Island	U
University of Regina	U
University of Saskatchewan	U, G
University of Toronto	U, G
University of Waterloo	U, G
University of Western Ontario	U
University of Windsor	U, G

CLASSICS & CLASSICAL LANGUAGES

Acadia University	U
Bishop's University	U
Brandon University	U, G
Brock University	U
Campion College	U
Carleton University	U
Concordia University	U
Dalhousie University	U, G
Huron College	U
Laurentian University	U
Malaspina University College	U
McGill University	U, G
McMaster University	U, G
Memorial University	U, G

Mount Allison University	U
Mount Royal College	U
Nipissing University	U
Queen's University	U, G
Redeemer College	U
Saint Mary's University	U
Saint Thomas More University	U
Trent University	U
Université de Montreal	U, G
University of Alberta	U, G
University of British Columbia	U
University of Calgary	U
University of Guelph	U
University of King's College	U
University of Lethbridge	U
University of Manitoba	U, G
University of New Brunswick	U, G
University of N. British Columbia	U
University of Ottawa	U, G
University of Prince Edward Island	U
University of Regina	U
University of Saskatchewan	U, G
University of Toronto	U, G
University of Victoria	U
University of Waterloo	U
University of Western Ontario	U, G
University of Windsor	U
University of Winnipeg	U
Wilfrid Laurier University	U
York University	U

CLOTHING & TEXTILES

University of Alberta	U, G
University of Manitoba	U, G
University of Prince Edward Island	U

COMMUNICATIONS

Athabasca University	U
Brock University	U
Cape Breton University	U
Carleton University	U, G
Concordia University	U, G
ECIAD	U
McGill University	U, G
McMaster University	U
Mount Royal College	U
NSCAD	U
Queen's University	U
Ryerson University	G
Simon Fraser University	U, G
Trinity Western University	U
Université de Moncton	U

Université de Montreal	U, G
Université de Sherbrooke	U
Université du Quebec	U
Université Laval	U
University of Calgary	U, G
University of Guelph	U
University of Lethbridge	U
University of Ottawa	U
University of Toronto	U
University of Victoria	U
University of Western Ontario	U, G
University of Windsor	U
University of Winnipeg	U
Wilfrid Laurier University	U
York University	U, G

COMPARATIVE LITERATURE

Brock University	U
Carleton University	U, G
McGill University	U
McMaster University	U
Mount Royal College	U
Université de Montreal	U
University of Alberta	U, G
University of British Columbia	U
University of Calgary	U
University of Lethbridge	U
University of Ottawa	U
University of Toronto	U, G
University of Victoria	U
University of Western Ontario	U, G
Wilfrid Laurier University	U, G
York University	U

COMPUTER & INFORMATION SCIENCES

Acadia University	U, G
Athabasca University	U, G
Bishop's University	U
Brandon University	U
Brock University	U
Campion College	U
Cape Breton University	U
Carleton University	U, G
Concordia University	U, G
Concordia University College	U
Dalhousie University	U
King's College	U
Kwantlen University College	U
Lakehead University	U
Laurentian University	U
Luther College	U
Malaspina University	U

McGill University	U, G
McMaster University	U, G
Memorial University	U, G
Mount Allison University	U
Mount Royal College	U
Nipissing University	U
Queen's University	U, G
Redeemer College	U
Ryerson University	U
Saint Francis Xavier College	U
Saint Mary's University	U
Simon Fraser University	U, G
The King's University College	U
Thompson Rivers University	U
Trent University	U, G
Trinity Western University	U
Université de Moncton	U, G
Université de Montreal	U, G
Université de Sherbrooke	U
Université du Quebec	U, G
Université Laval	U, G
University College of the Fraser Valley	U
University of Alberta	U, G
University of British Columbia	U
University of Calgary	U, G
University of Guelph	U, G
University of King's College	U
University of Lethbridge	U, G
University of Manitoba	U, G
University of New Brunswick	U, G
University of N. British Columbia	U, G
University of Ontario	U
University of Ottawa	U, G
University of Prince Edward Island	U
University of Regina	U, G
University of Saskatchewan	U, G
University of Toronto	U, G
University of Trinity	U
University of Victoria	U, G
University of Waterloo	U, G
University of Western Ontario	U, G
University of Windsor	U, G
University of Winnipeg	U
Wilfrid Laurier University	U
York University	U, G

COMPUTER ENGINEERING

Carleton University	U
Concordia University	U, G
Dalhousie University	U, G
Kwantlen University	U
McGill University	U

McMaster University   U, G
Queen's University   U, G
Ryerson University   U
Simon Fraser University   U
Université de Montreal   U
Université du Quebec   U, G
Université Laval   U, G
University of Alberta   U, G
University of British Columbia U
University of Calgary   G
University of Guelph   U
University of Manitoba   U, G
University of New Brunswick U
University of Ottawa   U
University of Saskatchewan   U
University of Toronto'   U, G
University of Victoria   U
University of Waterloo   U, G
University of Western Ontario U
York University

COUNSELING

Athabasca University   U, G
Bishop's University   U
Brandon University   U
McGill University   U, G
Memorial University   G
Mount Saint Vincent University G
Trinity Western University   G
Université de Montreal   U, G
Université de Sherbrooke   U, G
Université du Quebec   U, G
Université Laval   U, G
University of British Columbia U, G
University of Toronto   U, G
University of Winnipeg   U, G

CRIMINAL JUSTICE STUDIES

Athabasca University   U
Brock University   U
Campion College   U
Carleton University   U
Kwantlen University College U
Laurentian University   U
Luther College   U
Malaspina University   U
McGill University   U
Mount Royal College   U
Nipissing University   U
Queen's University   U, G
Ryerson University   U
Saint Mary's University   U

Simon Fraser University   U, G
St. Thomas University   U
Université de Montreal   U, G
University College of the Fraser Valley U
University of British Columbia   U
University of Calgary   U
University of Guelph   U
University of Ottawa   U, G
University of Prince Edward Island   U
University of Regina   U
University of Toronto   U, G
University of Trinity College   U
University of Victoria   U, G
University of Winnipeg   U
York University   U

DANCE

Corcordia University   U
University of Calgary   U, G
University of Western Ontario U
University of Winnipeg   U
York University   U, G

DENTAL HYGIENE

University of Alberta   U
University of British Columbia U
University of Toronto   U

DENTISTRY

Dalhousie University   G
McGill University   G
Université de Montreal   G
Université Laval   G
University of Alberta   G
University of British Columbia G
University of Manitoba   G
University of Toronto   G
University of Western Ontario G

DESIGN & APPLIED ARTS

ACAD   U
Concordia University   U
ECIAD   U
Mount Royal College   U
NSCAD   U
OCAD   U
Thompson Rivers University   U
Université de Montreal   U
Université du Quebec   U
University of Alberta   U
University of Lethbridge   U
University of Ottawa   U
York University   U, G

DIVINITY/MINISTRY

Concordia University	U, G
Huron College	U, G
Trinity Western University	G
University of Ottawa	G
University of Toronto	U
University of Trinity College	G
University of Winnipeg	G
Wilfrid Laurier University	G

DRAMA/THEATER ARTS

Acadia University	U
ACAD	U
Bishop's University	U
Brandon University	U
Brock University	U
Concordia University	U, G
Dalhousie University	U
Laurentian University	U
McMaster University	U
Memorial University	U
Mount Allison University	U
Mount Royal College	U
Mount Saint Vincent College	U
Queen's University	U
Redeemer College	U
Ryerson University	U
The King's University College	U
Thompson Rivers University	U
Trinity Western University	U
Université de Moncton	U
Université du Quebec	U, G
Université Laval	U
Université Sainte-Anne	U
University of Alberta	U, G
University of British Columbia	U
University of Calgary	U, G
University of Guelph	U, G
University of King's College	U
University of Lethbridge	U, G
University of Manitoba	U
University of Ottawa	U
University of Regina	U
University of Prince Edward Island	U
University of Saskatchewan	U, G
University of Toronto	U, G
University of Victoria	U, G
University of Waterloo	U
University of Windsor	U
University of Winnipeg	U
Wilfrid Laurier University	U
York University	U

EARTH & PLANETARY SCIENCES

Brock University	U, G
Carleton University	U
Dalhousie University	U, G
Laurentian University	U
McGill University	U, G
McMaster University	U
Memorial University	U, G
Simon Fraser University	U
University of Alberta	U, G
University of Guelph	U
University of King's College	U
University of Ottawa	U, G
University of Toronto	U, G
University of Victoria	U, G
University of Waterloo	U, G
University of Western Ontario	U
University of Windsor	U, G
York University	U, G

EAST ASIAN STUDIES

McGill University	U, G
University of Alberta	U, G
University of Calgary	U, G
University of Toronto	U, G
University of Waterloo	U
York University	U

ECOLOGY

Concordia University	U
McGill University	U
Nova Scotia Agricultural College	U
Thompson Rivers University	U
Université de Montreal	U
Université de Sherbrooke	U
Université du Quebec	U
University of Alberta	U, G
University of British Columbia	U
University of Calgary	U
University of Guelph	U
University of Lethbridge	U
University of Manitoba	U
University of Waterloo	U
University of Western Ontario	U

ECONOMICS

Acadia University	U
Athabasca University	U
Bishop's University	U
Brandon University	U
Brescia College	U
Brock University	U

Cape Breton University	U
Carleton University	U, G
Concordia University	U, G
Concordia University College	U
Dalhousie University	U, G
King's College	U
Kwantlen University College	U
Lakehead University	U, G
Laurentian University	U
Luther College	U
Malaspina University	U
McGill University	U, G
McMaster University	U
Memorial University	U, G
Mount Allison University	U
Mount Royal College	U
Mount Saint Vincent University	U
Nipissing University	U
Queen's University	U, G
Redeemer College	U
Ryerson University	U
Saint Francis Xavier College	U
Saint Mary's University	U
Saint Thomas More University	U
St. Thomas University	U
Simon Fraser University	U
The King's University College	U
Thompson Rivers University	U
Trent University	U, G
Trinity Western University	U
Université de Moncton	U, G
Université de Montreal	U, G
Université de Sherbrooke	U, G
Université du Quebec	U, G
Université Laval	U, G
University College of the Fraser Valley	U
University of Alberta	U, G
University of British Columbia	U, G
University of Calgary	U, G
University of Guelph	U, G
University of King's College	U
University of Lethbridge	U
University of Manitoba	U, G
University of New Brunswick	U, G
University of N. British Columbia	U
University of Ottawa	U, G
University of Prince Edward Island	U
University of Regina	U, G
University of Saskatchewan	U, G
University of Toronto	U, G
University of Victoria	U, G

University of Waterloo	U, G
University of Western Ontario	U, G
University of Windsor	U, G
University of Winnipeg	U
Wilfrid Laurier University	U
York University	U, G

EDUCATION

Acadia University	U, G
Athabasca University	U, G
Bishop's University	U
Brandon University	U, G
Brock University	U, G
Cape Breton University	U, G
Concordia University	U, G
Concordia University College	U
Lakehead University	U, G
Laurentian University	U
Luther College	U
Malaspina University	U
McGill University	U, G
McMaster University	U, G
Memorial University	U, G
Mount Allison University	U
Mount Royal College	U
Mount Saint Vincent University	U, G
Nipissing University	U, G
Queen's University	U, G
Redeemer College	U
Saint Francis Xavier College	U, G
Simon Fraser University	U, G
St. Thomas University	U
The King's University College	U
Thompson Rivers University	U
Trent University	U
Trinity Western University	U
Université de Montreal	U, G
Université de Sherbrooke	U, G
Université du Quebec	U, G
Université Laval	U, G
Université Sainte-Anne	U
University College of the Fraser Valley	U
University of Alberta	U, G
University of British Columbia	U, G
University of Calgary	U, G
University of Lethbridge	U, G
University of Manitoba	U, G
University of New Brunswick	U, G
University of Ontario	U
University of Ottawa	U, G
University of Prince Edward Island	U

University of Regina	U, G
University of Saskatchewan	U, G
University of Toronto	U, G
University of Victoria	U, G
University of Western Ontario	U, G
University of Windsor	U, G
University of Winnipeg	U
Wilfrid Laurier University	U
York University	U, G

ELECTRICAL/ELECTRONICS & COMM. ENGINEERING

Cape Breton University	U
Carleton University	U, G
Concordia University	U, G
Dalhousie University	U, G
Kwantlen University College	U
Lakehead University	U
Laurentian University	U
McGill University	U, G
McMaster University	U, G
Memorial University	U, G
Nova Scotia Agricultural College	U
Queen's University	U, G
Ryerson University	U, G
Simon Fraser University	U
Université de Moncton	U
Université de Montreal	U, G
Université de Sherbrooke	G
Université du Quebec	U, G
Université Laval	U, G
University of Alberta	U, G
University of British Columbia	U, G
University of Calgary	U, G
University of Manitoba	U, G
University of New Brunswick	U
University of Ontario	U
University of Ottawa	U, G
University of Regina	U
University of Saskatchewan	U, G
University of Toronto	U, G
University of Victoria	U, G
University of Waterloo	U, G
University of Western Ontario	U
University of Windsor	U, G
York University	U

ENGINEERING PHYSICS

Carleton University	U
Concordia University	G
McGill University	U
McMaster University	U, G

Queen's University	U, G
Simon Fraser University	U
University of Alberta	U
University of British Columbia	U
University of Toronto	U, G

ENGINEERING SCIENCES

Acadia University	U
Carleton University	U
Concordia University	U, G
Dalhousie University	U
Lakehead University	U, G
Laurentian University	U
Malaspina University	U
McGill University	U
McMaster University	U
Memorial University	U, G
Mount Royal College	U
Queen's University	U, G
Saint Francis Xavier University	U
Saint Mary's University	U
Simon Fraser University	U, G
Trinity Western University	U
Université de Moncton	U, G
Université de Montreal	U
Université de Sherbrooke	G
University of Alberta	U, G
University of Guelph	U
University of New Brunswick	U, G
University of Ottawa	U
University of Prince Edward Island	U
University of Regina	U, G
University of Toronto	U, G
University of Waterloo	U, G
University of Western Ontario	U, G
University of Windsor	U
University of Winnipeg	U
York University	U

ENGLISH LANGUAGE & LITERATURE

Acadia University	U, G
Athabasca University	U
Bishop's University	U
Brandon University	U
Brescia College	U
Brock University	U
Campion College	U
Cape Breton University	U
Carleton University	U, G
Concordia University	U, G
Concordia University College of Alberta	U

Dalhousie University	U, G
Huron College	U
King's College	U
Kwantlen University College	U
Lakehead University	U, G
Laurentian University	U, G
Luther College	U
Malaspina University	U
McGill University	U, G
McMaster University	U, G
Memorial University	U, G
Mount Allison University	U
Mount Royal College	U
Mount Saint Vincent College	U
Nipissing University	U
Queen's University	U, G
Redeemer College	U
Saint Francis Xavier College	U
Saint Jerome's University	U
Saint Mary's University	U
Saint Thomas More University	U
Simon Fraser University	U, G
St. Thomas University	U
The King's University	U
Thompson Rivers University	U
Trent University	U, G
Trinity Western University	U
Université de Moncton	U
Université de Montreal	U, G
Université de Sherbrooke	U
Université du Quebec	U
Université Laval	U, G
Université Sainte-Anne	U
University College of the Fraser Valley	U
University of Alberta	U, G
University of British Columbia	U, G
University of Calgary	U, G
University of Guelph	U
University of King's College	U
University of Lethbridge	U
University of Manitoba	U, G
University of New Brunswick	U, G
University of Northern British Columbia	U
University of Ottawa	U, G
University of Prince Edward Island	U
University of Regina	U, G
University of Saskatchewan	U, G
University of Toronto	U, G
University of Victoria	U, G
University of Waterloo	U, G

University of Western Ontario	U, G
University of Windsor	U, G
University of Winnipeg	U
Wilfrid Laurier University	U, G
York University	U, G

ENTOMOLOGY

McGill University	U
Trent University	U
University of British Columbia	U, G
University of Calgary	U
University of Manitoba	U
University of Toronto	U, G
University of Waterloo	U

ENTREPRENEURSHIP

Athabasca University	U
Brandon University	U
Brock University	U
Kwantlen University College	U
McGill University	U
Memorial University	U
Mount Royal College	U
Saint Mary's University	U
Université de Montreal	U
Université du Quebec	G
University of Alberta	U
University of British Columbia	U
University of Calgary	U
University of Manitoba	U
University of Ottawa	U
University of Toronto	U, G
University of Victoria	U
York University	U

ENVIRONMENTAL HEALTH ENGINEERING

Brock University	U
Cape Breton University	U
Carleton University	U, G
Concordia University College	U
Dalhousie University	U
McGill University	U
Redeemer College	U
Ryerson University	U
University of Alberta	G
University of Calgary	U
University of Guelph	U, G
University of Ottawa	U
University of Regina	U
University of Toronto	U, G

University of Waterloo	U
University of Western Ontario	U
York University	U

ENVIRONMENTAL HEALTH

Université de Montreal	G
University of British Columbia	U
University of Toronto	U, G
York University	U

ENVIRONMENTAL SCIENCES

Acadia University	U
Athabasca University	U
Brock University	U
Cape Breton University	U
Carleton University	U, G
Concordia University	U
Concordia University College	U
Dalhousie University	U, G
Lakehead University	U
Laurentian University	U
McGill University	U
McMaster University	U
Memorial University	U, G
Mount Allison University	U
Nipissing University	U
Nova Scotia Agricultural College	U, G
NSCAD	U
Queen's University	U
Redeemer College	U
Saint Mary's University	U
Simon Fraser University	U, G
The King's University College	U
Thompson Rivers University	U
Trent University	U, G
Trinity Western University	U
Université de Moncton	U, G
University of Alberta	U
University of Calgary	U, G
University of Guelph	U, G
University of Lethbridge	U
University of Manitoba	U
University of New Brunswick	U
University of N. British Columbia	U, G
University of Toronto	U, G
University of Victoria	U
University of Waterloo	U, G
University of Western Ontario	U, G
University of Windsor	U
University of Winnipeg	U
York University	U, G

EUROPEAN STUDIES

Carleton University	U, G
Simon Fraser University	U
University of Alberta	U
University of British Columbia	U, G
University of Guelph	U
University of Toronto	U

FAMILY & COMMUNITY STUDIES

Brescia University	U
King's College	U
Malaspina University College	U
Mount Royal College	U
Mount Saint Vincent University	U
Nova Scotia Agricultural College	U
Queen's University	U
St. Jerome's University	U
Université de Moncton	U, G
University of Alberta	U
University of British Columbia	U, G
University of Guelph	U, G
University of Manitoba	U, G
University of N. British Columbia	U
University of Toronto	U, G
University of Western Ontario	U

FASHION

Dalhousie University	U
Kwantlen University College	U
Ryerson University	U
Université du Quebec	U
University of British Columbia	U
University College of the Fraser Valley	U

FILM/CINEMA

Carleton University	U, G
Concordia University	U, G
Dalhousie University	U
ECIAD	U
Huron College	U
Luther College	U
Malaspina University	U
Queen's University	U
Ryerson University	U
Saint Mary's University	U
Université de Montreal	U, G
Université de Sherbrooke	U
Université du Quebec	U
Université Laval	U
University of Alberta	U, G

University of British Columbia	U, G
University of Calgary	U
University of Guelph	U
University of Manitoba	U
University of Regina	U
University of Toronto	U
University of Western Ontario	U
York University	U, G

FINANCE

Acadia University	U
Athabasca University	U
Bishop's University	U
Brock University	U
Cape Breton University	U
Carleton University	U
Concordia University	U
King's College	U
Lakehead University	U
Malaspina University College	U
McGill University	U, G
McMaster University	U
Memorial University	U
Queen's University	U
Saint Mary's University	U
Simon Fraser University	U
Thompson Rivers University	U
Université de Moncton	U
Université de Montreal	U
Université de Sherbrooke	U
Université du Quebec	U
University of Alberta	U, G
University of British Columbia	U, G
University of Guelph	U
University of Lethbridge	U
University of New Brunswick	U
University of Toronto	U, G
University of Windsor	U
Wilfrid Laurier University	U
York University	U

FINE/STUDIO ARTS

ACAD	U
Bishop's University	U
Brescia College	U
Concordia University	U, G
ECIAD	U
Kwantlen University College	U
McGill University	U
McMaster University	U

Memorial University	U
Mount Allison University	U
NSCAD	U
OCAD	U
Queen's University	U
Thompson Rivers University	U
Trinity Western University	U
University of British Columbia	U
University of Calgary	U, G
University of Guelph	U
University of Lethbridge	U, G
University of Manitoba	U
University of New Brunswick	U
University of Ottawa	U
University of Prince Edward Island	U
University of Toronto	U
University of Victoria	U
University of Waterloo	U, G
Wilfrid Laurier University	U
York University	U

FISHING & FISHERIES SCIENCES & MANAGEMENT

Malaspina University College	U
Nova Scotia Agricultural College	U
University of Guelph	U, G
University of British Columbia	U
University of N. British Columbia	U
University of Prince Edward Island	U, G

FOOD SCIENCES & TECHNOLOGY

Brescia College	U
Dalhousie University	U, G
McGill University	U, G
Memorial University	G
Ryerson University	U
Université de Moncton	U
University of Alberta	U, G
University of British Columbia	U, G
University of Guelph	U, G
University of Manitoba	U, G
University of Saskatchewan	U, G

FORENSICS

| Trent University | U |
| University of Ontario | U |

FORESTRY SCIENCES

Brandon University	U
Lakehead University	G
Malaspina University	U
NSAC	U

Thompson Rivers University	U
Université de Moncton	U, G
Université du Quebec	U, G
Université Laval	U, G
University of Alberta	U
University of British Columbia	U, G
University of Guelph	U, G
University of New Brunswick	U, G
University of N. British Columbia	U, G
University of Toronto	U, G

FRENCH LANGUAGE & LITERATURE

Acadia University	U
Athabasca University	U, G
Bishop's University	U
Brandon University	U, G
Brescia College	U
Brock University	U
Campion College	U
Carleton University	U, G
Concordia University	U, G
Concordia University College	U
Dalhousie University	U, G
Huron College	U
King's College	U
Kwantlen University	U
Laurentian University	U
Luther College	U
Malaspina University	U
McGill University	U, G
McMaster University	U, G
Memorial University	U, G
Mount Allison University	U
Mount Royal College	U
Nipissing University	U
Queen's University	U, G
Redeemer College	U
Saint Francis Xavier College	U
Saint Mary's University	U
Simon Fraser University	U, G
St. Jerome's University	U
St. Thomas University	U
Trent University	U
Trinity Western University	U
Université de Moncton	U, G
Université de Montreal	U, G
Université de Sherbrooke	U, G
Université du Quebec	U
Université Laval	U, G
Université Sainte-Anne	U
University of Alberta	U

University of British Columbia	U, G
University of Calgary	U, G
University of Guelph	U
University of King's College	U
University of Lethbridge	U, G
University of Manitoba	U, G
University of New Brunswick	U, G
University of Ottawa	U, G
University of Regina	U, G
University of Toronto	U, G
University of Victoria	U, G
University of Waterloo	U, G
University of Western Ontario	U, G
University of Windsor	U
University of Winnipeg	U
Wilfrid Laurier University	U
York University	U, G

GENETICS

Malaspina University College	U
McGill University	U
Nova Scotia Agricultural College	U
Thompson Rivers University	U
University of Alberta	G
University of British Columbia	G
University of Guelph	U, G
University of Manitoba	G
University of Toronto	G
University of Saskatchewan	U
University of Western Ontario	U

GEOGRAPHY

Athabasca University	U
Bishop's University	U
Brandon University	U, G
Brescia College	U
Brock University	U
Campion College	U
Carleton University	U, G
Concordia University	U
Huron College	U
King's College	U
Kwantlen University	U
Lakehead University	U
Laurentian University	U
Luther College	U
Malaspina University College	U
McGill University	U, G
McMaster University	U, G
Memorial University	U, G
Mount Royal College	U

Nipissing University	U
Queen's University	U, G
Redeemer College	U
Ryerson University	U
Saint Mary's University	U
Simon Fraser University	U, G
The King's University College	U
Thompson Rivers University	U
Trent University	U, G
Trinity Western University	U
Université de Moncton	U
Université de Montreal	U, G
Université de Sherbrooke	U
Université du Quebec	U, G
Université Laval	U, G
University College of the Fraser Valley	U
University of Alberta	U
University of British Columbia	U, G
University of Calgary	U, G
University of Guelph	U, G
University of Lethbridge	U, G
University of Manitoba	U, G
University of N. British Columbia	U, G
University of Ottawa	U, G
University of Regina	U, G
University of Saskatchewan	U, G
University of Toronto	U, G
University of Victoria	U, G
University of Waterloo	U, G
University of Western Ontario	U, G
University of Windsor	U
University of Winnipeg	U
Wilfrid Laurier University	U, G
York University	U, G

GEOLOGICAL ENGINEERING

Concordia University	G
Laurentian University	G
McMaster University	U
Queen's University	U, G
Université de Montreal	U
Université du Quebec	U
Université Laval	U
University of British Columbia	U, G
University of Calgary	U, G
University of Manitoba	U, G
University of New Brunswick	U, G
University of Saskatchewan	G
University of Waterloo	U
York University	U

GEOLOGY

Acadia University	U, G
Athabasca University	U
Brandon University	U, G
Cape Breton University	U
Carleton University	U
Kwantlen University College	U
Lakehead University	U, G
Laurentian University	U, G
Luther College	U
Malaspina University	U
McGill University	U
McMaster University	U, G
Memorial University	G
Mount Royal College	U
Nipissing University	U
Queen's University	U
Saint Frances Xavier University	U, G
Thompson Rivers University	U
Université du Quebec	U
University of Alberta	U, G
University of British Columbia	U, G
University of Calgary	U, G
University of Guelph	U
University of Lethbridge	U
University of Manitoba	U, G
University of New Brunswick	U, G
University of Ottawa	U
University of Regina	U, G
University of Toronto	U, G
University of Victoria	U, G
University of Waterloo	U
University of Western Ontario	U, G
University of Windsor	U

GEOPHYSICS & SEISMOLOGY

Carleton University	U
Kwantlen University College	U
McGill University	U
McMaster University	U
Memorial University	G
Queen's University	U
University of Alberta	U
University of British Columbia	U, G
University of Calgary	U, G
University of Guelph	U
University of New Brunswick	U, G
University of Western Ontario	G

GERMAN LANGUAGE & LITERATURE

Acadia University	U
Athabasca University	U
Bishop's University	U
Brandon University	U, G
Brescia College	U
Brock University	U
Campion College	U
Carleton University	U
Concordia University	U
Concordia University College	U
Dalhousie University	U, G
Huron College	U
Kwantlen University	U
Laurentian University	U
Luther College	U
Malaspina University	U
McGill University	U, G
McMaster University	U
Memorial University	U, G
Mount Allison University	U
Queen's University	U, G
Saint Mary's University	U
Trent University	U
Université de Montréal	U, G
Université Laval	U
University of British Columbia	U, G
University of Calgary	U, G
University of Guelph	U
University of King's College	U
University of Lethbridge	U, G
University of Manitoba	U, G
University of New Brunswick	U, G
University of Ottawa	U
University of Toronto	U, G
University of Trinity	U
University of Victoria	U, G
University of Waterloo	U, G
University of Western Ontario	U
University of Windsor	U
University of Winnipeg	U
Wilfrid Laurier University	U
York University	U

GERONTOLOGY

Lakehead University	G
Laurentian University	U
McGill University	U
McMaster University	U
Memorial University	G
Mount Royal College	U

Mount Saint Vincent College	U, G
Queen's University	U
Simon Fraser University	U, G
St. Thomas University	U
Université de Sherbrooke	G
Université du Quebec	U
Université Laval	U
University of Guelph	U
University of Manitoba	U
University of Regina	U
University of Toronto	U, G
University of Waterloo '	U, G

GREEK LANGUAGE & LITERATURE

Bishop's University	U
Luther College	U
Memorial University	U, G
Mount Allison University	U
University of Calgary	U, G
University of Lethbridge	U
University of New Brunswick	U
University of Victoria	U, G
University of Western Ontario	U
University of Windsor	U
Wilfrid Laurier University	U
York University	U

HEALTH SERVICE ADMINISTRATION

Athabasca University	G
Dalhousie University	U
Ryerson University	U
Université de Montréal	U
University of Alberta	U
University of British Columbia	U
University of Manitoba	U
University of N. British Columbia	U
University of Ottawa	U
University of Toronto	U

HEALTH SCIENCES

Athabasca University	U
Bishop's University	U
Brandon University	U
Brock University	U, G
Campion College	U
Dalhousie University	U
King's College	U
Kwantlen University	U
Luther College	U
Malaspina University College	U
McGill University	U

McMaster University	U, G
Mount Allison University	U
Mount Royal College	U
Queen's University	U
Ryerson University	U
Thompson Rivers University	U
Trinity Western University	U
Université de Montreal	U
University of Alberta	U, G
University of British Columbia	U, G
University of Calgary	U, G
University of Guelph	U
University of Lethbridge	U
University of Manitoba	U, G
University of New Brunswick	U
University of N. British Columbia	U, G
University of Ontario	U
University of Ottawa	U
University of Toronto	U, G
University of Saskatchewan	U, G
University of Victoria	U
University of Waterloo	U, G
University of Western Ontario	U, G
York University	U

HISTORY

Acadia University	U
Athabasca University	U
Bishop's University	U
Brandon University	U
Brescia College	U
Brock University	U
Campion College	U
Cape Breton University	U
Carleton University	U, G
Concordia University	U, G
Concordia University College of Alberta	U
Dalhousie University	U, G
Huron College	U
King's College	U
Kwantlen University	U
Lakehead University	U, G
Laurentian University	U, G
Luther College	U
Malaspina University College	U
McGill University	U, G
McMaster University	U, G
Memorial University	U, G
Mount Allison University	U
Mount Royal College	U
Mount Saint Vincent College	U

Nipissing University	U
OCAD	U
Queen's University	U
Redeemer College	U
Ryerson University	U
Saint Francis Xavier College	U
Saint Jerome's University	U
Saint Mary's University	U, G
Saint Thomas More University	U
Simon Fraser University	U, G
St. Thomas University	U
The King's University College	U
Thompson Rivers University	U
Trent University	U, G
Trinity Western University	U
Université de Moncton	U
Université de Montreal	U, G
Université de Sherbrooke	U, G
Université du Quebec	U, G
Université Laval	U, G
Université Sainte-Anne	U
University College of the Fraser Valley	U
University of Alberta	U, G
University of British Columbia	U, G
University of Calgary	U, G
University of Guelph	U, G
University of King's College	U
University of Lethbridge	U, G
University of Manitoba	U, G
University of New Brunswick	U, G
University of N. British Columbia	U, G
University of Ottawa	U
University of Prince Edward Island	U
University of Regina	U, G
University of Saskatchewan	U, G
University of Toronto	U, G
University of Victoria	U, G
University of Waterloo	U, G
University of Western Ontario	U
University of Windsor	U
University of Winnipeg	U, G
Wilfrid Laurier University	U, G
York University	U, G

HORTICULTURE SCIENCE

Brandon University	U
Kwantlen University College	U
McGill University	U
Nova Scotia Agricultural College	U, G
University of British Columbia	U, G
University of Guelph	U, G

University of Toronto	U
University of Saskatchewan	U, G
University of Western Ontario	U, G

HOSPITALITY/ADMINISTRATION MANAGEMENT

Laurentian University	U, G
Malaspina University College	U
Mount Royal College	U
Ryerson University	U
Université du Quebec	U
University of Calgary	U
University of Guelph	U, G
University of New Brunswick	U

HUMAN ECOLOGY

Brandon University	U
Brescia College	U
Mount Saint Vincent University	U, G
University of Alberta	U, G
University of Western Ontario	U

HUMAN RESOURCES MANAGEMENT

Acadia University	U
Athabasca University	U
Bishop's University	U
Brock University	U
Carleton University	U
Dalhousie University	U
King's College	U
Kwantlen University	U
McGill University	U
McMaster University	U
Memorial University	U
Queen's University	U
Saint Mary's University	U
Université de Montreal	U, G
Université du Quebec	U, G
University of Alberta	U
University of British Columbia	U
University of Calgary	U
University of Guelph	U
University of Lethbridge	U
University of Manitoba	U
University of New Brunswick	U
University of Ottawa	U
University of Regina	U
University of Toronto	U, G
University of Waterloo	U
Wilfrid Laurier University	U
York University	U

HUMANITIES/HUMANISTIC STUDIES

Athabasca University	U
Campion College	U
Carleton University	U
Concordia University	U
Dalhousie University	U
Kwantlen University College	U
Lakehead University	U
Laurentian University	U, G
Luther College	U
McGill University	U
McMaster University	U, G
Memorial University	U, G
Nipissing University	U
Queen's University	U
Simon Fraser University	U, G
Trinity Western University	U
University of Alberta	U
University of British Columbia	U
University of Calgary	U
University of Lethbridge	U
University of New Brunswick	U
University of Ottawa	U
University of Regina	U
University of Toronto	U
University of Victoria	U
University of Waterloo	U
University of Western Ontario	U
University of Windsor	U
Wilfrid Laurier University	U
York University	U, G

HUMAN KINETICS/KINESIOLOGY

Acadia University	U
Brock University	U
Concordia University	U
Dalhousie University	U, G
Huron College	U
King's College	U
Lakehead University	U, G
Laurentian University	U
McGill University	U
McMaster University	U
Memorial University	U, G
Redeemer College	U
Saint Francis Xavier University	U
Simon Fraser University	U, G
Trinity Western University	U
Université de Moncton	U
Université de Montreal	U
Université de Sherbrooke	U

University College of the Fraser Valley	U
University of Alberta	U
University of British Columbia	U, G
University of Calgary	U, G
University of Guelph	U
University of Lethbridge	U, G
University of New Brunswick	U, G
University of N. British Columbia	U
University of Ottawa	U, G
University of Regina	U, G
University of Saskatchewan	U
University of Victoria	U
University of Waterloo	U
University of Western Ontario	U
University of Winnipeg	U
York University	U

INDUSTRIAL/MANUFACTURING ENGINEERING

Cape Breton University	U
Concordia University	U
Dalhousie University	U, G
McMaster University	U
Ryerson University	U
University of British Columbia	U
University of Calgary	U
University of Manitoba	U
University of Regina	U
University of Toronto	U
University of Windsor	U, G

INFORMATION SCIENCES & SYSTEMS

Acadia University	U
Athabasca University	U, G
Cape Breton University	U
Carleton University	U, G
Concordia University	U
Concordia University College	U
Malaspina University College	U
McGill University	U, G
Mount Saint Vincent College	U
Nipissing University	U
Queen's University	U, G
Ryerson University	U
Trinity Western University	U
University College of the Fraser Valley	U
University of British Columbia	U, G
University of Guelph	U, G
University of Manitoba	U, G
University of Ottawa	U, G
University of Toronto	U, G
York University	U

INTERIOR DESIGN

Brandon University	U
Kwantlen University College	U
Malaspina University College	U
Mount Royal College	U
Ryerson University	U
University of Manitoba	U, G

INTERNATIONAL BUSINESS

Bishop's University	U
Brock University	U
Carleton University	U
Concordia University	U
McGill University	U, G
McMaster University	U
Mount Allison University	U
Mount Royal College	U
Ryerson University	U
Université de Moncton	U, G
Université de Montreal	U, G
Université du Quebec	U, G
University of Alberta	U, G
University of British Columbia	U, G
University of Calgary	U, G
University of Lethbridge	U
University of Manitoba	U
University of New Brunswick	U
University of Ottawa	U, G
University of Toronto	U, G
University of Waterloo	U

INTERNATIONAL RELATIONS & AFFAIRS

Brock University	U
Carleton University	U, G
Dalhousie University	U, G
Huron College	U
McGill University	U
Mount Allison University	U
Queen's University	U
Saint Mary's University	U, G
Trent University	U
Trinity Western University	U
Université Laval	G
Université de Sherbrooke	U
University of British Columbia	U, G
University of Calgary	U
University of Guelph	U, G
University of King's College	U
University of New Brunswick	U
University of N. British Columbia	U, G
University of Ottawa	U

University of Regina U
University of Toronto U, G
University of Trinity College U
University of Waterloo U
University of Western Ontario U
University of Windsor U
University of Winnipeg U
Wilfrid Laurier University U
York University U

ITALIAN LANGUAGE & LITERATURE

Brock University U
Carleton University U
Concordia University U
McGill University U, G
McMaster University U
Memorial University U
Queen's University U, G
St. Jerome's University U
University of British Columbia U
University of Calgary U, G
University of Guelph U
University of Manitoba U, G
University of Ottawa U
University of Toronto U, G
University of Victoria U, G
University of Western Ontario U
University of Windsor U
York University U

IRISH/CELTIC STUDIES

Cape Breton University U
Saint Francis Xavier University U, G
Saint Mary's University U
Trinity Western University U
University of Toronto U

JAPANESE LANGUAGE & LITERATURE

Campion College U
Kwantlen University College U
Luther College U
Malaspina University College U
McMaster University U
Mount Allison University U
University of Calgary U
University of Western Ontario U
York University U

JEWISH/JUDAIC STUDIES

Campion College U
Concordia University U

McGill University U, G
Queen's University U
University of Toronto U, G
University of Western Ontario U
York University U

JOURNALISM

Brandon University U
Campion College U
Carleton University U
Concordia University U, G
Luther College U
Malaspina University College U
Ryerson University U
St. Thomas University U
Thompson Rivers University U
Université Laval U
Université du Quebec U
University of British Columbia U, G
University of King's College U
University of Prince Edward Island U
University of Regina U
University of Toronto U
University of Western Ontario U, G
Wilfrid Laurier University U

LABOUR/PERSONNEL RELATIONS AND STUDIES

Athabasca University U
Brock University U
Carleton University U
Laurentian University U
McGill University U
McMaster University U, G
Queen's University U
Université Laval U, G
Université de Montreal U, G
Université du Quebec U, G
University of Alberta U
University of British Columbia U
University of Lethbridge U
University of Manitoba U
University of Ottawa U, G
University of Toronto U, G
University of Victoria U
University of Windsor U
York University U

LANDSCAPE ARCHITECTURE

Nova Scotia Agricultural College U
Université de Montreal U
University of British Columbia U, G

University of Guelph	U, G
University of Manitoba	U, G
University of Toronto	U

LATIN AMERICAN STUDIES

McGill University	U, G
McMaster University	U
Mount Allison University	U
Queen's University	U
Simon Fraser University	U, G
University College of the Fraser Valley	U
University of British Columbia	U, G
University of Calgary	U
University of Toronto	U
University of Victoria	U
York University	U

LATIN LANGUAGE & LITERATURE

Acadia University	U
Campion College	U
Luther College	U
McGill University	U
Mount Allison University	U
University of Calgary	U, G
University of Lethbridge	U
University of New Brunswick	U
University of Ottawa	U
University of Toronto	U
University of Western Ontario	U
University of Windsor	U
Wilfrid Laurier University	U
York University	U

LAW

Carleton University	G
Dalhousie University	G
McGill University	G
Queen's University	G
Université de Moncton	G
Université de Montreal	G
Université de Sherbrooke	G
Université du Quebec	G
University of Alberta	G
University of British Columbia	G
University of Calgary	G
University of Manitoba	G
University of Ottawa	G
University of Saskatchewan	G
University of Toronto	G
University of Western Ontario	G
York University	G

LEISURE & RECREATIONAL ACTIVITIES

Acadia University	U, G
Brock University	U
Concordia University	U
Dalhousie University	U, G
Lakehead University	U
Malaspina University College	U
Memorial University	U, G
Mount Royal College	U
Thompson Rivers University	U
Université de Moncton	U
Université du Quebec	U
University of Alberta	U, G
University of British Columbia	U
University of Calgary	U
University of Guelph	U
University of Lethbridge	U
University of Manitoba	U
University of N. British Columbia	U, G
University of Ottawa	U
University of Regina	U
University of Victoria	U
University of Waterloo	U, G

LIBRARY SCIENCE

Dalhousie University	U
Lakehead University	U
McGill University	U
Université de Montreal	U
University of Alberta	U
University of British Columbia	U, G
University College of the Fraser Valley	U
University of Lethbridge	U
University of Western Ontario	U

LINGUISTICS

Campion College	U
Carleton University	U, G
Concordia University	U
Dalhousie University	U
Kwantlen University	U
Luther College	U
Malaspina University	U
McGill University	U
McMaster University	U
Memorial University	U
Mount Saint Vincent University	U, G
Queen's University	U
Saint Mary's University	U
Simon Fraser University	U, G
Université Laval	U, G

Université de Moncton	U
Université de Montreal	U, G
Université du Quebec	U, G
University of Alberta	U, G
University of British Columbia	U, G
University of Calgary	U, G
University of Guelph	U
University of King's College	U
University of Lethbridge	U
University of Manitoba	U, G
University of New Brunswick	U
University of Ottawa	U, G
University of Regina	U, G
University of Saskatchewan	U, G
University of Toronto	U, G
University of Victoria	U, G
University of Waterloo	U
University of Western Ontario	U
Wilfrid Laurier University	U
York University	U, G

MANAGEMENT SCIENCE

Athabasca University	U, G
Brock University	U
Concordia University	U
Dalhousie University	U
McGill University	U, G
Mount Saint Vincent College	U
Ryerson University	U, G
Saint Mary's University	U
Simon Fraser University	U
Université de Montreal	U, G
Université de Sherbrooke	U
Université du Quebec	U, G
University of Alberta	U, G
University of British Columbia	U
University of Calgary	U, G
University of Guelph	U
University of Lethbridge	U, G
University of Manitoba	U, G
University of Ottawa	U, G
University of Saskatchewan	U, G
University of Toronto	U, G
University of Victoria	U
University of Waterloo	U, G
University of Windsor	U
York University	U

MANAGEMENT INFORMATION SYSTEMS

Athabasca University	U, G
Bishop's University	U

Carleton University	U
Concordia University	U
King's College	U
Lakehead University	U
McGill University	U
McMaster University	U
Nipissing University	U
Queen's University	U, G
Saint Francis Xavier University	U
Simon Fraser University	U
Université de Moncton	U
Université de Montreal	U
Université de Sherbrooke	U
Université du Quebec	U
University of Alberta	U
University of British Columbia	U
University of Calgary	U
University of Guelph	U
University of Lethbridge	U
University of Manitoba	U, G
University of Ottawa	U, G
University of Saskatchewan	U
University of Toronto	U, G
University of Victoria	U
University of Waterloo	U
Wilfrid Laurier University	U

MARINE/AQUATIC SCIENCES

Dalhousie University	U, G
Memorial University	U, G
Nova Scotia Agricultural College	U
Simon Fraser University	U
Thompson Rivers University	U
University of Alberta	U
University of Calgary	U
University of Guelph	U, G
University of King's College	U
University of New Brunswick	U
University of Toronto	U

MARKETING MANAGEMENT & RESEARCH

Acadia University	U
Athabasca University	U
Bishop's University	U
Brock University	U
Cape Breton University	U
Carleton University	U
Concordia University	U
King's College	U
Kwantlen University	U
Lakehead University	U

Malaspina University	U
McGill University	U
McMaster University	U
Mount Allison University	U
Queen's University	U
Saint Francis Xavier University	U
Saint Mary's University	U
Simon Fraser University	U
Thompson Rivers University	U
Université de Moncton	U
Université de Montreal	U
Université de Sherbrooke	U
Université du Quebec	U
University of Alberta	U
University of British Columbia	U, G
University of Calgary	U
University of Guelph	U
University of Lethbridge	U
University of New Brunswick	U
University of Ottawa	U, G
University of Regina	U
University of Saskatchewan	U
University of Toronto	U, G
University of Victoria	U
University of Waterloo	U
University of Windsor	U
Wilfrid Laurier University	U
York University	U

MATERIALS SCIENCE/ENGINEERING

Carleton University	U, G
McMaster University	U, G
McGill University	U
Queen's University	U
University of Alberta	U, G
University of British Columbia	U, G
University of Toronto	U
University of Western Ontario	U

MATHEMATICS

Acadia University	U
Athabasca University	U
Bishop's University	U
Brandon University	U, G
Brescia College	U
Brock University	U
Campion College	U
Carleton University	U, G
Concordia University	U, G
Concordia University College	U

Dalhousie University	U, G
Huron College	U
Kwantlen University	U
Lakehead University	U, G
Laurentian University	U
Luther College	U
Malaspina University	U
McGill University	U, G
McMaster University	U, G
Memorial University	U, G
Mount Allison University	U
Mount Royal College	U
Mount Saint Vincent College	U
Nipissing University	U
Nova Scotia Agricultural College	U, G
Queen's University	U, G
Redeemer University College	U
Ryerson University	U
Saint Francis Xavier College	U
Saint Mary's University	U
St. Jerome's University	U
St. Thomas University	U
The King's University	U
Thompson Rivers University	U
Trent University	U, G
Trinity Western University	U
Université Laval	U, G
Université de Moncton	U
Université de Montreal	U, G
Université de Sherbrooke	U, G
Université du Quebec	U, G
Université Sainte-Anne	U
University College of the Fraser Valley	U
University of Alberta	U, G
University of British Columbia	U, G
University of Calgary	U, G
University of Guelph	U, G
University of King's College	U
University of Lethbridge	U, G
University of Manitoba	U, G
University of New Brunswick	U, G
University of N. British Columbia	U, G
University of Ontario	U
University of Ottawa	U, G
University of Prince Edward Island	U
University of Regina	U, G
University of Saskatchewan	U, G
University of Toronto	U, G
University of Victoria	U, G
University of Waterloo	U, G
University of Western Ontario	U, G

University of Windsor	U, G
University of Winnipeg	U
Wilfrid Laurier University	U
York University	U, G

MECHANICAL ENGINEERING

Cape Breton University	U
Carleton University	U, G
Concordia University	U, G
Dalhousie University	U, G
Lakehead University	U
Laurentian University	U
Luther College	U
Malaspina University	U
McGill University	U, G
McMaster University	U, G
Memorial University	U
Nova Scotia Agricultural College	U
Queen's University	U, G
Ryerson University	U, G
Université Laval	U, G
Université de Moncton	U, G
Université de Montreal	U, G
Université de Sherbrooke	U, G
Université du Quebec	U, G
University of Alberta	U, G
University of British Columbia	U, G
University of Calgary	U, G
University of Manitoba	U, G
University of Ontario	U
University of New Brunswick	U, G
University of Ottawa	U, G
University of Saskatchewan	U, G
University of Toronto	U, G
University of Victoria	U, G
University of Waterloo	U, G
University of Western Ontario	U
University of Windsor	U, G

MEDICINE

Dalhousie University	G
McGill University	G
McMaster University	G
Memorial University	G
Queen's University	G
Université Laval	G
Université de Montreal	G
Université de Sherbrooke	G
University of Alberta	G
University of British Columbia	G
University of Calgary	G

University of Manitoba	G
University of Ottawa	G
University of Saskatchewan	G
University of Toronto	G
University of Western Ontario	G

MEDIEVAL & RENAISSANCE STUDIES

Memorial University	U
Queen's University	U
Université de Montreal	U, G
University of British Columbia	U
University of Manitoba	U
University of Ottawa	U
University of Toronto	U, G
University of Victoria	U
University of Waterloo	U

METALLURGICAL ENGINEERING

Dalhousie University	U, G
McGill University	U, G
Nova Scotia Agricultural College	U
Queen's University	U
Université Laval	U
Université de Montreal	U, G
Université du Quebec	U
University of British Columbia	U, G
University of Toronto	U, G

MICROBIOLOGY

Carleton University	U
Concordia University	U, G
Dalhousie University	U, G
Laurentian University	U, G
Malaspina University	U
McGill University	U, G
McMaster University	U
Memorial University	U
Mount Royal College	U
Nova Scotia Agricultural College	U
Queen's University	U
Thompson Rivers University	U
Université Laval	U, G
Université de Montreal	U
Université de Sherbrooke	U
Université du Quebec	U, G
University of Alberta	U, G
University of British Columbia	U, G
University of Calgary	U, G
University of Guelph	U, G
University of King's College	U
University of Manitoba	U, G

University of New Brunswick	U
University of N. British Columbia	U
University of Ottawa	U, G
University of Toronto	U, G
University of Saskatchewan	U, G
University of Victoria	U, G
University of Western Ontario	U, G

MIDDLE EASTERN LANGUAGES & STUDIES

Laurentian University	U
McGill University	U, G
University of Alberta	U
University of Toronto	U, G

MINING AND MINERAL ENGINEERING

Dalhousie University	U, G
Laurentian University	U, G
McGill University	U
Queen's University	U, G
Université Laval	U, G
Université de Montreal	U, G
University of Alberta	U
University of British Columbia	U, G
University of Toronto	U

MODERN LANGUAGES

University of Lethbridge	U, G
University of Prince Edward Island	U

MOLECULAR BIOLOGY

Concordia University	U, G
McMaster University	U
Université de Montreal	U, G
Université du Quebec	U
University of Guelph	U, G
University of Toronto	U, G

MUSIC

Acadia University	U
Athabasca University	U
Bishop's University	U
Brandon University	U, G
Brock University	U
Campion College	U
Carleton University	U
Concordia University	U, G
Concordia University College	U
Dalhousie University	U
Lakehead University	U
Laurentian University	U

Luther College	U
Malaspina University	U
McGill University	U, G
McMaster University	U, G
Mount Allison University	U
Mount Royal College	U
Queen's University	U
Redeemer University College	U
Saint Francis Xavier College	U
The King's University College	U
Trinity Western University	U
Université Laval	U, G
Université de Moncton	U
Université de Montreal	U, G
Université de Sherbrooke	U
Université du Quebec	U
University of Alberta	U, G
University of British Columbia	U, G
University of Calgary	U, G
University of Guelph	U
University of Lethbridge	U, G
University of Manitoba	U
University of Ottawa	U, G
University of Prince Edward Island	U
University of Regina	U, G
University of Saskatchewan	U, G
University of Toronto	U, G
University of Victoria	U, G
University of Waterloo	U
University of Western Ontario	U, G
University of Windsor	U
University of Winnipeg	U
Wilfrid Laurier University	U
York University	U, G

NATURAL RESOURCES MANAGEMENT

McGill University	U, G
Nova Scotia Agricultural College	U
Simon Fraser University	U
Thompson Rivers University	U
University of British Columbia	U
University of Guelph	U, G
University of Manitoba	U, G
University of New Brunswick	U
University of N. British Columbia	U

NATIVE STUDIES

Athabasca University	U
Brandon University	U
Cape Breton University	U
Laurentian University	U
Luther College	U

McMaster University	U
Memorial University	U
Nipissing University	U
St. Thomas University	U
Thompson Rivers University	U
Trent University	U, G
University of Alberta	U
University of British Columbia	U
University of Calgary	U
University of Lethbridge	U, G
University of Manitoba	U, G
University of N. British Columbia	U, G
University of Regina	U, G
University of Saskatchewan	U, G
University of Toronto	U

NEUROSCIENCE

Brock University	U
Carleton University	U, G
Corcordia University	U
Dalhousie University	U, G
McGill University	U, G
Memorial University	G
Queen's University	U
Université Laval	G
University of Alberta	U, G
University of Calgary	G
University of British Columbia	U
University of Lethbridge	U
University of Manitoba	G
University of Ottawa	G
University of Toronto	U, G
University of Western Ontario	G

NUCLEAR ENGINEERING

University of Ontario	U

NURSING

Athabasca University	U, G
Brandon University	U, G
Brock University	U
Cape Breton University	U
Dalhousie University	U, G
Kwantlen University	U
Lakehead University	U
Laurentian University	U
Malaspina University	U
McGill University	U, G
McMaster University	U, G
Memorial University	U, G
Mount Royal College	U

Nipissing University	U
Queen's University	U, G
Ryerson University	U
Saint Francis Xavier College	U
Thompson Rivers University	U
Trent University	U
Trinity Western University	U
Université Laval	U, G
Université de Moncton	U, G
Université de Montreal	U, G
Université de Sherbrooke	U
Université du Quebec	U, G
University College of the Fraser Valley	U
University of Alberta	U, G
University of British Columbia	U, G
University of Calgary	U
University of Lethbridge	U
University of Manitoba	U, G
University of New Brunswick	U, G
University of N. British Columbia	U
University of Ontario	U
University of Ottawa	U, G
University of Prince Edward Island	U
University of Saskatchewan	U, G
University of Toronto	U, G
University of Victoria	U
University of Waterloo	U
University of Western Ontario	U, G
University of Windsor	U, G
York University	U

NUTRITIONAL SCIENCES

Acadia University	U
Athabasca University	U
Brescia College	U
McGill University	U, G
Mount Saint Vincent College	U, G
Ryerson University	U
Saint Francis Xavier University	U
Université Laval	U, G
Université de Moncton	U, G
Université de Montreal	U, G
University of British Columbia	U, G
University of Guelph	U, G
University of Manitoba	U, G
University of Prince Edward Island	U
University of Saskatchewan	U, G
University of Toronto	U, G
University of Western Ontario	U

OCCUPATIONAL THERAPY

Dalhousie University	U, G
McGill University	U, G
McMaster University	U, G
Queen's University	U
Université de Montreal	U
University of Alberta	U, G
University of Ottawa	U
University of Toronto	U
University of Western Ontario	U, G

OCEANOGRAPHY

Dalhousie University	U, G
McGill University	U, G
Memorial University	U, G
Nova Scotia Agricultural College	U
Université Laval	U
Université de Montreal	U
University of British Columbia	U, G
University of Victoria	U, G

OPERATIONS MANAGEMENT & SUPERVISION

Brock University	U
Carleton University	U
Concordia University	U
King's College	U
McGill University	U
Saint Francis Xavier University	U
Université de Moncton	U, G
Université de Montreal	U
Université du Quebec	U
University of Alberta	U
University of British Columbia	U
University of Calgary	U
University of Guelph	U
University of Lethbridge	U
University of Manitoba	U
University of New Brunswick	U
University of Ottawa	U, G
University of Regina	U
University of Saskatchewan	U
University of Toronto	U
University of Waterloo	U
Wilfrid Laurier University	U

OPTHALMOLOGY

University of Alberta	G

OPTOMETRY

Université de Montreal	G
University of Waterloo	G

ORGANIZATIONAL BEHAVIOR STUDIES

Athabasca University	U
Bishop's University	U
McGill University	U
Université de Sherbrooke	U
Université du Quebec	U
University College of Cape Breton	U
University of Alberta	U
University of British Columbia	U
University of Calgary	U
University of Guelph	U
University of Ottawa	U, G
University of Saskatchewan	U
University of Toronto	U
University of Victoria	U
Wilfrid Laurier University	U

PACIFIC AREA STUDIES

Mount Royal College	U
University of British Columbia	U, G
University of Calgary	U
University of Toronto	U
University of Victoria	U

PAINTING

ACAD	U
Concordia University	U
NSCAD	U
OCAD	U
Thompson Rivers University	U
University of Toronto	U

PALEONTOLOGY

University of Alberta	U
University of Saskatchewan	U
University of Toronto	U

PETROLEUM ENGINEERING

Cape Breton University	U
University of Alberta	U
University of Calgary	U
University of Regina	U

PHARMACY/PHARMACOLOGY

Dalhousie University	U, G
Memorial University	G
Queen's University	G
Université Laval	U, G
University of Alberta	U, G
University of British Columbia	U, G
University of Manitoba	U, G

University of Saskatchewan	U, G
University of Toronto	U, G
University of Western Ontario	U, G

PHILOSOPHY

Acadia University	U
Athabasca University	U
Bishop's University	U
Brandon University	U
Brescia College	U
Brock University	U, G
Campion College	U
Cape Breton University	U
Carleton University	U, G
Concordia University	U, G
Concordia University College	U
Dalhousie University	U, G
Huron College	U
King's College	U
Kwantlen University	U
Lakehead University	U
Laurentian University	U
Luther College	U
Malaspina University	U
McGill University	U, G
McMaster University	U, G
Memorial University	U, G
Mount Allison University	U
Mount Royal College	U
Mount Saint Vincent College	U
Nipissing University	U
Queen's University	U, G
Redeemer College	U
Saint Francis Xavier College	U
Saint Jerome's University	U
Saint Mary's University	U, G
Saint Thomas More University	U
Simon Fraser University	U
St. Thomas University	U
The King's University	U
Trent University	U, G
Trinity Western University	U
Université Laval	U
Université de Moncton	U, G
Université de Montreal	U, G
Université de Sherbrooke	U, G
Université du Quebec	U, G
University of Alberta	U, G
University of British Columbia	U, G
University of Calgary	U, G
University of Guelph	U, G

University of King's College	U
University of Lethbridge	U, G
University of Manitoba	U, G
University of New Brunswick	U, G
University of Ottawa	U, G
University of Prince Edward Island	U
University of Regina	U
University of Saskatchewan	U, G
University of Toronto	U, G
University of Waterloo	U, G
University of Western Ontario	U, G
University of Windsor	U, G
University of Winnipeg	U
Wilfrid Laurier University	U, G
York University	U, G

PHYSICAL EDUCATION TEACHING & COACHING

Brock University	U
Cape Breton University	U
Huron College	U
Malaspina University	U
McGill University	U, G
Memorial University	G
Mount Royal College	U
Queen's University	U, G
Université de Sherbrooke	U
University of Alberta	U, G
University of British Columbia	U
University of Calgary	U
University of Lethbridge	U
University of Manitoba	U, G
University of Winnipeg	U
Wilfrid Laurier University	U
York University	U

PHYSICAL THERAPY

Dalhousie University	U
McGill University	U, G
McMaster University	U, G
Memorial University	U
Queen's University	U
Thompson Rivers University	U
Université Laval	U
Université de Montreal	U
University of Alberta	U, G
University of Manitoba	U
University of Ottawa	U
University of Regina	U
University of Saskatchewan	U
University of Toronto	U
University of Western Ontario	U, G

PHYSICS

Acadia University	U
Athabasca University	U
Bishop's University	U
Brock University	U, G
Campion College	U
Cape Breton University	U
Carleton University	U, G
Concordia University	U, G
Dalhousie University	U, G
Kwantlen University	U
Lakehead University	U, G
Laurentian University	U, G
Luther College	U
Malaspina University College	U
McGill University	U
McMaster University	U, G
Memorial University	U, G
Mount Allison University	U
Mount Royal College	U
Mount Saint Vincent College	U
Nipissing University	U
Nova Scotia Agricultural College	U, G
Queen's University	U, G
Redeemer University College	U
Saint Francis Xavier College	U, G
Thompson Rivers University	U
Trent University	U
Université Laval	U, G
Université de Moncton	U, G
Université de Montreal	U, G
Université de Sherbrooke	U, G
Université du Quebec	U, G
Université Sainte-Anne	U
University College of the Fraser Valley	U
University of Alberta	U, G
University of British Columbia	U, G
University of Calgary	U, G
University of Guelph	U, G
University of King's College	U
University of Lethbridge	U, G
University of Manitoba	U, G
University of New Brunswick	U
University of N. British Columbia	U, G
University of Ottawa	U, G
University of Prince Edward Island	U
University of Regina	U, G
University of Saskatchewan	U, G
University of Toronto	U, G
University of Victoria	U, G
University of Waterloo	U, G
University of Western Ontario	U, G
University of Windsor	U, G
University of Winnipeg	U
Wilfrid Laurier University	U
York University	U, G

PHYSIOLOGY

Dalhousie University	U, G
Kwantlen University College	U
Laurentian University	G
McGill University	U, G
Nova Scotia Agricultural College	U
Trent University	U
Université Laval	U, G
Université de Montreal	U, G
University of Alberta	G
University of British Columbia	U, G
University of Guelph	
University of Lethbridge	G
University of Manitoba	G
University of N. British Columbia	G
University of Regina	G
University of Toronto	U, G
University of Western Ontario	U, G

PLANT SCIENCES

Kwantlen University	U
McGill University	U, G
Nova Scotia Agricultural College	U
Thompson Rivers University	U
University of British Columbia	U, G
University of Guelph	U, G
University of Manitoba	U, G
University of N. British Columbia	U, G
University of Ottawa	U, G
University of Toronto	U
University of Saskatchewan	U, G
University of Western Ontario	U

PLAYWRITING & SCREENWRITING

Bishop's University	U
Concordia University	U

POLITICAL SCIENCE

Acadia University	U, G
Athabasca University	U
Bishop's University	U
Brandon University	U
Brescia College	U
Brock University	U, G
Campion College	U

Cape Breton University	U
Carleton University	U, G
Concordia University	U, G
Concordia University College	U
Dalhousie University	U, G
Huron College	U
King's College	U
Kwantlen University College	U
Lakehead University	U
Laurentian University	U
Malaspina University	U
McGill University	U, G
McMaster University	U, G
Memorial University	U, G
Mount Allison University	U
Mount Royal College	U
Mount Saint Vincent College	U
Queen's University	U, G
Redeemer University College	U
Saint Francis Xavier College	U, G
Saint Mary's University	U
Saint Thomas More University	U
Simon Fraser University	U, G
St. Thomas University	U
The King's University College	U
Thompson Rivers University	U
Trent University	U
Trinity Western University	U
Université Laval	U, G
Université de Moncton	U
Université de Montreal	U, G
Université de Sherbrooke	U, G
Université du Quebec	U, G
University of the Fraser Valley	U
University of Alberta	U, G
University of British Columbia	U, G
University of Calgary	U, G
University of Guelph	U, G
University of King's College	U
University of Lethbridge	U
University of Manitoba	U, G
University of New Brunswick	U
University of N. British Columbia	U, G
University of Ottawa	U
University of Prince Edward Island	U
University of Regina	U, G
University of Saskatchewan	U, G
University of Toronto	U, G
University of Victoria	U, G
University of Waterloo	U, G
University of Western Ontario	U

University of Windsor	U, G
University of Winnipeg	U
Wilfrid Laurier University	U, G
York University	U, G

PORTUGUESE LANGUAGE & LITERATURE

University of Toronto	U, G
York University	U

PRE-DENTISTRY

Mount Allison University	U
Trinity Western University	U
University of British Columbia	U
University of Toronto	U

PRE-MEDICINE

Mount Allison University	U
Queen's University	U
Simon Fraser University	U
Trinity Western University	U
University of British Columbia	U
University of Guelph	U
University of Toronto	U

PRE-VETERINARY SCIENCE

Mount Allison University	U
Trinity Western University	U
Université Sainte-Anne	U
University of British Columbia	U
University of Guelph	U
University of Prince Edward Island	U
University of Toronto	U

PSYCHOLOGY

Acadia University	U, G
Athabasca University	U, G
Bishop's University	U
Brandon University	U
Brescia College	U
Brock University	U, G
Campion College	U
Cape Breton University	U
Carleton University	U, G
Concordia University	U, G
Concordia University College	U
Dalhousie University	U, G
Huron College	U
King's College	U
Kwantlen University College	U
Lakehead University	U, G
Laurentian University	U

Malaspina University College	U
McGill University	U, G
McMaster University	U, G
Memorial University	U, G
Mount Allison University	U
Mount Royal College	U
Mount Saint Vincent University	U, G
Nipissing University	U
Queen's University	U, G
Redeemer College	U
Saint Francis Xavier College	U
Saint Jerome's College	U
Saint Mary's University	U, G
Saint Thomas More University	U
Simon Fraser University	U
St. Thomas University	U
The King's University College	U
Thompson Rivers University	U
Trent University	U, G
Trinity Western University	U, G
Université de Moncton	U, G
Université de Montreal	U, G
Université de Sherbrooke	U
Université du Quebec	U
University College of the Fraser Valley	U
University of Alberta	U, G
University of British Columbia	U, G
University of Calgary	U, G
University of Guelph	U, G
University of King's College	U
University of Lethbridge	U
University of Manitoba	U, G
University of New Brunswick	U, G
University of N. British Columbia	U, G
University of Ottawa	U, G
University of Prince Edward Island	U
University of Regina	U, G
University of Saskatchewan	U, G
University of Toronto	U, G
University of Victoria	U, G
University of Waterloo	U, G
University of Western Ontario	U, G
University of Windsor	U, G
University of Winnipeg	U
Wilfrid Laurier University	U, G
York University	U, G

PUBLIC ADMINISTRATION

Athabasca University	U, G
Brock University	U
Carleton University	U, G
Concordia University	U
Dalhousie University	U, G
Kwantlen University	U
Lakehead University	U
Queen's University	G
Université Laval	G
Université de Moncton	U, G
Université de Montreal	U
Université du Quebec	U, G
University of Guelph	U
University of Lethbridge	U
University of Manitoba	G
University of Ottawa	U
University of Prince Edward Island	U
University of Toronto	U
University of Victoria	G
University of Windsor	U
University of Western Ontario	G
University of Winnipeg	G
York University	U

PUBLIC HEALTH

Brock University	U
Kwantlen University College	U
Mount Royal College	U
Ryerson University	U
University of British Columbia	U
University of Manitoba	U
University of Toronto	U, G

PUBLIC RELATIONS & COMMUNICATIONS

Kwantlen University	U
McGill University	U
Mount Saint Vincent University	U
Queen's University	U
Ryerson University	U
Université Laval	U
Université du Quebec	U, G
University of British Columbia	U
University of Guelph	U
University of Ottawa	U, G
University of Regina	U
University of Victoria	U

RADIO & TELEVISION BROADCASTING

King's College	U
Ryerson University	U
University of British Columbia	U
University of Regina	U

RELIGION/RELIGIOUS STUDIES

Athabasca University	U
Bishop's University	U
Brandon University	U
Brescia College	U
Campion College	U
Carleton University	U, G
Concordia University	U, G
Concordia University College	U
Dalhousie University	U
Huron College	U
King's College	U
Kwantlen University College	U
Lakehead University	U
Laurentian University	U
Luther College	U
Malaspina University	U
McGill University	U, G
McMaster University	U, G
Memorial University	U, G
Mount Allison University	U
Mount Royal College	U
Mount Saint Vincent University	U
Nipissing University	U
Queen's University	U
Redeemer College	U
Saint Francis Xavier University	U
Saint Mary's University	U
Saint Thomas More University	U
St. Jerome's University	U
St. Thomas University	U
Trinity Western University	U, G
Université Laval	U, G
Université de Montreal	U, G
Université du Quebec	U
University of Alberta	U, G
University of British Columbia	U, G
University of Calgary	U, G
University of King's College	U
University of Lethbridge	U
University of Manitoba	U, G
University of Ottawa	U, G
University of Prince Edward Island	U
University of Regina	U, G
University of Saskatchewan	U, G
University of Toronto	U, G
University of Trinity College	G
University of Waterloo	U
University of Western Ontario	U
University of Winnipeg	U, G
Wilfrid Laurier University	U, G
York University	U

RESPIRATORY THERAPY

Thompson Rivers University	U
University of New Brunswick	U

RUSSIAN & SLAVIC AREA STUDIES

Campion College	U
Carleton University	U, G
Dalhousie University	U
Huron College	U
Kwantlen University	U
McGill University	U, G
Memorial University	U
Université Laval	U
Université de Montreal	U, G
University of Calgary	U
University of Guelph	U
University of King's College	U
University of New Brunswick	U
University of Toronto	U, G
University of Victoria	U
University of Waterloo	U
University of Western Ontario	U
York University	U

RUSSIAN LANGUAGE & LITERATURE

Campion College	U
Carleton University	U, G
Dalhousie University	U
Kwantlen University	U
Luther College	U
Memorial University	U
St. Thomas University	U
Université de Laval	U
University of British Columbia	U
University of Calgary	U
University of Toronto	U, G
University of Western Ontario	U
York University	U

SCANDINAVIAN LANGUAGE & LITERATURE

Athabasca University	U, G
Memorial University	U
University of British Columbia	U
University of Western Ontario	U

SLAVIC LANGUAGES & LITERATURE

Kwantlen University College	U
McGill University	U
University of Calgary	U, G
University of Manitoba	U, G
University of Ottawa	U

| University of Toronto | U, G |
| University of Victoria | U |

SCULPTURE

ACAD	U
Concordia University	U
NSCAD	U
OCAD	U
Thompson Rivers University	U
University of Toronto	U

SOCIAL WORK

Campion College	U
Carleton University	U
Concordia University	U
Dalhousie University	U, G
King's College	U
Lakehead University	U, G
Laurentian University	U, G
Luther College	U
Malaspina University College	U
McGill University	U, G
McMaster University	U, G
Memorial University	U, G
Mount Royal College	U
Nipissing University	U
Redeemer University College	U
Ryerson University	U
St. Thomas University	U
Thompson Rivers University	U
Trinity Western University	U
Université de Laval	U, G
Université de Moncton	U, G
Université de Montreal	U, G
Université de Sherbrooke	U, G
Université du Quebec	U, G
University College of the Fraser Valley	U
University of British Columbia	U
University of Calgary	U, G
University of Manitoba	U, G
University of N. British Columbia	U, G
University of Ottawa	U, G
University of Regina	U, G
University of Toronto	U, G
University of Victoria	U
University of Waterloo	U
University of Western Ontario	U
University of Windsor	U
Wilfrid Laurier University	U, G
York University	U, G

SOCIOLOGY

Acadia University	U
Athabasca University	U, G
Bishop's University	U
Brandon University	U
Brescia College	U
Brock University	U
Campion College	U
Cape Breton University	U
Carleton University	U, G
Concordia University	U
Concordia University College	U
Dalhousie University	U, G
Huron College	U
King's College	U
Kwantlen University	U
Lakehead University	U, G
Laurentian University	U, G
Luther College	U
Malaspina University	U
McGill University	U, G
McMaster University	U, G
Memorial University	U, G
Mount Allison University	U
Mount Royal College	U
Mount Saint Vincent University	U
Nipissing University	U
Queen's University	U, G
Redeemer College	U
Ryerson University	U
Saint Francis Xavier College	U
Saint Mary's University	U
Saint Thomas More University	U
St. Jerome's University	U
Simon Fraser University	U, G
The King's University College	U
Thompson Rivers University	U
Trent University	U
Trinity Western University	U
Université Laval	U, G
Université de Moncton	U, G
Université de Montreal	U, G
Université de Sherbrooke	U
Université du Quebec	U, G
University College of the Fraser Valley	U
University of British Columbia	U, G
University of Calgary	U, G
University of Guelph	U, G
University of King's College	U
University of Lethbridge	U, G
University of Manitoba	U, G

University of New Brunswick	U, G
University of Ottawa	U, G
University of Prince Edward Island	U
University of Regina	U, G
University of Saskatchewan	U, G
University of Toronto	U, G
University of Victoria	U, G
University of Waterloo	U, G
University of Western Ontario	U, G
University of Windsor	U, G
University of Winnipeg	U
Wilfrid Laurier University	U
York University	U, G

SOFTWARE ENGINEERING

Carleton University	U, G
Concordia University	U
Lakehead University	U
McGill University	U
McMaster University	U
University of Alberta	U
University of British Columbia	U
University of Calgary	U
University of Ontario	U
University of Ottawa	U, G
University of Regina	U
University of Toronto	U, G
University of Victoria	U
University of Waterloo	U
University of Western Ontario	U

SPANISH LANGUAGE & LITERATURE

Acadia University	U
Athabasca University	U
Brescia College	U
Brock University	U
Campion College	U
Carleton University	U
Concordia University	U
Concordia University College	U
Dalhousie University	U
Huron College	U
Laurentian University	U
Malaspina University	U
McGill University	U
Memorial University	U
Mount Allison University	U
Mount Royal College	U
Mount Saint Vincent College	U

Queen's University	U, G
Saint Mary's University	U
St. Thomas University	U
Trent University	U
Université Laval	U
Université de Montreal	U, G
Université de Sherbrooke	U
Université du Quebec	U
University of British Columbia	U
University of Calgary	U, G
University of Guelph	U
University of King's College	U
University of Lethbridge	U, G
University of Manitoba	U, G
University of New Brunswick	U
University of Ottawa	U, G
University of Toronto	U, G
University of Waterloo	U
University of Western Ontario	U, G
University of Windsor	U
University of Winnipeg	U
Wilfrid Laurier University	U
York University	U

SPEECH LANGUAGE PATHOLOGY & AUDIOLOGY

Dalhousie University	U, G
Kwantlen University	U
Mount Royal College	U
Saint Francis Xavier University	U
Université de Montreal	U, G
University College of the Fraser Valley	U
University of Alberta	U, G
University of British Columbia	U, G
University of Manitoba	U
University of Toronto	U, G
University of Waterloo	U
University of Western Ontario	U

SPORT & FITNESS ADMINISTRATION

Brock University	U
Concordia University	U, G
Lakehead University	U, G
Laurentian University	U
University of British Columbia	U
University of New Brunswick	G
University of Ottawa	U, G
University of Toronto	U
University of Victoria	U
University of Winnipeg	U

STATISTICS

Acadia University	U
Campion College	U
Carleton University	U, G
Concordia University	U
Dalhousie University	U, G
Kwantlen University	U
Luther College	U
McGill University	U
McMaster University	U, G
Memorial University	U, G
Nova Scotia Agricultural College	U, G
Queen's University	U, G
Saint Francis Xavier University	U
Simon Fraser University	U
Thompson Rivers University	U
Université Laval	U, G
Université de Montreal	U, G
Université du Quebec	U, G
University College of the Fraser Valley	U
University of Alberta	U
University of British Columbia	U, G
University of Calgary	U, G
University of Guelph	U
University of King's College	U
University of Lethbridge	U
University of Manitoba	U, G
University of New Brunswick	U, G
University of N. British Columbia	U, G
University of Prince Edward Island	U
University of Ottawa	U
University of Regina	U, G
University of Saskatchewan	U, G
University of Toronto	U, G
University of Victoria	U, G
University of Waterloo	U, G
University of Western Ontario	U, G
University of Windsor	U, G
University of Winnipeg	U
York University	U, G

TEXTILE SCIENCES

Kwantlen University College	U
NSCAD	U, G
University of Manitoba	U, G
University of N. British Columbia	G

THEOLOGY/THEOLOGICAL STUDIES

Acadia University	U, G
Campion College	U
Concordia University	U, G
Concordia University College	U
Huron College	U, G
Queen's University	U, G
The King's University College	U
U Trent University	U
Trinity Western University	U, G
Université Laval	U
Université de Montreal	U
Université du Quebec	U, G
University of Trinity College	G
University of Winnipeg	U, G
Wilfrid Laurier University	U, G

TOXICOLOGY

Kwantlen University College	U
Memorial University	G
Université de Montreal	G
Université du Quebec	U
University of Guelph	U, G
University of N. British Columbia	G
University of Ottawa	U, G
University of Saskatchewan	U, G
University of Toronto	U, G
University of Western Ontario	U

TOURISM

Acadia University	U
Brock University	U
Cape Breton University	U
Concordia University	U
Dalhousie University	U
Lakehead University	U
Malaspina University	U
Memorial University	U
Mount Royal College	U
Mount Saint Vincent College	U
Thompson Rivers University	U
University of Alberta	U
University of British Columbia	U
University of Calgary	U
University of Guelph	U
University of New Brunswick	U
University of N. British Columbia	U, G
University of Prince Edward Island	U
University of Victoria	U

TRANSLATION

Concordia University College	U
Laurentian University	U
Université Laval	U, G
Université de Moncton	U

Université de Montreal	U, G
Université de Sherbrooke	U
Université du Quebec	U
University of Ottawa	U
University of Toronto	U
University of Winnipeg	U
York University	U

URBAN AFFAIRS/STUDIES

Concordia University	U
Concordia University College	U
McGill University	U, G
Queen's University	U, G
Ryerson University	U
Université de Montreal	U, G
University of British Columbia	U, G
University of Calgary	U
University of Lethbridge	U
University of Toronto	U, G
University of Winnipeg	U
Wilfrid Laurier University	U
York University	U

VETERINARY MEDICINE

Université de Montreal	G
University of Guelph	G
University of Prince Edward Island	G
University of Saskatchewan	G

VISUAL & PERFORMING ARTS

ACAD	U
Bishop's University	U
Brock University	U
Concordia University	U
Concordia University College	U
Dalhousie University	U
ECIAD	U
Huron College	U
Lakehead University	U
Laurentian University	U
Luther College	U
Malaspina University	U
Memorial University	U
Nipissing University	U
NSCAD	U
Redeemer College	U
Thompson Rivers University	U
Université Laval	U, G

Université de Moncton	U
Université de Montreal	U
Université de Sherbrooke	U
Université du Quebec	U
University College of the Fraser Valley	U
University of British Columbia	U, G
University of Calgary	U
University of Guelph	U
University of King's College	U
University of Lethbridge	U, G
University of New Brunswick	U
University of Ottawa	U
University of Prince Edward Island	U
University of Regina	U
University of Toronto	U
University of Trinity	U
University of Victoria	U, G
University of Western Ontario	U, G
University of Windsor	U, G
University of Winnipeg	U
Wilfrid Laurier University	U
York University	U, G

WATER RESOURCES ENGINEERING

Lakhead University	U
University of Guelph	U
University of British Columbia	U, G
University of New Brunswick	U, G

WOMEN'S/GENDER STUDIES

Acadia University	U
Athabasca University	U
Bishop's University	U
Brandon University	U
Brock University	U
Carleton University	U
Concordia University	U
Concordia University College	U
Dalhousie University	U, G
Huron College	U
Lakehead University	U, G
Laurentian University	U
Luther College	U
Malaspina University College	U
McGill University	U
McMaster University	U
Memorial University	U, G
Mount Royal College	U

Mount Saint Vincent University	U, G
Nipissing University	U
Queen's University	U
Saint Francis Xavier College	U
Saint Mary's University	U, G
Simon Fraser University	U, G
Trent University	U
Université Laval	U
Université du Quebec	U
University of Alberta	U
University of British Columbia	U, G
University of Calgary	U
University of Guelph	U, G
University of King's College	U
University of Lethbridge	U
University of Manitoba	U
University of New Brunswick	U
University of Northern British Columbia	U
University of Ottawa	U
University of Prince Edward Island	U
University of Regina	U
University of Saskatchewan	U, G
University of Toronto	U, G
University of Victoria	U
University of Waterloo	U
University of Western Ontario	U
University of Windsor	U
University of Winnipeg	U
Wilfrid Laurier University	U
York University	U, G

WOOD SCIENCES

Campion College	U
Concordia University College	U
Kwantlen University College	U
McGill University	U
University of British Columbia	U, G
University of New Brunswick	U
University of N. British Columbia	U, G
University of Toronto	U, G

Con...	
King's ...	
Kwantlen ...	
Malaspina U...	
McGill Universi...	
Mount Royal Colle...	
University of Alberta	
University of British Colu...	
University of Ottawa	
University of Toronto	
University of Victoria	
University of Western Ontario	
University of Windsor	
University of Winnipeg	

ZOOLOGY

Brandon University	U
Laurentian University	G
McGill University	U
Mount Royal College	U
Nova Scotia Agricultural College	U
University of Alberta	U
University of British Columbia	U, G
University of Calgary	U
University of Guelph	U, G
University of Lethbridge	U
University of Manitoba	U, G
University of N. British Columbia	U, G
University of Toronto	U, G
University of Western Ontario	U, G

MAJORS INDEX

A-Z INDEX